"Down-to-earth, sensible, wise, inspira for anyone who preaches. This fine nev plainspoken approach to life, will be a boon for both pastors, preachers, and anyone who considers themselves 'hearers of the word.'"

> —James Martin, SJ
> Author of *The Jesuit Guide to (Almost) Everything*

"The title *Between the Ambo and the Altar* could have been extended to include Summoned to Mission. Fr. DeBona provides the reader not only with insights into understanding God's word, but also offers 'tactics' on how to translate the word into everyday life. What a great service this volume is to preachers and students of Scripture."

> —Bishop Robert Morneau
> Auxiliary Bishop of Green Bay, Wisconsin

"A wise, timely, and practical resource for liturgical preachers! Reminding homilists that the Scriptures and the liturgy form a single banquet of the word of God, Guerric DeBona, OSB, offers a creative recipe for moving from Scripture, to liturgical texts and rituals, to the homily. The challenge for the preacher is clear: to serve 'fresh bread' rather than 'stale crumbs' to those who hunger for richer fare from the pulpit."

> —Mary Catherine Hilkert, OP
> Professor of Theology
> University of Notre Dame

"A ground breaking and much needed commentary on the Sunday Liturgy that will benefit presiders, deacons, and all involved in liturgical ministry and liturgical preparation. Insightful commentaries on the scripture readings accompanied, where appropriate, by comments on the prayers and prefaces of the day. A method for homily preparation and keen insights about the day's liturgy offered but never forced, suggestions offered but nothing demanded. This is a mature work that serves up things to ponder and pray about, that respects and even encourages the reader to go beyond what is so well stated here to serve the diversity of the Catholic parish today."

> —Rev. Msgr. Kevin Irwin
> Ordinary Professor of Liturgical Studies and Sacramental Theology
> Author of *Serving the Body of Christ*
> The Catholic University of America

Between the Ambo and the Altar

Biblical Preaching and The Roman Missal,
Year B

Guerric DeBona, OSB

LITURGICAL PRESS
Collegeville, Minnesota

www.litpress.org

1	2	3	4	5	6	7	8	9

Library of Congress Cataloging-in-Publication Data

DeBona, Guerric, 1955–
    Between the Ambo and the altar : biblical preaching and the Roman missal, year a / Guerric DeBona.
        pages   cm.
    ISBN 978-0-8146-3459-2 (alk. paper) — ISBN 978-0-8146-3484-4 (e-book)
    1. Church year sermons.   2. Lectionary preaching—Catholic Church.
3. Catholic Church—Sermons.   4. Catholic Church. Lectionary for Mass
(U.S.). Year A.   5. Catholic Church. Missale Romanum (1970)   I. Title.

BX1756.A1D43 2013
251'.6—dc23   2013008345

For the priests of the
Archdiocese of Indianapolis
and the people they serve

"He loved his own in the world, and he loved them to the end."
—John 13:1b

Contents

Holy Week

Easter Time

Ordinary Time

Solemnities of the Lord during Ordinary Time

Introduction: Biblical Preaching and the New *Roman Missal*

The Geography of the Homily

It is no exaggeration to say that we live in a world choked with words. From texting with smartphones to blogging on the Internet, we face a glut of language day after day. Paradoxically, we strain to establish relationships with one another that really connect. Indeed, this age of global messaging has been far from communicative. Instead, we are a culture of individual selves, more often isolated than not by the very words we form, longing for true community and reconciliation. In the end, no multiplication of words or virtual encounters via the latest technology will satisfy the human yearning for connecting to the deepest center of our being and the lives of others. Only the Word made visible will satiate that terrible hunger.

That is the mission of Christian preaching when the community of faith gathers as the eucharistic assembly: to unearth a liberating Word to the weary, the downtrodden, and the alienated. As Christ tells those gathered to hear the words of Scripture broken open to them in the synagogue at Nazareth at the beginning of his ministry in Galilee, God has sent him "to proclaim liberty to captives / and recovery of sight to the blind, / to let the oppressed go free, / and to proclaim a year acceptable to the Lord" (Luke 4:18-19, NAB). The liturgical homily exists, then, for the purpose of deepening the faith of the baptized. In the often quoted words from *Sacrosanctum Concilium* of the Second Vatican Council, "By means of the homily, the mysteries of the faith and the guiding principles of the christian life are expounded from the sacred text during the course of the liturgical year" (52). Preaching is meant to guide the Christian community into a deeper celebration of the Eucharist and engage the faith community in the "richer fare"

1

of the Scriptures as they unfold in the Sunday Lectionary and in the experience of the faith community.

This banquet of God's saving word served at the eucharistic celebration emerges from the Scriptures and the church's liturgy itself. As the *General Instruction of the Roman Missal* says, the homily "is necessary for the nurturing of the Christian life. It should be an explanation of some aspect of the readings from Sacred Scripture or of another text from the Ordinary or the Proper of the Mass of the day and should take into account both the mystery being celebrated and the particular needs of the listeners" (65). The preacher, then, engages the assembly in its particular historical horizon with the language of faith and tradition in order to draw the congregation into the paschal mystery of Christ's sanctification for his church. Preaching is a grace-filled convergence among preacher, text, and God's people. As a constitutive component of the liturgy, the homily "points to the presence of God in people's lives and then leads a congregation into the Eucharist, providing, as it were, the motive for celebrating the Eucharist in this time and place."[1] As the USCCB document *Preaching the Mystery of Faith: The Sunday Homily* enjoins us, "Every homily, because it is an intrinsic part of the Sunday Eucharist, must therefore be about the dying and rising of Jesus Christ and his sacrificial passage through suffering to new and eternal life for us."[2] The preacher facilitates the congregation's discovery of the Word unfolding in the very midst of sacred space and, in so doing, discloses the mystery of God's faithful love, together with the thanks and praise that is at the heart of the Eucharist, the height and summit of our worship as the people of God. As Pope Benedict XVI writes in *Verbum Domini*, quoting *Sacrosanctum Concilium*,

> Here one sees the sage pedagogy of the Church, which proclaims and listens to sacred Scripture following the rhythm of the liturgical year. This expansion of God's word in time takes place above all in the Eucharistic celebration and in the Liturgy of the Hours. At the center of everything the paschal mystery shines forth, and around it radiate all the mysteries of Christ and the history of salvation, which become sacramentally present: "By recalling in this way the mysteries of redemption, the Church opens up to the faithful the riches of the saving actions and the merits of her Lord, and makes them present to all times, allowing the faithful to enter into contact with them and to be filled with the grace of salvation." For this reason I encourage the Church's Pastors and all engaged in pastoral

work to see that all the faithful learn to savor the deep meaning of the word of God which unfolds each year in the liturgy, revealing the fundamental mysteries of our faith. This is in turn the basis for a correct approach to sacred Scripture.[3]

I have titled this preaching commentary *Between the Ambo and the Altar* in order to locate the liturgical geography of the homily and call attention to the place of preaching as the site for the faithful "to savor the deep meaning of the word of God which unfolds each year in the liturgy, revealing the fundamental mysteries of our faith." As is well known, for many years the sermon functioned as a kind of misplaced little island at the Roman liturgy; it became a harbor for boatloads of parish announcements or themes that were loosely drifting out to sea. Most of these were well-intentioned sermons but something like castaways unmoored, poorly integrated into the liturgy itself. When the restoration of the ancient *homilia* was promulgated with the Second Vatican Council, the character of preaching the Word shifted from a lone island adrift in a vast ocean to a strategic bridge connecting two vast continents. The purpose of the homily in the age of the new evangelization is to preach the Good News of Christ's saving work as it is disclosed in the entire Bible, God's living Word among us, and this disclosure is to lead the baptized assembly to praise, thanksgiving, and mission. "The homily is a means of bringing the scriptural message to life in a way that helps the faithful to realize that God's word is present and at work in their everyday lives. It should lead to an understanding of the mystery being celebrated, serve as a summons to mission, and prepare the assembly for the profession of faith, the universal prayer and the Eucharistic liturgy. Consequently, those who have been charged with preaching by virtue of a specific ministry ought to take this task to heart" (*Verbum Domini* 59). By accounting for God's activity in Christ throughout salvation history, the homily deepens the faith of the Christian assembly, instilling in the faithful a heartfelt desire to gather at the eucharistic sacrifice. So by definition, the homily exists for the sake of the hearer of the Good News, to transition this congregation from Word to sacrament, from the ambo to the altar. And from the altar to mission.

The present series, which begins with this volume, is meant to be an application of preaching in the context of the church's Lectionary inside the language of the Sunday liturgy. From the perspective of the Sunday homily and the interests of those who preach week after week, I think that there remains a marvelous opportunity to discover a dialogue that exists between the liturgical texts—the presidential prayers and eucharistic prayers, the prefaces for Ordinary Time as well as feasts and solemnities—and the Scriptures themselves. I think we should view our dialogue with the Sunday liturgy as both culturally local and broadly universal. Just as the Scriptures have been passed down to us and are made applicable for our day by exegetical methods such as historical criticism and other ways of study, so too are we able to draw in the church's liturgical tradition for the homily as a constitutive dialogue partner. As of this writing, there have already been some fine introductions to the translation and implementation of the new *Roman Missal* (2011), such as Paul Turner's *Pastoral Companion to the Roman Missal* (WLP, 2010). Indeed, the probing of the vast resources of the liturgy and the Scriptures from which this celebration has emerged allows for what Louis-Marie Chauvet calls *"la Bible liturgique."*[4] Drawing from Chauvet and echoing the *GIRM*, Edward Foley and Jon Michael Joncas remind us that the preacher may explore further resources for the homily, among them the "liturgical bible," which "may refer to all liturgical texts apart from the lectionary." These include the major and minor euchologies such as the eucharistic prayers, prefaces, collects, the invariable (e.g., the "Holy, Holy"), and optional texts for the day (e.g., prayers for the blessing of an Advent wreath or newly restored Blessing over the People during Lent), "as well as the words of the hymns, songs and acclamations that are sung during worship."[5] I hasten to add that this liturgical language is not simply a resource for the preacher, but the living text of the faith community that has unfolded over the centuries. Yes, we are a historical, culturally specific faith community but always in dialogue with sacred history and how God has shaped us through the mediation of the church. The liturgy and the Scriptures that are the spine of the Body of Christ, as it were, form a marvelous dialectic for the preacher to witness the proclamation of the Good News of Jesus Christ.

The Homiletic Arc

In addition to providing a resource for the preacher by way of commentary, my hope is that the present text will contribute to an understanding of homiletic process as well. After teaching preaching to seminarians for over a dozen years and giving workshops to priests, deacons, and other ministers, I can say that one of the most difficult concepts to grasp—but one of the most essential to learn—is the essential organic unity of the homily. The late Ken Untener and others have stressed the frustration present in hearers in the congregation who complain about the homily having too many ideas and failing to challenge the call to mission in the world on a practical level.[6] Every preacher should certainly have some kind of method that serves as a kind of armature for the text, moving the homily along and structured around the listener. We cannot rely on our subjective, privatized voice to preach to a community of believers. All of us have been trained as solitary writers from an early age, but those who preach write for a congregation of ears, not a single pair of eyes. In this regard, homiletic strategy is very much in order so that the baptized assembly might listen to the word of God with faith and understanding, unencumbered by the personal eccentricities of the preacher. For those who are interested in developing a method of homiletics more fully, I would recommend the works of David Buttrick, Eugene Lowry, and Paul Scott Wilson, all of whom have written extensively on crafting the homily.[7]

With *Between the Ambo and the Altar*, I have in mind something less like a method and more like process, moving from Scripture to liturgical text to homily. Therefore, I have structured the book around three coordinates that seem to me to be the most productive way of engaging a preaching dialogue between the Sunday Lectionary readings and the liturgical texts that surround them. The first section is meant to be a prayerful reflection on the Lectionary for the day. I have avoided commentaries but used only some (minor) native ability in biblical languages, together with a good study Bible. Over the years, I have found that scholarly biblical commentaries are quite useful but usually only *after* a kind of naïve reading of the text, a precritical reflection, which Paul Ricoeur has called "the first naiveté" or "the spontaneous immediacy of reader to subject matter."[8] Such reading of the sacred text allows me to sink deeply into the word of God without a gloss. At the same time, a study Bible with adequate footnotes affords the opportunity to make very general historical and textual connections that aid in the life of prayer and contemplation. I am suggesting, then, that this first section of exploring the biblical text become the initial starting point for the homily, best accessed about a week before the homily is to be delivered and, ideally, integrated into Morning or Evening Prayer.

The second section is devoted precisely to establishing a substantial connection with the liturgical texts and making some links with the Scripture. "Connecting the Bible and the Liturgy" is rather subjective and personal, and it is my hope that the preacher will bring a wealth of associations to such a process of connections between Scripture and the liturgy, or between the ambo and the altar. These musings on the prayers in the liturgy are meant to be pastoral suggestions for homiletic building blocks rather than formal theoretical arguments. To this end, I have taken each of the Lectionary cycles (A, B, C) and evinced some connection with the liturgical texts for that particular Sunday. My goal here is certainly not exhaustive; in fact, it is far from that. As every seasoned preacher knows, homiletics relies on making associations and connections for an increasingly diverse congregation of listeners. My aim is that preachers, new and experienced alike, will begin to mine the wealth of material already present in the liturgy and the Scriptures for a multicultural and multigenerational assembly. Although there are numerous elements in the "liturgical Bible" to consider, as well as many possible partners for establishing the homiletic text, I have confined myself mostly to the newly revised translation of the presidential prayers and prefaces of *The Roman Missal* in an effort to glean material for preaching. There is a wealth of potential present in these texts for reflection. I have avoided historical explanations of the prayers, but simply recommend what might be considered a point of departure for constructing the liturgical homily. In some rare instances, I have alluded to the previous (revised) *Sacramentary*'s (1985) translation or, again, sometimes averted to the original Latin itself as a way of mining the depth of the church's liturgy. So saying, the wise homilist's attention to these prayers demonstrates an attention to what *Fulfilled in Your Hearing* (1982) refers to as the preacher's unique role as "mediator of meaning." The preacher stands in the midst of the Christian assembly as an interpreter of the Word within a particular culture articulating a powerful witness, nurtured by the faith of the church. As Daniel McCarthy has demonstrated with his commentaries on selected Collects originally published in *The Tablet*, the liturgy itself is a catalyst to such preaching.[9] Careful meditation on the liturgical prayers in the manner of *lectio divina*, while reflecting on a given Sunday, solemnity, or feast that celebrates these days, will undoubtedly assist the preacher not only in the homily itself but also with the entire Eucharistic Liturgy for the various needs of these particular hearers of the gospel.

Finally, I have included a third section on "Strategy for Preaching" as a kind of point of homiletic integration for each Sunday. As with the previous two sections, I hardly expect that each reader will come to the same homiletic text as I did in the course of this process, but I simply recommend one that strikes me as a plausible outcome of my own engagement with the texts. The paradigm remains the same, though, for each of the Sundays, feasts, and solemnities presented in the liturgical year. If we follow the process for preaching in this book, we move from a meditation on Scripture as it is given in the Lectionary then on to a connection of these texts with the liturgical prayers for the given Sunday (or perhaps some other relevant liturgical text) to the emergence of the homily itself. In terms of a watershed moment in preaching preparation, I regard the primary task of this third stage of the homiletic process a narrowing down to a single declarative sentence, which I have called here the homiletic core idea, but which has also been termed by others a "focus sentence."[10] Discovering a homiletic core idea, a foundation for an uncluttered, pristine armature from which to hang eight to ten minutes of words each week, is not easy, but absolutely necessary. It is the sentence that should be in the mind of every congregant after the homily is over in answer to the question, "What did you hear?"

Having come to a core homiletic sentence, the preacher will then need to develop practical tactics as to how this idea will become a reality for the congregation. For most Sundays, feasts, and solemnities, the best guide to understanding tactics is posing the question: What are some concrete images, relevant stories, or illustrations that will make the core homiletic idea a reality in the heart of the hearer? Tactics are culturally specific and will have strong pastoral application. The preacher ought to instinctively know that the day-to-day activity of the parish and the world at large will, by and large, inform tactics. If one is preaching to a youth group, there is no sense using stories, vocabulary, or illustrations that are more appropriate to the retired members of the parish. Then again, parishioners will be directly affected by the economic and political happenings around them, which will inflect the meaning of the homiletic core. If there has been a tragic death in the parish family, the homiletic event for the next Sunday (let's say, it is the Fifth Sunday of Lent, Year A, the gospel for which is the raising of Lazarus) will carry a different freight than if such sadness were not part of the community. Again, these homiletic strategies are only meant to be suggestive and not prescriptive.

As every seasoned preacher knows very well, abstractions are the kiss of death when it comes to homilies, and so the tactics for achieving a core homiletic idea should be as concrete as possible and structured in a way that the congregation may follow it with ease, with a logic that is slow and available. Remember—tactics are practical actions with measured goals; in this case there is a single target: the core homiletic idea. What must be done to achieve that goal? As I have suggested earlier, homiletic methods are designed to organize a structure around the listener. We cannot presume that simply because I am speaking the fruits of my meditation and study that the congregation is unpacking the homily and getting to the depth of the core homiletic idea. The homiletic idea gives something precious to the baptized, enfleshing the word of God; it is a deepening of the reality of faith, a pondering of the mysteries of Christ, an exploration into God's creation. So in order to get to a theological understanding of the word of God, we ought to taste the aroma of fresh bread in that language.

In a word: the people of God don't want our stale crumbs in our preaching. "Homilies are inspirational when they touch the deepest levels of the human heart and address the real questions of human experience."[11] The worst possible response anyone can evince after preaching the word of God is for a faithful member of the congregation to respond, "So what?" Good tactics in homilies, like creative strategic planning, ensure that there is a measurable outcome. "So what?" Homilists should take care that this primary question is the subtext of every preaching event because no congregation should walk away from the Eucharist with that question lingering in their hearts. If we don't have a method or a structure of some kind to achieve the incarnation of our words, then we may have a great private meditation, but not much by way of evangelization. Jesus did not preach in parables for nothing: they are stories designed around the hearer to challenge, affirm, and unfold the kingdom of God.

It is a great privilege to stand in the midst of the baptized assembly and mediate meaning for those who have faithfully gathered at the Eucharist. Our preaching begins long before we come to the ambo and remains in the hearts of the congregation well after we leave the altar. Pray God that our own words become sown in the field of the Lord and reap a bountiful harvest.

Feast of St. Gregory the Great
Saint Meinrad School of Theology and Seminary, 2012

Notes

1. USCCB, *Fulfilled in Your Hearing: The Homily in the Sunday Assembly* (Washington, DC: USCCB, 1982), 23.

2. United States Conference of Catholic Bishops, *Preaching the Mystery of Faith: The Sunday Homily* (Washington, DC: USCCB Publishing, 2012), 15.

3. Benedict XVI, Post-Synodal Apostolic Exhortation, *The Word of the Lord (Verbum Domini)* (Boston: Pauline Books, 2010), 52.

4. Louis-Marie Chauvet, "*La Dimensions bibliques des texts liturgiques,*" *La Maison-Dieu* 189 (1992): 131–47. Chauvet demonstrates the foundational influence of the biblical text on the Christian liturgy, citing just some of the more obvious examples.

5. Edward Foley, Capuchin, "The Homily beyond Scripture: *Fulfilled in Your Hearing* Revisited," *Worship* 73, no. 4 (1999): 355.

6. Cf. Kenneth Untener, *Preaching Better* (Mahwah, NJ: Paulist Press, 1999).

7. Cf. David Buttrick, *Homiletic* (Philadelphia: Fortress Press, 1987); Eugene Lowry, *The Homiletic Plot* (Louisville: Westminster John Knox, 2001); Paul Scott Wilson, *The Four Pages of the Sermon* (Nashville: Abingdon, 1999 [1980]).

8. Cf. Paul Ricoeur, *The Symbolism of Evil*, trans. Emerson Buchanan (Boston: Beacon Press, 1967), 347–53.

9. Daniel McCarthy, *Listen to the Word: Commentaries on Selected Opening Prayers of Sundays and Feasts with Sample Homilies* (London: Tablet Publishing, 2009).

10. Cf. Thomas Long, *The Witness of Preaching*, 2nd ed. (Louisville: Westminster John Knox, 2005 [1990]), 99–116.

11. United States Conference of Catholic Bishops, *Preaching the Mystery of Faith*, 15.

ADVENT

First Sunday of Advent

Readings from the Ambo

Isa 63:16b-17, 19b; 64:2-7; Ps 80:2-3, 15-16, 18-19; 1 Cor 1:3-9; Mark 13:33-37

The portrait of the community in the **First Reading** for the First Sunday of Advent by the author commonly referred to as Third Isaiah (about 535–20 BC, or sometime after the return from exile) is adrift and searching. "Why do you let us wander, O Lord, from your ways, / and harden our hearts so that we fear you not?" The passage is something like a penitential lament (like Psalm 80), asking the Lord to be yoked back into a more familial relationship with him. If the return from exile has already occurred and the rebuilding of the temple has subsequently begun or (as some have argued) even been completed, then what is missing is a divine center pole, a compass pointing to the divine. There seems to be a loss of the memory of God when the prophet cries, "There is none who calls upon your name, / who rouses himself to cling to you." The lament, then, is that God's deeds have been forgotten, and so common memory, collective memory or what we might call the religious imagination, has failed to unite the community. The sadness and intensity of the cry becomes heightened with the prophet assuming the voice of the people and represents a substantial shift in tone from the other oracles in the corpus we know as Third Isaiah. Vanished is the eschatological hope of Second Isaiah previous to these oracles, and yet this present text, with its plaintive cry, wants to gather us into its fold and take us into Advent, accompanied by the prophet.

The **Responsorial Psalm** reinforces the urgency of Isaiah's prayer: "Lord, make us turn to you; let us see your face and we shall be saved." The prayer for both Isaiah and psalmist is urgent. There is no longer any more time for wandering. The petition is for a father, not a patriarch who is powerful enough to "rend the heavens and come down, / with the mountains quaking."

The necessity for action and zeal has been absorbed by Jesus in his admonition to the disciples in Mark's Gospel to be watchful. Be alert! The passage comes at the end of a string of apocalyptic prophecies in chapter 13 and just before the events leading up to Jesus' passion, death, and resurrection were about to unfold, beginning in chapter 14. Being alert and awake and not wandering into sleep is obviously an applicable irony for the soon-to-be dozing disciples in the Garden of Gethsemane (in Mark 14:37-42) as it is for an eschatological forecast for the church during Advent. Jesus takes on a prophetic role here, moving us toward the Day of the Lord. There is a tonal shift from the **First Reading** present in this **Gospel**: the invitation to stay away is hope for the future precisely because of the engine of zeal with which Jesus captures the need to stay awake. Far from a lament, this **Gospel** sets a tone that is a summons to action, a trumpet blast before the final chords will be sounded at the end-time.

Perhaps Paul would say that every one of us is drowsy except God, who is "faithful, / and by him you were called to fellowship with his Son, Jesus Christ our Lord." That fidelity is the other side of a God who will come quickly and is near at hand. And it seems to be a divine virtue that Isaiah is counting on as well—the father whom we await to be our shepherd, since we are the clay and he is the potter. All is the work of his hands.

Connecting the Bible and the Liturgy

If the Isaiah text might be characterized as something like a sad lamentation for a people who are wandering after a period of exile and are now in a period of collective amnesia about God and his works, the church's prayers represent a kind of counterpoint to the Isaiah text, inviting the assembly to hasten toward Christ. In this regard, the alertness that Jesus demands in the **Gospel** is illuminated in a brilliant way through the liturgy. As a baptized assembly, we must be ready and keep watch. The implication is that the reign of God is for neither the slow of foot nor the faint of heart. "Resolve" is what the **Collect** will ask of God in order to cure our sloth. "Grant your faithful, we pray, almighty God, / the resolve to run forth to meet your Christ / with righteous deeds at his coming." Even while we are urged to gather to the future kingdom, Isaiah's lament reminds the Christian assembly of the potential loss of community, especially marshaling of the just into the kingdom of God. Isaiah's text has a crucial function of naming the deep sin of separation, fragmentation, and forgetfulness present in every community. At the same time, the liturgy provides the impetus to want to be of one heart and one mind, "worthy to possess the heavenly Kingdom." The liturgical prayers, then, disclose the redeemed community for which Isaiah longs: all the faithful are invited to be gathered in hope and promise, to leave the wandering and restless heart behind, even as the church pours forth its prayers to be gathered into one sheepfold, the person of Christ himself. The image of being gathered at his right hand (*eius dexterae sociati*) deployed in the Collect conjures the landscape of the righteous shaped by the potter's hand at the end-time.

Paul himself is quite sanguine and confident about the sanctifying role of our redemption and clear about where true fidelity resides: in the God who continues to call not only for the future, but now. So too, the **Prayer after Communion** urges the faithful to remember that "we walk amid passing things" and asks God to teach us by the mysteries we celebrate "to love the things of heaven / and hold fast to what endures." This advice from Paul is sound teaching for keeping vigil. It is one thing to will ourselves to watch, but it is quite another to remember that we live amid passing things and intend to keep our eyes on what endures. To observe the latter causes us to desire to keep watch and maintain vigil out of a hunger for what we long for—the things of heaven.

Strategy for Preaching

In 2003 Peter Steinfels published a provocative book called *A People Adrift*, which projected a potential crisis for the American Catholic Church. Steinfels says that American Catholicism is on the verge of either an irreversible decline or a thoroughgoing trans-formation. Folks may disagree with the apocalyptic tone, but there is a way in which we might read the state of affairs in American Ca-tholicism as the equivalent to exile, some of which is self-imposed to be sure. If we find ourselves in a state of exilic wandering—and who does not at one time or another—perhaps we might consider the powerful line in the **Collect** that encapsulates the Sunday liturgy and is echoed throughout the readings: "Grant your faithful, we pray, almighty God, / the resolve to run forth to meet your Christ." I am reading "resolve" here, the *voluntatem* as the Latin text puts it, is another way of expressing the "good zeal" that Benedict reminds the monk in chapter 72 of the Rule is so crucial for keeping us honest and headed toward seeking God. If we have lost that zeal, or worse, turned to wicked zeal, then setting our minds on righteous deeds and remembering God's works in our lives and the lives of others is very much in order this Advent.

It is probably not an accident that Benedict is so strongly weighted toward the good zeal; he gets this quality from God himself. Recall that the prophet says when it comes to the Messianic Promise that so envelopes this season: the zeal of the Lord of hosts will do this. The question of maintaining zeal over the long run (or even the short run, for that matter) in running the ways of God's commands is not easy. When we add to this strain on perseverance the reality of more and more members of the Christian community losing heart and drifting off, then mustering the good zeal becomes even more difficult to embrace. A good question to ask during Advent, then, is how can my zeal be ignited at God's coming? Returning to Steinfels' observations, a question that the American Catholic Church might consider is: where is the center of our life in Christ that will set the ignition on a nonpolarized, nonadversarial, noncynical mission? That is the good zeal.

There may be a tendency for the preacher to begin the homily with "watch and stay ready." Fair enough. But how does this warning get the congregation to love the things of heaven and keep vigil for the one who is to come? Further, beginning with watching deflates the narrative tension that should be building in the homily throughout the text. The preacher should presume that keeping watch is a kind of "aha" moment toward which the homily is headed, a kind of climax to a homiletic narrative. Therefore an interesting homiletic core would be: if we know what really mattered in life, we'd be more aware than ever of God's gifts and even more of his own presence that has yet to come.

I. We might begin with a question to start the ball rolling. Did you ever hear the story about someone who found out that he had just a day to live? What do you suppose he thought about? Examples of possibilities, which should be specific and colorful, even poignant.

II. This is followed by the challenge of what our own list might be. Name the specifics that might impact the parish locally.

III. These are values that endure. God will come with all of these in his arms, because we are the things most precious to him.

    A. God wants to gather us in also from our exile, even more than we want the things that are precious to us.

    B. Image here: a mother and her newborn, a child first coming home from school, a reunion between siblings or friends.

IV. So we can resolve to keep vigil to meet Christ because in him all our desires will be fulfilled. We are that close during Advent (Second Reading).

Second Sunday of Advent

Isa 40:1-5, 9-11; Ps 85:9-10, 11-12, 13-14;
2 Pet 3:8-14; Mark 1:1-8

Comfort my people! The word "comfort" in Isaiah 40:1 is the demarcation line between First and Deutero-Isaiah, a fulcrum that negotiates us into the Second Sunday of Advent. As is well known, this oracle is addressed to the people of Israel during the end of the exilic period in Babylon. The emphasis throughout that book will be on restoration and hope because Israel's penalty is paid off big time by her own suffering. "[S]he has received from the hand of the LORD / double for all her sins." The passage is certainly filled with the good news of the future rebuilding when "the glory of the LORD shall be revealed, / and all people shall see it together; / for the mouth of the LORD has spoken." There is a vision of a unified humanity coming together as one. No wonder this text has been quoted by the likes of Franz Joseph Haydn in the celebrated *Messiah* to announce the impending presence of the future king.

But there is something else, which the lectionary omits. Verses 6–8 demonstrate the prophet's hesitancy because he has seemed to glimpse the mortality of human flesh. He says, "All mankind is grass, / and all their glory like the flower of the field" (v. 6, NAB). This vocational insight to a glimpse of human limitation is not an erasure to a revelation of God's glory. In fact, the point seems to be that God will visit us *despite* our limitation, since the word of the Lord endures forever and that "the Lord GOD . . . rules by his strong arm." Therefore, 2 Peter speaks of God's transcendence, the Lord for whom "one day is like a thousand years / and a thousand years like one day." God will come without delay and because of our own

17

fragility, we will be incapable of understanding how he will come and when. That insight equips our shaky humanity with a sturdy hope and trust in God's power to redeem time itself, a poignant reminder of the Advent season at hand.

From a Christian perspective, that Day of the Lord was best expressed by the herald of glad tidings, John the Baptist. Mark's Gospel uses Isaiah as a platform to announce the Baptist's mission in Judea and as a way of linking the prophetic tradition of Isaiah and exile with the people who long for a messianic future. Mark weaves in John's version of the coming of the future King when he says that "One mightier than I is coming after me." John's baptism of repentance is a sign of the kingdom that is about to come, indeed, that is at hand; it is a call to righteousness and repentance. This same admonition is echoed in 2 Peter when he says this: "since [we] await these things, / be eager to be found without spot or blemish before him, at peace." It is telling that 2 Peter connects being found without spot or blemish with peace. It would seem that the result of preparation is peace, or a self that is utterly at rest in God with good conscience, but also a community at peace because all wait eagerly for the Lord with anticipation and not dread. The anticipation for the Day of the Lord is clearly a call to conversion, a recognition that the kingdom of God is at hand, as John the Baptist proclaims. At the same time, conversion is not a time to wail over the past but to look to the future, to remember the possibility of peace in God's almighty presence. Recognition of our own mortality frees us from a preoccupation with our self-interests and self-determination: the day belongs to the Lord, and indeed, every day belongs to Almighty God who will bring it into fulfillment according to the rule of his strong arm. Advent is there to remind us of the approaching time, but this time it is a gift from God and no one else.

Connecting the Bible and the Liturgy

If the First Sunday of Advent gathered the church into a fold of urgent longing for the King, the following Sunday focuses the assembly's collective mind on ways to gain access to that heavenly home. The prayers initiate a congregation already in process to meet the Lord in the pursuit of humility, wisdom, and prudence—virtuous avenues of conversion that will find a trace in the biblical readings themselves. The liturgy sets a tone of an Advent church already in progress and moving toward the promised one. That progress is best expressed in **Preface I** for Advent that reminds us that the people of God straddle a time that commemorates the one who "assumed at his first coming / the lowliness of human flesh" but awaits that future time "when he comes again in glory and majesty / and all is at last made manifest."

Throughout Advent, the church is identified with the Heavenly City of Jerusalem. The **Entrance Antiphon**, taken from Isaiah 30:19, proclaims: *"Populus Sion, ecce Dominus veniet ad salvandas gentes"* ("O people of Sion, behold, / the Lord will come to save the nations"). While the **Communion Antiphon** says, *"Ierusalem, surege et sta in excelso"* ("Jerusalem, arise and stand upon the heights"). Additionally, it seems clear enough that the operative word from Second Isaiah is "comfort"—that is, the imperative call that God has given the prophet to speak to the heart of Jerusalem. It is also the pastoral task of the church during Advent so that, as it says in the **Preface I of Advent**, "we who watch for that day / may inherit the great promise / in which now we dare to hope." That is our comfort. To this end, the Eucharist is the site of that sublime restoration and hope, the eschatological meal that is the foretaste and promise of the Heavenly Banquet. So we find ourselves in the **Prayer after Communion** beseeching the Lord that we be "[r]eplenished by the food of spiritual nourishment." That feeding is the hope of God's future. At the same time, that full restoration has not come because we still have one foot very much on earth. The Baptist cries for repentance, a *metanoia* as we await the one who is to come quickly. How is this accomplished? The redeemed community can count on celebrating the Eucharist but also the "learning of heavenly wisdom / [to] gain us admittance to his company," as it says in the **Collect** for this day. Indeed, we must rely on God's mercy to help us continue the journey in haste. This prayer is a frank admission that we come into God's company in poverty and ask for the virtues to proceed on the journey. As the **Prayer over the Offerings** says, "we have no merits to plead our cause."

Strategy for Preaching

If the thematic question of zeal on the First Sunday of Advent concerns how we engage Christian life on its deepest level, then the

Second Sunday of Advent seeks conversion or how God engages us. We might consider that *metanoia* is somehow registering a catalogue of our failings, but the quality of conversion is surely more than that, unless we are mired in Jansenism. Reforming our ways is really a matter of grasping our limitations in the context of God's love. That love means recognizing that Almighty God has a plan for us. Comfort my people. We can talk rather glibly about God's will for us, but what does this mean, exactly, for us as individuals? Open to God's future is an Advent posture meant to guide our entire lives, a comfort that we are loved but also called into mission. To this end, the core homiletic idea could be drawn from the **Collect** and supported by Scripture and further imaged in the liturgy, particularly the **Entrance Antiphon** and the **Preface I of Advent**. This is the church in expectation and longing for the promised time to come when we meet the Messiah. Each day we set out to run as we meet Christ wherever we find him—as individuals, as a family, as a church—and that encounter will lead us to a discovery of our mission.

Moreover, the **Gospel** for today offers an unusually powerful connection for preaching and missiology through the witness of John the Baptist. The preacher should seize the opportunity to identify with this unique messenger during Advent, making straight the Lord's ways. That modeling happens first in prayer and then at the ambo.

A thoughtful opening image for the homily today (and one that helps unfold the core idea) is the colorful illustration of Olympic torchbearers. They are the folks who literally pass on the light; they run with haste preparing the way; they make straight the paths of what is to come. Those torchbearers are John the Baptist all rolled up into one, for he reminds us of the excitement of running the Gospel way, as well as the excitement of the new event that is to come. Isaiah expresses this wonder in exquisite comfort. For 2 Peter, God will not delay, so neither should we. Why would we not want to run, like the Baptist, to meet Christ at his coming? That is a question to nicely round off this homily in a potential conclusion.

Third Sunday of Advent

Readings from the Ambo

Isa 61:1-2a, 10-11; Luke 1:46-48, 49-50, 53-54;
1 Thess 5:16-24; John 1:6-8, 19-28

The **First Reading** is a very familiar one, taken from one of the oracles forming Trito-Isaiah. As we might suspect, these prophetic writings, when taken together, do not crystalize around an organic theme or unity. Unlike the selection from Third Isaiah that faced us in the First Sunday of Advent, the present reading stands out as part of three collections (60:1-22; 61:1-11; 62:1-12) that are highly charged with optimism and the expectation of immediate restoration for Israel. As such, the reading from Third Isaiah is a perfect choice for this Gaudete Sunday in Advent, with its heightened anticipation of the nativity of the Lord.

The promised renewal for Israel after the exile appears to be instilled in the prophet himself as he experiences the Spirit anointing him—the only instance of which occurs in the prophetic writings. And so first and foremost we might say that the reading discloses a God who renovates the human subject into future service, animating and anointing the prophet into a proclamation of the Good News of restoration to others, "to bring glad tidings to the poor, / to heal the brokenhearted, / to proclaim liberty to the captives / and release to the prisoners, / to announce a year of favor from the LORD / and a day of vindication by our God." It is this text in particular, of course, that Jesus lays claim to in Luke 4:16-21, when he begins his Galilean ministry at the synagogue at Nazareth. Jesus echoes God's plan for a new restoration by proclaiming Isaiah's oracle that becomes fulfilled in their hearing.

The **Gospel** for this Sunday gives us a slice from one squarely in the Isaiah prophetic line as well. Indeed, the passage from John is precisely about prophetic identity and vocation, as the priests and religious leaders come to grill the Baptist about who he is: the Christ? Elijah? A prophet (Isaiah)? All of these have some reason to account themselves as charged into mission from God. Interestingly enough, the Baptist identifies himself with (Second) Isaiah by quoting him not, however, as the anointed one but as *"the voice of one crying out in the desert"* (cf. Isa 40:3). In a sense, it would seem that all we need to know about John is that he is the voice, the one who baptizes with water, the one who makes straight the way of the Lord, the one who says, "I am not the Christ." Paradoxically, John's voice, far from bringing him into the **Gospel** as a major character in a drama, gradually disappears like an echo in a vast cavern. Only the voice and its memory remains, the backbone of proclamation. From a narrative perspective, John the Baptist will diminish as Jesus arrives on the scene; even his disciples (one of whom was Andrew, Simon Peter's brother) followed Jesus along the way. Ultimately, the **Gospel** underlines the role of the prophet as a self-effacing witness for the Lord, a model for discipleship.

The humility of the disciple as prophet modeled on John's witness allows the voice of the Lord—indeed the actions of the Lord—to be fulfilled in the hearing of all who will hear with the ears of faith. As Paul tells the Thessalonians, "The one who calls you is faithful, / and he will also accomplish it." Paul can tell this community to rejoice and pray always without ceasing and "[i]n all circumstances give thanks, / for this is the will of God for you in Christ Jesus." If we follow the Baptist's lead, we simply allow the faithful God to accomplish what he wills as we consent to what will be made manifest. We all will become self-effacing, prophetic witnesses to the manifestation of God in Christ.

Connecting the Bible and the Liturgy

On this Gaudete Sunday, the church aspires to be one with the prophet Isaiah who rejoices "heartily in the LORD, / in my God is the joy of my soul." This interior disposition of ecstatic wonder voiced by the prophet is the result of thanksgiving for his vocation; he has been anointed and sent to "announce a year of favor from the LORD." In a similar way, the baptized assembly exalts at their own anointing; they are the more elated because their salvation has come within arm's length. Still, the community of love asks for the grace "to attain the joys of so great a salvation" and "with solemn worship and glad rejoicing" (**Collect**). While seizing on the joy of the season of Advent and the apprehension of the coming of the Lord that is so very near, the Christian assembly accounts for its own distinct vocation as baptized members of the Body of Christ. To this end, the congregation is asking for a deepened awareness of the joy, *ut valeamus ad tantae salutis gaudia prevenire*—to be enabled "to attain the joys of so great a salvation." This desire for *gaudium* can only occur if such joy is deepened in the present moment; that is the reason for Gaudete Sunday, an anticipation of the solemnity ahead. We celebrate now *"ad festa ventura nos praeparent"* and "prepare us for the coming feasts" (**Prayer after Communion**). I see this joy leading into joy as nothing less than the approach of the interior contemplation of the call of the anointed. In a real sense, then, the Collect is preparing the assembly for the close proximity of the solemnity of the Lord's nativity, but also beckons those who worship to understand the interior impact the feast claims on the baptized anointed in Christ.

There is an important theological understanding that ought to be underlined, especially on Gaudete Sunday: Christ has already come in the flesh. We are not awaiting an event that has yet to occur, but celebrating and shouting "gaudete" because we have already been clothed in baptism. **Preface II of Advent** echoes this important liturgical and theological reality when it acknowledges John the Baptist's role of proclaiming Christ's presence when he came in history and therefore "[i]t is by this gift that we already rejoice at the mystery of his Nativity, so that he may find us watchful in prayer and exultant in his praise." It is our very gift in Christ that, to echo Paul, enables us to "[r]ejoice always" and to "[p]ray without ceasing. / In all circumstances give thanks."

Strategy for Preaching

In my years of teaching homiletics to Roman Catholic seminarians (and I think I can speak for my colleagues in the same profession), it is a rare instance when a student says that he first felt called to ministry by preaching the Gospel. That tends to be untrue for those called to other religious confessions, where the call to preach is often the first spur to move a candidate on to ministerial life. "Preaching comes with priesthood" is often the most common refrain heard in classes on Foundational Homiletics. Soon enough seminarians will hear the *Rite of Ordination* tell them that preaching the Gospel is the first duty of the priest. The ministry of preaching is clearly an anointing accomplished by the Holy Spirit for the sake of the universal church, a gift at ordination that bestows on the candidate the grace of proclamation as a primary vocation. We need look no further than Isaiah 61:1ff. and Jesus' appropriation of that moment in the life of the prophet in Luke 4:16ff.

Even more intensely than last week, the readings for Gaudete Sunday compel the preacher to access the gift of the vocation of proclaiming the Word. First and foremost this Sunday, then, the preacher's witness ought to be filled with rejoicing, a voice like the Baptist announcing that the Lord is very near at hand. How near? This question gets to the heart (literally) of the theological and liturgical understandings for the Sunday. The core homiletic idea, then, could be: if we think the Lord is near, he is closer to us than we might imagine. Here are some general categories that might serve as something of an outline for constructing a homily.

I. The Word has already given us the promise announced by prophetic witness through Isaiah and John the Baptist. Together with the church, we acknowledge the God who has already entered history and our lives in baptism.

II. And so like Mary, the church is already pregnant with anticipation and senses Christ's presence deep within her (Responsorial Psalm—*Magnificat*). This is a love beyond all telling that awaits only further joy (Preface II of Advent).

A. The Eucharist deepens our joy of anticipating the nearness of Christ.

III. Therefore the nearness of Christ can already be sensed at this very moment in the celebration of Gaudete Sunday (Preface II of Advent), and so we "pray always" and continually "give thanks" celebrating our anointing as children of God, called to announce a year of favor from the Lord, with the whole church as the Body of Christ.

Fourth Sunday of Advent

Readings from the Ambo

2 Sam 7:1-5, 8b-12, 14a, 16; Ps 89:2-3, 4-5, 27, 29;
Rom 16:25-27; Luke 1:26-38

The **First Reading** spotlights King David, that one-of-a-kind monarch, now at the height of his powers. We catch him here having just made Jerusalem his capital and defeating the Philistines. What could be left to do? There is one thing that remains: the Davidic dynasty. We might recall that God's subjugation of a monarchical procession of generations to follow Saul angered that first king. But by contrast, the dynastic house seems less of a concern to David than building a dwelling for the ark, the presence of God, before which David danced when it was brought into the city of Jerusalem. In a marvelous reversal, God tells the prophet Nathan that God will build David a house, "And when your time comes and you rest with your ancestors, / I will raise up your heir after you, sprung from your loins . . . Your house and your kingdom shall endure forever before me; / your throne shall stand firm forever."

It is hard to resist the obvious entanglements God had established with King David. Although the Lord had originally disapproved of an Israelite monarchy, he reluctantly allowed Samuel to choose Saul, who was subsequently rejected. David, despite his obvious shortcomings and sins, harbors a single-minded devotion to God throughout the texts concerning him in the Hebrew Scriptures. And it is God's love for David (that is clearly reciprocated by the king's desire to build a house for the ark) which, like the promise given to Abraham, contains the power of generativity and continuance. From a Christian perspective, the "throne" that "stand[s] firm forever" is the line that will bring forth the Savior, Jesus Christ, who will be housed in the womb of the virgin.

The **Gospel** echoes the covenant God made to David and is clearly made a companion piece to the **First Reading** in this regard. Indeed the angel's reference point in the annunciation to Mary is precisely that the Lord God will give the Son she is to bear the throne of David, and he will rule over the house of Jacob forever. That Christ's kingdom will not end is yet another covenant, a new one that will be established when the true King comes sitting on his royal throne. That new kingdom will be established at the price of the King's blood. But for the moment, the angel only tells the virgin what she can bear—quite literally—that the child to be born will come from God as an enduring sign of the divine remembrance and salvation from a House he established long ago with David. Mary is to be the new house that initiates a lasting covenant. A bit later in Luke's **Gospel**, Mary's Magnificat will echo the gratitude of her entire people at the house of her cousin, Elizabeth.

The **Second Reading** gives us a perspective on the passage from 2 Samuel and Luke. These are the stunning closing words of Paul to the Romans, often referred to as a benediction or final doxology. Paul is able to see the grace unfolding in the context of salvation history, the "revelation of the mystery kept secret for long ages / but now manifested through the prophetic writings." At the same time, this mystery of God's manifestation is not kept silent in any human dwelling place, but "according to the command of the eternal God, / made known to all nations to bring about the obedience of faith." This is Paul's mission: to make known the message not only to David's house but to the Gentiles and, to echo a major theme in the Letter to the Romans, to allow that revelation to become actualized by the obedience of faith. This faith will find a home in God's house.

Connecting the Bible and the Liturgy

The **Entrance Antiphon** is taken from Isaiah 45:8, which will be familiar to some as a famous chant melody for the season, *Rorate Caeli*: "Drop down dew from above, you heavens, / and let the clouds rain down the Just One; / let the earth be opened and bring forth a Savior." In poetic ways, the passage from Isaiah forms a congregational response for the Lukan Gospel text of the Annunciation. Once we hear the news that the Savior will come to be born of Mary, she becomes the earth waiting to bud forth the Just One, the earth longing to receive heavenly dew from above. Additionally, there is something quite urgent about the hope for the Just One. In a parallel way, in the **Collect** the congregation begs the Lord for grace: "Pour forth, we beseech you, O Lord, / your grace into our hearts." This is the earnest prayer of the church responding to the Angelus, of course, asking "that we, to whom the Incarnation of Christ your Son / was made known by the message of an Angel, may by his Passion and Cross / be brought to the glory of his Resurrection." The petition is as familiar as it is economical in its expression of what is to be the blossoming of salvation history. Interestingly, the text keeps before our eyes the purpose, ultimately speaking, of the upcoming nativity of the Lord (something that Mary was not told at the annunciation): our redemption will occur through the passion and the cross, yielding to the glory of the resurrection.

There is something very future-oriented about this Fourth Sunday of Advent, perhaps expectedly so. David is promised a house as a dynasty that will endure. Paul contemplates for the Romans "the revelation of the mystery kept secret for long ages, / but now manifested." The angel Gabriel announces that Mary's Son "will rule over the house of Jacob forever, / and of his kingdom there will be no end." The liturgy directs the assembly to look to the heavens, the locus of the *Rorate Caeli*—open up heavens! We await the Just One. The Fourth Sunday of Advent is not a countdown to Christmas but a journey into the expectation of the Savior. Christmas only makes sense when we recognize that this nativity is coterminous with the birth of the Just One who will rule forever and free his people from their sins. If there is one emotion that sums up the church's attitude this day, that feeling is holy desire, a longing for the Promised One. So the **Prayer after Communion** says that "as the feast day of our salvation draws ever nearer, / so we may press forward all the more eagerly / to the worthy celebration of the mystery of your Son's Nativity." It is the longing for our redemption that compels the church forward.

Strategy for Preaching

At this very busy time of year, it is often possible for Catholic grammar schools and other Christian religious organizations to have something like "Keep Christ in Christmas" art contests. The tactic here is to get the participants to fashion artwork of various kinds—posters, watercolors, oils, sculpture—that centers on the real meaning of Christmas, which is often snowed under by plastic Santas, eight tinseled tiny reindeer, and department stores that have held red-tag sales and had tacky, trashy ornaments out since September.

Remembering the Lord's gift to us this season is absolutely crucial and worthy of intense catechesis during all of Advent. But the greater gift is recognizing that God has remembered us in Christ. This divine recollection becomes the centerpiece to the mystery of the incarnation and Mary's heart-felt proclamation in the *Magnificat*. God has entered history for the purpose of our redemption, where he will live as a human being and will die and be raised up. All three readings focus on the astonishing way that God has intervened in our history: building a house, a dynasty for David, and finally crowning that lineage with Christ, the Son of God and Savior and true King. The mystery once kept secret has now been revealed to the nations.

The **Responsorial Psalm** says it all: "Forever I will sing the goodness of the Lord." This refrain captures not only our response to God's wonders, in the Incarnate Word, but also the resounding echo of Mary's responding to that same divine intervention. "He has helped Israel his servant, / remembering his mercy, / according to his promise to our fathers, / to Abraham and to his descendants forever" (Luke 1:54-55, NAB). So the core homiletic idea could be rooted in the preacher's own witness of a response not unlike the psalmist and Mary: "Forever I will sing the goodness of the Lord." In order to create narrative tension, though, this idea and its biblical and theological support will have to be the climax of the homily and not its starting point. Indeed, the Annunciation itself is filled with this tension, a mystery about who the angel is, what the message could be, and what the consequences are.

A possible structure will begin with ways that we are distant from seeing God's goodness (i.e., the secular Christmas drowns out our listening to the Word). But the turning point in recognizing Christ is near comes in the liturgy and Scripture that remind us of the hope we have in God (all the readings, the **Entrance Antiphon** and the **Collect** testify to God's intervention in the incarnation). Therefore, we can only respond in the wonder of God's goodness. This last movement in the text should be highly visual and particular, like a child captured in surprise at the sight of new snow; it should instill a longing for the heavens to be opened to pour forth the Christ (Entrance Antiphon, the Collect).

# CHRISTMAS TIME

The Nativity of the Lord
The Mass during the Day

Readings from the Ambo

Isa 52:7-10; Ps 98:1, 2-3, 3-4, 5-6; Heb 1:1-6; John 1:1-18

The majestic Prologue of John's Gospel echoes the beginning of the book of Genesis insofar as we are witnessing a new world come into being. The presence of the Word from the dawn of creation has been made flesh and "made his dwelling among us." The incarnation becomes the mystery in which we celebrate God pitching his tent among us at our rather untidy human campground. The legacy of that sacred canopy stretches all the way back to the Ark of the Covenant, the place where the Law made its home. Now, the fulfillment of the Law has come to make his own dwelling, not to live apart, enshrined in a separate place, but among human beings. This is indeed the Light, begotten and not made, but not one who is unapproachable; he has come to illuminate all things because he himself is the reflection of the Holy.

The role of proclamation finds a strong emphasis with the **Gospel's** account of the testimony of John the Baptist. That witness appears to be especially crucial because John came to testify to the light, "[t]he true light, which enlightens everyone." The whole play of light and darkness in the Prologue gives the reality of the Incarnate word a cosmic feel. So then John the Baptist appears to have knowledge of the transcendent nature of the word. "The one who is coming after me ranks ahead of me / because he existed before me."

Along with the passage from Isaiah in the **First Reading**, the **Gospel** sets the tone of the power of witness; it will be the hallmark of the Baptist and Christ himself to testify to the truth of God. John will testify to the light of truth, but the Light will give testimony to the source of light, from whom all things came into being. In a way, Isaiah's words are equally applicable to John or Jesus: "How beautiful upon the mountains / are the feet of him who brings glad tidings, / announcing peace, bearing good news, / announcing salvation, and saying to Zion, / 'Your God is King!' " In some sense, it may be that we are to see the restoration of humanity communicated by the voice of proclamation, by virtue of the Prince of Peace who brings glad tidings. This day is about the message and the Messenger. The **Gospel** at midnight carried the message of the Gloria by angels; today we can see John the Baptist announcing the coming restoration because he testified to the light.

The Letter to the Hebrews sees the restoration through the lens of salvation history, particularly in the legacy of the Judaic prophetic tradition. From the perspective of the author, God is the voice speaking first through the prophets, but "in these last days, he has spoken to us through the Son." Again, we hear of the one "who brings glad tidings." I think we should read "these last days" as the interpretation of the definitive word of proclamation or expression of God's Almighty Word, whom he has made "heir of all things" and is "the refulgence of his glory." There is an echo of John the Baptist's statement that "he existed before me" in the Letter to the Hebrews, a reminder that the Son is the *apaugasma*, or brightness, or (even better) *reflection* of his glory, the "very imprint" (*charakter*) of God's being. The One who existed from the beginning has now come in our days to proclaim and to be proclaimed.

Connecting the Bible and the Liturgy

Preface II of the Nativity of the Lord captures the intense, high christological tones in the readings for Christmas Day: "For on the feast of this awe-filled mystery, / though invisible in his own divine nature, / he has appeared visibly in ours." The language here highlights Christ as Son, who is the brilliant "refulgence of [God's] glory." The Word made flesh is set before the congregation this morning, "begotten before all ages, / he has begun to exist in time; / so that, raising up in himself all that was cast down, / he might restore unity to all creation / and call straying humanity back to the heavenly Kingdom."

In celebrating the Mass during the Day, the nativity has a different sort of character than the Mass at Midnight, an impression created by the biblical texts, the liturgical prayers, and indeed, the very environment of worship itself. It is as if the church is not reflecting on the unfathomable theological moment that has already been celebrated just that early morning. This is a pondering of the gift that has not been unwrapped and so, like the Letter to the Hebrews, the **Collect** also praises the God who "created the dignity of human nature / and still more wonderfully restored it." It may be too obvious a point to even mention, but this is the Mass during the *Day*, after all; it sheds clear light on the mystery of the incarnation so that "all the ends of the earth will behold / the salvation of our God."

An interesting expression for Christmas is used in the **Prayer over the Offerings** when it says that God "manifested the reconciliation / that makes us wholly pleasing in your sight." The Letter to the Hebrews hints at the same kind of reconciliatory power when it speaks of the "purification of sins." This is obviously the language of sanctification and atonement, so prominent in Hebrews. That we should hear this on the Nativity suggests that what we see transpiring at this liturgy will set in motion a course for salvation history. Yes, the incarnation has a trajectory: the cross and resurrection. In a sense, the nativity of the Lord can never be isolated from salvation history because the entrance of God into human history is the pivot that initiates the rest of God's saving action. To return to the **Collect** in this regard: God "wonderfully created the dignity of human nature / and still more wonderfully restored it."

Strategy for Preaching

Ideally speaking, it is clear that there should be two separate preaching events for the Mass at Midnight and the Mass during the Day. The Scriptures and the liturgical texts set the preacher and the hearer on separate courses, which, admittedly, arrive at the same station. The strategic action taken in the **Gospel** proclaimed at midnight matches the character of the liturgy for a people gathering from a cold dark night into the warmth of the church community gathered at the crib of the Messiah, together with Mary and Joseph. By contrast, the Mass during the Day is filled with light, quite literally: it is a theological and mystical reflection pondering the incarnation, the content of which could not be held until the broad daylight in all its radiance cast its knowing glow upon the church, now in possession of its Incarnate Word.

It is important to give the Mass during the Day its due—and indeed, to exegete this particular assembly as quite different from the one that gathered in the middle of the night. To this end, the homily ought to engage the hearers in something like "a moment to catch one's breath," or a chance to gain a theological or catechetical perspective on the incarnation. The very proclamation of the beginning of John's Gospel suggests that this is a chance to reflect, like the Evangelist himself, upon the reality of the gift God has bestowed on his people.

The homiletic core idea could be that this solemnity celebrates an eternal God made visible and human for our sake so that we might become children of the eternal kingdom. This may sound like a huge theological task on Christmas morning, but the structure for such a homiletic core or focus is already in place in **Preface II of the Nativity of the Lord**, which, together with some judicious editing, allows for a cohesive structure to emerge.

I. God has appeared in our history, though he is outside of time.
   A. John's Prologue.
   B. Consider the limits of space and God beyond that (illustration: a planetarium).

II. Yet God took on the limits of human flesh and "has begun to exist in time."
   A. Letter to the Hebrews.
   B. *Catechism of the Catholic Church* (various sections on the incarnation).
   C. *Philippians Hymn.*
   D. Creed: "the Word became flesh" (we genuflect as a sign that everything has changed at that moment because God has entered into human history; there is a new thing on the earth).

III. God accomplished this for the sake of our redemption so that we might become one with each other and partake of his kingdom.
   A. This is the love that cannot be silent, which both Isaiah and John the Baptist spoke as heralds of the Good News.

B. Our redemption is born today, carried by the feet of one who is beautiful on the mountain.

C. That is the very mountain that God asks us to climb so that we might be led into the kingdom.

Holy Family of Jesus, Mary, and Joseph

Readings from the Ambo

Gen 15:1-6; 21:1-3; Ps 105:1-2, 3-4, 5-6, 8-9;
Heb 11:8, 11-12, 17-19; Luke 2:22-40

Chapter 15 from the book of Genesis marks a seminal moment for the Judeo-Christian community, disclosing God's promise of fecundity to Abraham and Sarah and their descendants, making them as numerous as the stars in the sky. This vision of the Lord to Abraham returns to the call first made to the patriarch in chapter 12, when God said that he would make of him a "great nation." Once again, Abraham has to place his trust in the Lord, even as he left his fatherland and his strange domestic gods in order to follow this one lone Deity calling out to him in love. It is this very moment of relationship that grounds Abraham in faith, which is credited to him "as an act of righteousness."

It is hard to imagine this in our own day, but childlessness in antiquity was a curse, a sign that divine favor had surely been evacuated from the lives of those who were condemned to spend their lives without hope of an heir. So the promise to Abraham is, for good reason, considered a "blessing." But more than that, God has disclosed himself as the one who breaks into human history by means of everyday human intercourse. In this regard, the family becomes the mediator of the wonderful works of God, the sign that God continues to do a new thing. As we move into chapter 21 of Genesis in this lectionary selection, it is clear that God has fulfilled his promise to Abraham and Sarah. "The LORD took note of Sarah as he had said he would; / he did for her as he had promised." That the Promise Keeper demonstrates his love also discloses God's act of righteousness as well as Abraham's. As the **Responsorial Psalm** says, "The Lord remembers his covenant forever." If we are credited as righteous, it is only because we are *imago Dei*. As the Letter to the Hebrews reminds us, Abraham's act of faith brought about a renewal by the God who raises us to new life. So when the time came for Abraham to put his full trust in God once again when asked to offer his only son (thereby seeming to negate the very promise of chaps. 12 and 15), "[h]e reasoned that God was able to raise even from the dead, / and he received Isaac back as a symbol."

That God works in our ordinary history to do great things becomes apparent in the account of Jesus' birth and, as reflected in today's **Gospel**, the Presentation in the Temple in Luke. This child who was born of a woman would become "the fall and rise of many in Israel." This is the beginning of the new generation into which God has once again inserted himself, this time definitively in his own person. This is the generation that will truly regard itself as a blessing.

Connecting the Bible and the Liturgy

The **Collect** for this feast offers us some interesting issues to ponder, when, in regard to the Holy Family, it asks that God "graciously grant that we may imitate them / in practicing the virtues of family life and in the bonds of charity, / and so, in the joy of your house, / delight one day in eternal rewards." The locus of sacred domesticity, of the Christian family, is God's house, and we imitate the Holy Family insofar as we draw together in love as brother and sister in Christ. To this end, there is a *letitia domus tua* that gives an exuberating feeling to all true worship. This Latin word *letitia*, which the *Missal* translates as "joy," carries with it a sense of abundance, which, in its richness, threatens to burst the bounds of the house itself. It seems that the liturgy positions us at this moment much like Abraham and his descendants—blessed with innumerable progeny and family. As we are united with one another in the One Bread and the One Chalice, we come together in love, using the Holy Family as our model. As the **Prayer after Communion** reminds the faithful, "Bring those you refresh with this heavenly Sacrament, / most merciful Father, / to imitate constantly the example of the Holy Family, / so that, after the trials of this world, / we may share their company for ever."

There is yet another way in which the Christian community finds itself in the joy of God's house: as part of a Holy Family, or Holy Dynasty, which began with the incarnation. We trace our family tree to the Holy Family because in them God initiated a new cycle of humanity, where the long reign of sin would be ended. Christians who reckon themselves from this tree long to be free from the fateful tree from which our first parents plundered. In this New Dynasty established by God through the righteousness of Christ, we have become partakers of another family system, born of water and blood on the cross. **Preface III of the Nativity of the Lord** looks back in gratitude to the roots of the Christian family when it says that "For through him the holy exchange that restores our life / has shone forth today in splendor: / when our frailty is assumed by your Word / not only does human mortality receive unending honor / but by this wondrous union we, too, are made eternal."

Strategy for Preaching

For years, the Holy Family has been the subject of endless pious sermons about aspiring to become nice Christian families. But surely this feast is more than an ideal domestic establishment. Without doubt, the family unit is to be treasured and honored, but the Scriptures point us in the direction of God's activity within the generations of humankind to break the cycle of shame (Abraham) and then reestablish a family born of a virgin who was free from the taint of original sin. This is a feast of the Lord, not about our attempts to become a virtuous family unit, as admirable as that may be in other contexts. Anything we do shrinks by comparison with God's activity in history. So the core homiletic idea for today might be that even in the midst of our shame and sin, God has promised us a new generation, knit together by Christ as head of our family of believers.

God works out our salvation in the midst of generations of humanity, often subverting "the mighty from their thrones," to paraphrase Mary's *Magnificat*. Isabel Allende's splendid novel, *The House of the Spirits* (1982) is the portrait of a family saga, dominated by an oppressive and repressive *patrón*. But in the course of his long life, he sees his wife, sons, and daughters usher in a new reality, one of imagination and magic and freedom. The novel is meant to be a critique of the Pinochet legacy in Chile and how that regime—and all tyrannical systems—might be subverted. Healing comes in the course of generations—not without pain—as it did for those who remembered God's promises in the Bible.

We might consider a homily that helps the congregation to understand the newness of God's restoration of generations in Christ. The **Collect** suggests that it is in the liturgy where we might find a new Holy Family, while **Preface III for the Nativity** further validates the Incarnate presence among us as an historical reality. The Christian community is the Holy Family with Christ as the Head, even as he himself is subjected to the Law, with Simeon as a witness. God speaks to us now in his Son.

Solemnity of Mary, the Holy Mother of God (Years ABC)

Readings from the Ambo

Num 6:22-27; Ps 67:2-3, 5, 6, 8; Gal 4:4-7; Luke 2:16-21

The choice gleaned from the book of Numbers occurs at the end of a section in that book dealing with the Nazirites, particularly the laws governing Naziriteship, the most familiar of which to us is Samson's promise to not cut his hair. But the benediction at the end of chapter 6 seems fairly unconnected to the rest of the text and functions something like a coda just before a description of the leaders' offerings commences in chapter 7. In a certain sense, the prayer of blessing is not so much an instruction on proper behavior (contrasting with the specific ones that we have been seeing in the instructions to the Nazirites) than it is God's own promise for a benediction when his name is invoked. Here, we might recall the importance of the name in ancient Israel, particularly how YHWH, or the Lord, was so transcendent and wholly other that this "G-d" could not be represented, and then only obliquely in an unutterable, unpronounceable symbol. As far as antiquity is concerned, knowledge of the divine name implies ownership and control. This episode recorded in the **First Reading** is an interesting development when the life of Moses is examined from our own horizon. Indeed, when Moses first encountered the Lord on Mount Horeb in chapter 3 of the book of Exodus, God told Moses that he would not give him his name (*shem*) in a parlance of what is really the Semitic equivalent to "It's none of your business." In the current passage, though, the Lord is telling Moses that the priestly lineage connected with Aaron (and Moses himself, also traditionally reckoned as a Levite) has access to the name, suggesting the sacred character of the Levitical priesthood (cf. Exod 28:1) and its zeal for God. Additionally, God's granting access to his name for the purpose of a blessing guarantees a future cultic legacy for Israel in its covenant with the Lord. We might speculate that this movement on God's part to grant Moses and Aaron a certain amount of ownership when it comes to invoking the Lord's name suggests a divine willingness to enter even more deeply into a covenant of love with his people.

That sacred bond becomes definitively expressed in the incarnation, a promise that is sealed with the name Jesus. The Gospel of Luke here recollects "the name given him by the angel / before he was conceived in the womb." The circumcision of the child itself resonates with Israel's covenant with God and so plunges into our humanity at its deepest level by taking on flesh and being subject to the law of Moses. Mary is the witness of all of these things, "reflecting on them in her heart," and so, in some sense, she is the holder of memory of the sacred pact precisely because of her own motherhood. The name given by the angel at the annunciation was whispered to her at the most intimate of maternal moments, a mystery she alone would hold claim. Undoubtedly, in this early reference to the Mother of God, Paul's letter to the Galatians ratifies the maternity of Mary in the **Second Reading**, when he recalls God's pact with humanity and its ripening through the very act of birth: *"genomenon ek gunaikos, genomenon upo nomon,"* or "born of a woman, born under the law." Furthermore, the connection with the Christian community is clearly evident, since we have received the Spirit of God's Son in our hearts, "Crying out, 'Abba, Father!' " Thus Mary makes possible our own adoption as God's children, "an heir, through God," even as the church initiates its own children into the maternal womb of baptism.

Connecting the Bible and the Liturgy

The **Preface I of the Blessed Virgin Mary** that is to be used on the Feast of the Mother of God is a bit more biblical (and darker) in its references than the previous translation. *The Roman Missal* uses a more direct reference to the annunciation with "the overshadowing of the Holy Spirit," which reflects Luke's use of the verb *episkiazo*, meaning to cast a shadow upon. The emphasis clearly suggests a potential heavy burden, possibly hinting at Mary's future contemplation of these mysteries in her heart, or the passion of the

Lord, which the angel Gabriel fails to mention. The *Sacramentary* used the expression "the power of the Holy Spirit," also present in Luke, but that rendering lacks the haunting encumbrance implied by the Spirit's power "to overshadow." Moreover, the new translation of the Preface demonstrates, in miniature, Mary's role as mother and an instrument of the incarnation: "For by the overshadowing of the Holy Spirit she conceived your Only Begotten Son, and without losing the glory of virginity, brought forth into the world the eternal Light, Jesus Christ our Lord." The singing of the Preface places the celebrant and the congregation in the same arena as the shepherds, who are also witnesses to the Christ-event; all return "glorifying and praising God." Therefore the Preface underlines the praise and thanksgiving of the eucharistic assembly in a very powerful way by invoking the unseen witnesses to the nativity, the heavenly hosts. "Through him the Angels praise your majesty, Dominions adore and Powers tremble before you. Heaven and the Virtues of heaven and the blessed Seraphim worship together with exultation." These are the same vocal instruments of praise, the angels and shepherds, who at the birth of Jesus in Luke 2:1-15, some lines earlier than the **Gospel** for this Sunday, became the first evangelists with "Glory to God in the highest and on earth peace to those on whom his favor rests." **The Prayer after Communion** emphasizes the congregational response in praise and exaltation when it says that "we rejoice to proclaim the blessed ever-Virgin Mary Mother of your Son and mother of the Church." This praise is proclaimed not as a slave crying out to its master, but as a child by adoption speaking its first words of love, "Abba, Father." The Body of Christ, then, expresses the Spirit of Jesus in its heart in praise with the angels and all the heavenly hosts. On the Octave of Christmas, we are onlookers and witnesses of the Son, "born of a woman, born under the law" for the sake of our salvation, which made us children of the living God. That is the New and Eternal Covenant that allows us to call upon God by name, "Abba, Father!" and made possible by the Mother of God.

Strategy for Preaching

This feast figures within a range of Marian celebrations, but its position in the Christmas season guarantees it special prominence. In this celebration of the Christmas Octave, the eucharistic assembly has come prepared and visually catechized to ponder these things in their hearts. Images of Mary as Mother abound during the Christmas season on postage stamps, Christmas cards, and in mangers large and small. The Mother of God remains without doubt the most represented face in Western art, with the exception of Jesus himself. The reason for this extraordinary phenomenon may well be that the sharing of divine life has reached into the most basic and essential aspect of humanity: motherhood. It may be too obvious to point out, but everyone in the congregation will be touched in some way by a maternal relationship. This most common of experiences draws the assembly intrepidly close to this solemnity. The question for the preacher is how to lend this most sacred image a new life and meaning.

The day is marked also by the secular calendar, which is one of the few times that the liturgical season is underlined by a popular cultural event. Millions of people have celebrated the New Year, and the preacher should work this reality into the homiletic arc as a way of unfolding the praise and thanksgiving before us in contemplating the motherhood of God. Indeed, a core homiletic idea could focus on the new life that greets us always as a grace, always in mystery, always in blessing. These three areas could be unpacked as we see them marvelously disclosed in the Christmas season: the grace of God's intervention in history, which granted to Mary, as it does to us, an opportunity to cooperate with God's will, even under potentially difficult circumstances; the mystery of understanding that gift (maybe something like a single mother trying to deal with the difficulties of raising a child alone); and the blessing that may lie underneath whatever God places before us, a blessing because even in the most trying of circumstances God has whispered his name to us in the darkness and is with us in the presence of his Son.

The congregation should leave the Eucharist with a sense of God's continued activity in their lives, something that they share with the Mother of God herself. This is grace in action. As the mystery of the incarnation expresses itself in the **Prayer over the Offerings**, "grant to us, who find joy in the Solemnity of the holy Mother of God, that, just as we glory in the beginnings of your grace, so one day we may rejoice in its completion."

Second Sunday after the Nativity
(Years ABC)

Readings from the Ambo

Sir 24:1-2, 8-12; Ps 147:12-13, 14-15, 19-20 (John 1–4);
Eph 1:3-6, 15-18; John 1:1-18

The magnificent beginning of chapter 24 in the book of Sirach sets the tone for this Sunday, which is one of awestruck wonder at the power of God. Psalm 147 is a festive response to the celebration of Wisdom, the mysterious presence at God's right hand. The author's exultation of the Wisdom tradition in Israel and its relationship with God reflects the overall concern of Ben Sira in developing a school of thought to wean the Hellenistic Jews away from their Greek neighbors and their growing influence on God's chosen people in the Near Eastern world. In a certain sense, the personification of *Sophia* as a kind of companion to the Most High suggests the intimate relationship that the transcendent Hebrew God has with the depths of wisdom. That chaste companionship stands in sharp contrast to the mischievous and carnal behavior of the Greek gods. The passage we have here should be read in the larger context of chapter 24 in order to grasp the full force of Wisdom's place as a ubiquitous, abiding presence who announces that "Before all ages, in the beginning, he created me, / and through all ages I shall not cease to be. / In the holy tent I ministered before him, / and in Zion I fixed my abode."

Christians might read Jesus as the personification of wisdom, with some important differences, which will be clarified in the Prologue of John's **Gospel**. The *Logos* was present (though uncreated) at the dawn of time, collaborating in fashioning creation with the Eternal Father and, though like Wisdom dwelling in highest heaven, became flesh. The Word has made his home with humanity. A haunting line in this regard is in verses 6-7 from the book of Sirach: "Over waves of the sea, over all the land, / over every people and nation I held sway. / Among all these I sought a resting place; / in whose inheritance should I abide?"

If we think of the Prologue to John's **Gospel** as a hymn, its contours become more lucid, its insights more penetrating. Clearly, the language in John allows for a kind of resplendent praise augmenting the creation narrative itself in Genesis, one that is now informed by the Word becoming flesh. In contrast to Ben Sira, John substantiates not ethereal Wisdom, but the Word become Light in the world. Moreover, the presence of the Word engages testimony (from John the Baptist), which then lives among us in proclamation even though "his own people did not accept him." The plea from Paul to the Ephesians, then, is for "a Spirit of wisdom and revelation / resulting in knowledge of him."

Connecting the Bible and the Liturgy

Like the Scriptures, the liturgy for the Second Sunday after the Nativity emphasizes the sublime mystery of the Incarnation and offers the congregation an opportunity to delve into its richness. The **Entrance Antiphon**, even if it is unused in the liturgy itself, is especially evocative for reminding us of the connection between the Eternal Word leaping from heaven's royal throne down to earth at midnight. The **Collect** picks up on the presence of the Eternal Word becoming flesh in our world precisely as light, revealing to the world the glory of God "to all peoples by the radiance" of his "light." But perhaps the most available liturgical language for drawing out the scriptural readings remains any of the three **Prefaces for the Nativity of the Lord**. For instance, **Preface I**, though rather brief, picks up very nicely on the "mystery of the Word made flesh" by echoing John's Prologue and its imagery of light when it says that "a new light of your glory has shone upon the eyes of our mind (*nova mentis nostrae oculis lux tuae claritatis infulsit*), so that, as we recognize in him God made visible, we may be caught up through him in love of things invisible." There are notes here of the recognition (*cognoscimus*) and discernment enlightening the mind, which, we might remember, Paul emphasizes in his letter to the church at Ephesus and a homage to the place of wisdom in gaining understanding. Similarly, **Preface II** emphasizes the Word becoming flesh and dwelling among us and our response "on the feast of this awe-filled mystery." In fact, most of this **Preface** might be considered as a theological commentary on the Christmas event, certainly one that fits neatly as a companion to the Prologue. "Though invisible in his own divine nature, he has appeared visibly in ours; and begotten before all ages, he has begun to exist in time." Yet the Preface does not end there but suggests the work of redemption and, as the Prologue puts it, makes us the recipients of his fullness, "grace in place of grace." Our nature has been thus taken up in Christ, "so that, raising up in himself all that was cast down, he might restore unity to all creation and call straying humanity back to the heavenly Kingdom." This last section, in particular, discloses the mission of the Word made visible, not simply for our edification but for divine reconciliation. Lastly, **Preface III** focuses on "the holy exchange" implied in the Prologue and in Paul's letter to the Ephesians, the latter of which says that this exchange "destined us for adoption to himself through Jesus Christ." The Preface affirms the same since, "when our frail humanity is assumed by your Word not only does human mortality receive unending honor but by this wondrous union we, too, are made eternal," or as Paul might say, we receive "the riches of glory in his inheritance among the holy ones."

Strategy for Preaching

With Christmas having been celebrated only a few days before, the homily on this Second Sunday after that solemnity should focus on a concrete theological expression of the incarnation. Most congregations are really waiting for a more searching interrogation of the mystery of God made flesh. That task is not easy, since all the readings, beautiful as they are, speak rather abstractly about Wisdom and its place before all ages, together with the Word present from the beginning and its appearance among us as Light. Even Paul seems a bit like a systematic theologian at times in the letter to the Ephesians. How can the preacher make the Word made visible really *visible* to the Sunday assembly? Of all days, it would seem that our task as homilists remains, to paraphrase novelist Joseph Conrad out of context, "to make them see."

A combination of catechetical and practical rhetorical strategy is recommended for the homily. A prime resource to keep in mind here and elsewhere is *The Catechism of the Catholic Church* (chapter 2, article 3), which deals with the creedal affirmation: "He was conceived by the power of the Holy Spirit, and born of the Virgin Mary"

(456–83 might be particularly useful in addressing that statement). Now the assembly will not hear a string of quotations strung along without any force or context, but a homiletic core idea could be posing the question simply as "Why did God choose to dwell among us, and how is he re-creating us day by day?" The readings and the liturgy help to fill out this theological query because they are full of images of light, "wisdom sings," "opens her mouth," and ministers before God "in the holy tent." Ironically, John's Prologue seems much removed from the common experience where men and women toil and love, but it is the preacher's responsibility to be what *Fulfilled in Your Hearing* calls, "the mediator of meaning" for the assembly and unfold the Word made visible.

So then the issue to confront is simply this: what does John's Prologue look like? Are there appropriate windows into the text? Yes, undoubtedly. The coming of the Word is like opening the window in a dusty attic on a brilliant spring day, or a sudden yank of some heavy and dusty drapes in a room filled with decay. (A good reference might be the closing chapters of Charles Dickens's *Great Expectations* in which the protagonist, Pip, lets in the sunlight on old Miss Havisham's frightful room, where, with mice as her companions, she has sat for decades with her rotting wedding cake for a day that never came.) The coming of the Word is also like a wonderful secret that was first whispered in the dark but now takes on new life when it is proclaimed. We know the negative side of spreading gossip and rumors, the useless words we throw away every day on our mobile gadgets, but what about good news that travels? This witnessing was what John the Baptist did, even though he was not the Light. His testimony and ours can multiply the presence of the Word among us. The coming of the Word is also like the Word we speak back to God through Christ in the liturgy. This suggestion encourages the assembly to intentionally embrace the language of praise and live inside faith, hope, and love. Since the Preface will soon follow, getting the congregation to listen closely to that text and to own the responses at the **Preface Dialogue** as well as other congregational responses, such as the Mystery of Faith, is an unfailing homiletic tactic that blesses the faithful with the same thoughtful intention contained in the words of Paul: "May the eyes of your hearts be enlightened, that you may know what is the hope that belongs to his call, what are the riches of glory in his inheritance among the holy ones."

The Epiphany of the Lord (Years ABC)

Readings from the Ambo

Isa 60:1-6; Ps 72:1-2, 7-8, 10-11, 12-13;
Eph 3:2-3a, 5-6; Matt 2:1-12

The inspiring selection from the book of the prophet Isaiah to celebrate the solemnity of Christ's manifestation among the nations belongs to the larger frame of Isaiah 56:1–66:24, often referred to as "Third Isaiah." The scholarly community generally dates the text somewhere around 520 BC, marking this section as contemporary with the return of Israel from the Babylonian exile. Generally speaking, Third Isaiah shares some common features with Second Isaiah (some believe the author to be a disciple of his forerunner) and is informed by a somewhat disillusioned reality because the jubilant expectations of Israel have not come to pass. Chapters 56–59 are strikingly strident in their admonitions to Judah after their return from exile in 539 BC, which include warnings about idolatry, false worship, and injustice.

The current passage, however, shows itself to be a bit of an exception to the content and the tone present earlier in Third Isaiah and even includes a promise for rebuilding by foreigners, which is not part of this selection (v. 10). Notable from the first verse is an address to Jerusalem itself and the promise to become the carrier of light. We might mention the importance of the corporate salutation, a feature of community joy and responsibility that will run through all of the readings. Third Isaiah is here paying special attention to the homage of earthly powers to God's kingdom of light: "Nations shall walk by your light, / and kings by your shining radiance," specifically Midian, Ephah, and Sheba, all of them from eastern Arabia. From the point of view of the present solemnity, these tributes from the diverse nations become especially evocative, right down to the bearing of "gold and frankincense" imagined in the Isaiah text, an echo of the gifts of the eastern visitors in Matthew's gospel. These two texts reveal an interesting little intertextual dynamic at work, but the parallel should not be overdrawn. There is more to tell, especially when it comes to the corporate share of responsibility. Where Third Isaiah represented Jerusalem as the splendor of the Lord, that city is implicated in the **Gospel** by resisting the new light in the heavens, together with its king, Herod, who was *"etarachthe kai pasa Ierosoluma met autou"* (greatly troubled / and all Jerusalem with him). I think Matthew is reminding his hearers that corporate opposition has its associations with the remarkable global call of "the wealth of the nations" brought to the poor. Bethlehem of Judea, then, the least of cities, eclipses Jerusalem as the city of light because God has rested beneath the light; it is now the new light of nations and owns a child as its king.

Meanwhile, Paul is at work with his own reversals in his letter to the Ephesians and begins to sketch out what he reads as God's revelation to the Gentiles, a theological insight that will become one of the dominant threads in the unmatched preaching tapestry. This mission to the Gentiles highlights yet another significant color in the Pauline theological weaving: unity in Christ. A few verses earlier, at the end of chapter 2, for instance, Paul speaks of Christ as the cornerstone that holds the whole dwelling together and into which we are all drawn into participation. So Paul sees the Gentiles as "coheirs, members of the same body, / and copartners" and *"sugkleronoma kai sussoma kai summetocha"* in God's unfailing promise in Christ. The call to unity in *sussoma*, the same body, sets up a wider discussion of the unity of the Body in chapter 4 to follow.

Connecting the Bible and the Liturgy

This liturgy occasions a Vigil Mass as well as a Mass during the Day; the readings are the same for both. The solemnity is unusual in that it is well integrated in terms of the symbolic structure present in both Word and sacrament, even in its cultural ambiance. As with the Mass during the Night at Christmas, the Vigil Mass for the Epiphany already presents the Christian community with the natural symbols to be accessed for the solemnity: darkness, light, and, of course, the stars. The texts themselves highlight each other as well. The **Collect** for the vigil implores the "splendor" of the Lord's majesty to "shed its light upon our hearts that we may pass through the shadows of this world and reach the brightness of our eternal home." The coming of the Lord makes this day like a New Jerusalem, where God's light is shining in Christ.

A very interesting (and hard to avoid) parallel exists between the liturgy and the action of the gospel registered in the **Prayer over the Offerings** for both the vigil and the day Masses. "In honor of the appearing of your Only Begotten Son," the presider asks on behalf of the congregation that the Lord accept "the first fruits of the nations" (Vigil). The allusion here is to the corporate body, the nations bringing tributes from afar in Third Isaiah, but also the *ethnoi* in Paul who are now incorporated into one Body, one partnership. The presidential prayer and the gospel fit nicely together here. Along these lines, the **Prayer over the Offerings** in the Mass during the Day transforms this parallel action of the magi and the congregation into a theological statement about the work of Christ: "Look with favor, Lord, we pray, on these gifts of your Church, in which are offered now not gold or frankincense or myrrh, but he who by them is proclaimed, sacrificed and received, Jesus Christ." The sentence structure is a bit awkward here, but the christological moment should not be lost. Christ is the new gift being offered, who in receiving them also proclaims our redemption. The prayer recalls Christ's grace of reconciliation, which fully takes up all gifts preceding it, even as the nations come toward the Light. The **Preface of the Epiphany of the Lord** picks up on this mystery when it says that "when he appeared in our mortal nature, you made us new by the glory of his immortal nature." That "*nova nos immortalitatis eius Gloria reparasti*" of the great exchange between God and humanity reminds us that the Lord is the true giver of gifts, transforming our own.

Strategy for Preaching

With the Solemnity of the Epiphany of the Lord, the readings and liturgical prayers shift the axis of the congregation's worship from contemplation to action. The days after Christmas, including the Solemnity of the Mother of God (as well as the Second Sunday after the Nativity), are continued reflections and deep ponderings of the mystery of the nativity. Now the church has hardly ceased its meditation on the incarnation, but the Scriptures for today bring into focus the implications of God taking on human flesh in a public and, indeed, global way. In this regard, the liturgical pattern from the Nativity to the Epiphany follows Paul's own movement in the Spirit, who tells us that he first received the mystery "by revelation" but has now become a promise to all. The Light that has dawned will not and cannot be encased in darkness. So God's outreach shines even to the ends of the earth, where nations will come streaming. That same light shatters distinctions between Jew and Gentile for Paul.

Preaching on this solemnity, then, has global signification, and its symbols have a very contemporary feel. With our instant communication, our own world is itself becoming more and more like a large village. Moreover, this solemnity's corporate emphasis raises the issue of national boundaries, which God has erased. The social implications of following the gospel become clear from the trek of the magi who "departed for their country by another way." Some, like the magi, may choose to follow the light; others, like "all Jerusalem," may find themselves allied with earthly powers instead of God's kingdom.

A core homiletic idea might consist of challenging the congregation to consider the social realities of God taking on our human flesh. If we are to take the **Preface of the Epiphany of the Lord** at its word, or that we have been made "new by the glory of his immortal nature," then a new star has appeared on our horizon implicating us in God's splendor. Are we willing to see the transformation of our earthly reality into the gift of witness to the incarnation? And if so, what would that testimony look like in the public square? Here, the homily might start to name the contemporary gifts all of us bring to be unwrapped by grace. Needless to say, the more specific we can be in the homiletic text, the better the hearers of the Word will be able to become copartners with the preacher. Some bring gifts of diversity that are golden in their poetic expressions of Hispanic song and praise. Others offer the frankincense of their hard work, after a long day at the accounting firm; they come to offer their time by helping with parish bookkeeping. Still others bring the myrrh of bereavement ministry to their brothers and sisters, by cooking dishes after funerals or spending time with the children of loss. All of these gifts are testimony to the global reach of the incarnate Word into which the Christian faithful have been drawn this season. That witness will have public consequences in and out of the parish. These are specific challenges to ratify the promise God made in Christ, an invitation to enflesh what has already been made Incarnate.

The Baptism of the Lord

Readings from the Ambo

Isa 55:1-11; Isa 12:2-3, 4bcd, 5-6; 1 John 5:1-9;
Mark 1:7-11 (or alternative readings from Year A)

Although the **First Reading** is clearly recognizable as a renewal for those living at the margins of exile—something Second Isaiah has of course celebrated throughout his prophetic ministry—the summons to come to the waters obviously has special meaning around this feast of the Lord's Baptism. As God invites the people of Israel to renew the covenant, the conditions are plain enough: there are no conditions; this is a free and everlasting gift, a bond that will never be broken. Typically, we know that covenants usually involve equals mutually observing a bargain. But Isaiah says that the waters that God pours forth with the Word are completely gratis. "[C]ome, without paying and without cost, / drink wine and milk!" The historical reality behind God's promise to Israel living at the margins is nothing less than a restoration among the nations. The Babylonian captivity that began in 587 BC crushed a nation and shamed Israel in the eyes of other people. This corporate poverty God also intends to raise up: "nations that knew you not shall run to you, / because of the LORD, your God, / the Holy One of Israel, who has glorified you."

From a Christian perspective, the feast of the Lord's Baptism reminds the church that God in Christ has sanctified the waters, taking away our shame and sin, and restoring us to his likeness. We witness this transformation in a manifestation of God during the baptism of Jesus. In a very real sense, Mark's account of Jesus' entering the waters of baptism is an account of Jesus' glorification by the Father with the descent of the Holy Spirit. This Trinitarian moment is a revelation of God's renewal of the covenant with Israel through the one who would renew that divine pledge with his own blood. The new bond that God established in Christ in baptism will endure forever because the Father is "well pleased" or takes great pleasure—*eudokesa*. That Jesus, acknowledged by the Father as the Beloved Son, has established a renewal, yoking us from the exile of sin and into the sanctified world of the children of God, will become clearer as the Gospel of Mark unfolds. Jesus, Beloved, is the faithful witness at the epiphanic moment in the Jordan but will become "Son of God" at the moment of his death on the cross as well.

John addresses the church as the Beloved, which accentuates the connection the Beloved Son has with all of us. Where Christ is the Beloved Son by his own divine nature, we become adopted children in the free gift of baptism and faith. As John puts it, "Everyone who believes that Jesus is the Christ is begotten by God, / and everyone who loves the Father / loves also the one begotten by him." So it is that when we enter into the waters of baptism by faith in Jesus Christ we conquer the world even as he did. This victory over the world as expressed by John seems a bit at odds with the emphasis the Second Vatican Council (particularly *Gaudium et Spes*) places on being in dialogue with the world. In this regard, however, we ought to remember that the Johannine vision is establishing a new world built not on condemnation but on love and faith—that is, the restoration from exile into which belief in Christ has brought us. The true enemy of the human heart is not the world but sin, from which baptism has delivered us. Christ has sanctified the world by his presence, and the waters of baptism have made this a reality for all Christian people. Therefore we can say with Isaiah that we can "draw water joyfully from the springs of salvation."

Connecting the Bible and the Liturgy

The alternative prayer today for the **Collect** nicely gathers the theological spectra for this feast into a single, bright ray: "O God, whose only Begotten Son / has appeared in our very flesh, / grant, we pray, that we may be inwardly transformed / through him whom we recognize as outwardly like ourselves." This Collect prepares the congregation for the transformative encounter with Jesus in the Jordan, the recognition that it is in the baptized that God sees and loves in us what he sees and is well pleased with in his Son. The **Second Reading** comes to mind here as well, since we are made beloved and recognize our gift in Christ when the Father acknowledges that this Son is his pleasure. I wonder if we sense God's own happiness as members of Christ's body in the baptized assembly. In a way, this feast is a celebration of the congregation as a corporate Body of worship, the liturgical assembly doing the work of God and acting in prayer and thanksgiving to the Father. We know the Spirit comes upon us at the very beginning of the Eucharist when the presider says, "The Lord be with you." That is a greeting that asks us to believe that the Spirit has come down upon the assembly like a dove, urging us to have faith in Christ and making us begotten by God. We are born by water and blood, a testimony nowhere more visible than at the Eucharist itself.

The feast of the Baptism of the Lord offers the faithful an opportunity to recommit lives of faith and love. The liturgy, as always, becomes a dynamic dialogue through Christ to the Father and in the Holy Spirit, a singular moment in prayerful worship engaging a Trinitarian moment. Additionally, the **Prayer over the Offerings** reminds us that in the oblation of the faithful we "may be transformed into the sacrifice of him / who willed in his compassion / to wash away the sins of the world." It is Christ's own gift of sanctifying the waters for the church that so clearly expresses itself in the action of the Pascal Mystery and that began to be revealed in the waters of the Jordan: these are the waters that have washed us clean from sin and made us beloved of God. It is telling that the Prayer over the Offerings says that Christ "willed in his compassion / to wash away the sins of the world" (*mundi voluit peccata miseratus abluere*). The difference between Christian baptism and Christ's baptism in the Jordan is that the sinless Jesus is not acted upon but is the actor: he willed to sanctify us, a revelatory statement concerning the Savior's infinite love for all God's children. Surely, the recognition of Christ's love in baptism makes faith in him a matter of love. We obey the commandments of Christ, as the **Second Reading** suggests, out of a response for Christ's love for us—not for fear of punishment. So as Christ enters the waters of the Jordan this day, he shores up our human nature but not our sinful condition: he desires us to be children of God, his brother and sister in the same baptism.

Strategy for Preaching

The homily for this feast cannot emphasize conversion enough, especially when it comes to renewing the baptized assembly in the work of Christ's sanctification. The **Prayer over the Offerings** expresses the intention present in the faithful to be "transformed into the sacrifice of him / who willed in his compassion / to wash away the sins of the world." This portion of the prayer forms a splendid homiletic core idea that might be unfolded for the congregation in a variety of ways.

As an initial consideration, start with the **First Reading** from Second Isaiah that invites everyone to come to the waters without cost. The connection to Christian baptism is hard to miss. Christ's compassion invites us to come out of the exile of our sins (already accomplished for us and given to the faithful in baptism). The reading has a theological connection and is already on its way to a visual image. What does it mean *visually* to be asked to come to the waters without price today? To be given a drink by a stranger on a hot day when we were far from any other resource? Mmm . . . what does that look like?

Second, there is a crucial rejoinder to this first foray into the invitation to come to the waters: we have to *want* to come to those waters and respond to Christ's love. Indeed, we might say that many in the Christian community fall short or fall between the cracks between coming to the waters and the ongoing desire for sanctification. Do we have the intention of living out our baptismal commitment day after day? At this point, the preacher already has an original (visual) image in the first section, and the homily can now continue with this same construction. We would never hesitate to run to quench our thirst on a hot day; our bodies long for that water or else we faint. The same is true for our spiritual life as well: how badly do we long for God, now that we have put on Christ in baptism? At this point, I think an allusion to the Gospel text and the call of the Beloved is appropriate enough, and some catechesis drawn from either the *Catechism of the Catholic Church* or patristic or modern authors can underline the theological point.

Third, we therefore come to this feast of the Baptism of the Lord and every Eucharist sanctified by Christ's saving act and ready to love even more by obeying his teaching. (The **Second Reading** can be deployed to illustrate how obedience to Christ's words connects with love.) As a visual example, we can imagine a child who moves beyond rules of being punished to one who does the right thing for the sake of love of the family.

LENT

First Sunday of Lent

Readings from the Ambo

Gen 9:8-15; Ps 25:4-5, 6-7, 8-9; 1 Pet 3:18-22; Mark 1:12-15

In this First Sunday of Lent, the **First Reading** finds the Christian community very much awash in the familiar story of the Great Flood. As is well known, the account of the flood in Genesis, woven together by the Yahwistic and Priestly traditions, is almost certainly part of a larger Near Eastern culture that also shares a flood narrative history, such as the epic of Gilgamesh and the epic of Atrahasis written in Akkadian. Generally speaking, we might say that from the earliest days of storytelling, there has been some kind of understanding concerning sinful humanity and its transgressions of divine authority. The focus in the Christian tradition, and on this First Sunday of Lent in particular, is what God chooses to do after the flood has subsided. The Yahwistic tradition parts company with the Priestly author at this point, the latter of which reckons a series of three covenants beginning here with Noah, then following with Abraham (Gen 17:1-27), and finally with Israel as a nation at Mount Sinai (Exod 31:12-17).

Clearly, the biblical author wishes the reader to understand that this covenant is first of all initiated by God. Second, it is a promise made to all creation. Third, this covenant is everlasting. That the covenant has been established by God reminds us of the power of this relationship: "never again shall all bodily creatures be destroyed / by the waters of a flood." All creation is sacred. The First book of Peter will use the flood story this Sunday in Genesis as an allegory for baptism, which saves through water rather than kills. Indeed, initiating a long line of patristic readings about those destructive waters in the Hebrew Scriptures, the flood *prefigured* baptism, "which saves." The First Letter of Peter uses covenantal language to describe the work of Christ who suffered for the sins of humanity once and for all, "the righteous for the sake of the unrighteous." We should see 1 Peter itself as a testimony to the rainbow of God's own covenant, a redeeming text: this is God's covenant played out, a witness to Christ's saving all creation from the destructiveness of sin and death.

That covenant is renewed by Jesus who encounters the forces of evil in the desert. Mark's Gospel account of the temptation of the Lord is quite brief compared to the other synoptic writers, Matthew and Luke. And yet Mark's very terseness reveals the boldness of Jesus' action in the desert as he is *"ekballei eis ten eranon,"* or literally pushed out into the desert (after his baptism by the Spirit and tempted). Especially striking is this phrase: "He was among wild beasts." The rawness of the incarnation stares at us directly in the face as Christ must stare down the natural inclinations of the flesh, the wild beasts of our nature. At the same time, though, God is present: *hoi aggeloi diekonoun auto.* The angels coming to minister or serving Jesus presents a nice contrast to those gnarling beasts. We see a mix here of darkness and light, temptation and salvation, injury and its remedy; this is the kind of dialectic that will inform Jesus' Gospel of proclamation and repentance: yes, there is sin in the world, but with repentance and belief in the Good News, this flood of transgression can be taken away. The wild beasts are at our door, but the way into our house has been sealed by divine covenant. This is the coming of the kingdom, now at hand. So it is with this First Sunday of Lent. The Markan Jesus brokers no delay but, obedient to the Spirit, immediately intends to remedy the fallen world with God's promise of redemption.

Connecting the Bible and the Liturgy

Although the **Gospel** for the First Sunday of Lent focuses on the temptation in the desert, the text reminds us of the power of baptism, since Jesus' encounter with Satan occurs immediately after the Savior's own immersion in the waters of the Jordan. With their eyes on the baptismal waters that will cover the church anew at the end of the Lenten season, most parishes will invest this season with the addition of catechumens, living witness of the Pascal mystery unfolding before us. The First Letter of Peter places special emphasis on baptism by connecting the flood account in Genesis with the saving waters of that mystic bath. That New Testament author sees baptism as an appeal to God for living out a clear conscience, through the resurrection of Jesus Christ. The liturgy for today says as much when the **Collect** implores God for the sake of the congregation, "that we may grow in understanding / of the riches hidden in Christ / and by worthy conduct pursue their effects." The appeal asks that *"ad intellegendum Christi proficiamus arcanum"* or continue the ongoing process of growth toward understanding Christ and his hidden treasures; it is an effort for a lifetime of Sundays, but a purposeful act as well—a prayer to realign ourselves with our baptismal commitment. The Collect, then, recognizes our own part in the covenant that God has established through divine promise, renewed by Christ the celebration of which occurs in the Easter Vigil at the end of this holy season.

Similarly gesturing toward congregational conversion, the **Prayer over the Offerings** asks for "the right dispositions . . . to make these offerings." The offerings at the Eucharist, then, becomes an act of will, a site for new beginnings as we participate in Christ's saving work. The urgency for a proper disposition helps set the tone for "this sacred time" and offers an opportunity for the baptized assembly to unite themselves with the catechumens who are preparing for baptism. The right disposition is the gift of grace to strengthen our resolve, often amid the wild beasts of our nature. We also need the "true and living Bread" so that we might "strive to live by every word / which proceeds from [God's] mouth." Although this excerpt from the **Prayer after Communion** is a clever allusion to Matthew's Gospel (4:11), the prayer remains an appropriate one for those who have just received the Eucharist and long to grow in holy charity, service to one another, together with faith and hope.

Fittingly, the **Prayer over the People** (a newly restored addition to the last edition of the *Roman Missal*) reinforces hope, a virtue that all the readings this day emphasize, owing to the gift of God's covenantal renewal in Christ, who, although he clothed himself with our human flesh and faced temptation in the wilderness, remained sinless. We know that we are sinners but ask God's blessing "that hope may grow in tribulation, / virtue be strengthened in temptation, / and eternal redemption be assured." We ask that God's angels come to minister to us in our journey through the desert.

Strategy for Preaching

The First Sunday of Lent is an invitation to see the whole season before us. Preachers should see that all of Lent culminates in the Triduum and the Pascal Mystery; otherwise we miss an important pastoral opportunity. The good news is that the people of God are usually aware of the holy season as a time of preparation and sacrifice, and these attributes are underlined in the readings and in the liturgical prayers throughout. The bad news is that sometimes the beginnings of Lent can be more about what "I am giving up this year" rather than a celebration of God's renewed covenant, our conversion, and the saving work of Christ, whose first steps after baptism encountered the wild beasts of the desert for our sake.

The homiletic core idea might guide the congregation into thinking more broadly about Lent and where they would like to be at the celebration of Easter. This challenge could be both personal and corporate: Are there issues that should be tackled in regard to growth in virtue? As individuals or a parish? What does it mean to recognize God's covenant and renewal for me and my family? The catechumens are the living symbols of those seeking conversion and baptism, and they should be acknowledged as such to the assembly throughout the season of Lent. The catechumens' presence also accentuates the importance of hospitality, the cornerstone of charity. Together, all the members of the congregation will journey toward the mysteries hidden in Christ, the mystery of the community that is his Body, awaiting eagerly the joys of Easter.

The readings are quite vivid, and so the preacher ought to draw from the wealth of the literary and theological insight embedded in these scriptural and liturgical texts. Here is a suggestion for a starting point for a homily.

I. Introduction: One of the most recognizable songs in popular ballads over the last century is recognized by young and old alike: Harold Arlen (music) and E. Y. (Yip) Harburg (lyrics) composed "Over the Rainbow" to express a young girl's wish to leave her troubles behind in Kansas and to find the perfect land beyond the horizon. Dorothy got her wish when she landed in Munchkinland and then journeyed to Oz.

II. But we don't need to search over the rainbow; God has painted
one in the sky for us as a lasting covenant of love for us here
and now.

Consider the tactics operative here: getting right into things with
an appropriate introduction that leads *immediately* into the body of
the homiletic text. Second, note that the first sentence of the body
of the homily is a contrasting point with the introduction, "But we
don't need to search. . . ." Third, this new turn has a definite direction and ample theological and biblical mandates, supported by
the liturgical texts; these should be used as counterbalances to the
introduction: what particular promise has God given us so that we
do not have to go searching "over the rainbow?" (Christ's victory
over sin and death, particularly emphasized in his battle with Satan
in the desert). What does the divine covenant look like? (Image: a
rainbow not only of color but of virtues into which we participate
throughout Lent). Do we have the resolve to carry out this invitation
to covenant? When it comes to a conclusion, the preacher could pick
up on the introduction again, perhaps with a contrasting example of
the mystery hidden in Christ that we discover in our baptism, versus
a child's fantasy to look over the rainbow for the answer.

Second Sunday of Lent

Readings from the Ambo

Gen 22:1-2, 9a, 10-13, 15-18; Ps 116:10, 15, 16-17, 18-19;
Rom 8:31b-34; Mark 9:2-10

Known in the Jewish tradition as the *Akedah* or "binding" of Isaac, the **First Reading** presents the modern hearer of the word with one of the most troubling moral and religious problems in the Hebrew Scriptures: God demanding human sacrifice for the sake of obedience. Early rabbinic midrash responses to this text have sought to explain it on the level of symbol (as the patristics would later on in the Christian era) or even that Abraham got carried away. Contemporary listeners of the Lectionary should, as always, examine the full text of this passage in the Bible as a whole, which is full of rich nuances and implications. That said, we are still left with a text that interpreters have been attempting to explain for centuries on this Second Sunday of Lent. And as if this were not enough, the passage will appear again, of course, during the Easter Vigil. Why would God ask such a thing from Abraham, which is not only wrong and cruel but utterly negates the divine promise making Abraham and his offspring the generators of countless people as numerous as the stars in the heavens?

One of the most fruitful enterprises when encountering any difficult text in the Scriptures is to pay close attention to our initial reaction, which may attempt to domesticate God or seek an alternative motif for this holocaust. Ancient and modern readers have suggested that the story serves to argue against child sacrifice in the ancient world, since a ram was eventually offered in Isaac's place. And yet the Elohist tradition from which this story emerges clearly evinces a history of testing the patriarchs, which, in the end, seems to be the bottom line of the narrative. If we bracket the considerable ethical dimensions of the scene, we might ask how far will Abraham go in order to obey God—even to the extent of obliterating the promise foretold guaranteeing numerous progeny?

We know that the patristic authors were creative in their reading of this passage from Genesis, which became an allegory for God sacrificing his own Son. Isaac, then, is a figure for Christ himself. The subtext, though, suggests the ambiguous role that God plays in acting as both the one who surrenders his son but also demands him in sacrifice. The **Second Reading** participates in a more benign, innocent reading of the *Akedah*, bringing God's sacrifice of his Son into high relief: "He who did not spare his own Son / but handed him over for us all, / how will he not also give us everything else along with him?" The Greek verb used here is *paradidomi*, a word that will become the operative action for the Lord's passion and death, when Jesus is *paredoken*, "handed over" to the religious authorities and the powers seeking his death. In the Pauline corpus, the word is also used when God hands over those who have sinned to the power of their own vices. So Jesus is handed over for our sins to the power of death and other people's sins. For Paul, God's supreme generosity in handing over his Son becomes the theological justification for our acquittal from sin and guilt and will lay the foundation for a doctrine of the atonement for the likes of St. Anselm and St. Thomas Aquinas in later centuries.

The paternal relationship between the Father and the Son is further underlined in the **Gospel** when the voice from the cloud overshadows those present at the transfiguration of the Lord and speaks: "This is my beloved Son. Listen to him." It is not coincidental that the moment of Jesus' transfiguration and revelation through Moses and Elijah also becomes the occasion for our own call to obedient listening. From this perspective, the transfiguration pericope in Mark might strike us as a bit late, because nobody seems to be listening to Jesus throughout the narrative. Perhaps the proximate relationship of this occurrence on Mount Tabor and the ensuing passion and death of the Lord makes an argument that the disciples are given an obvious command to be listeners of the word before it is too late. As contemporary hearers, though, we are in line with Abraham who becomes the model of the utterly obedient listener.

Connecting the Bible and the Liturgy

The **Entrance Antiphon** immediately draws us into the Gospel narrative with an ironic twist, imploring the Lord, *"Ne avertas faciem tuam a me"*—"hide not your face from me." We certainly sense the disciples' desire to be with the Master, but, paradoxically enough, it is they who hide their faces from the theophany at Mount Tabor. All the more are we encouraged in the **Collect** for today to open our ears (perhaps when we are blinded and fail to see God's glory transfigured before us in the Son) "to listen to your beloved Son" so that "we may rejoice to behold" his glory.

At the same time, though, we may also sense that the **Entrance Antiphon** also belongs to Abraham whose experience belongs to the mysterious eclipse of God in the command to sacrifice Isaac. To this end, Abraham becomes a kind of Everyman at the celebration of this liturgy, who faces confusion and wonder at God's presence—again, not unlike the disciples and, of course, the people of God gathered to celebrate the sacred mysteries in the Eucharist. The Entrance Antiphon gathers the confused and names their frustration, a reality that the glory of the resurrection is hidden in the cross of Christ, that the transfiguration will also be the foreshadowing of the passion, death, and resurrection of the Lord. The **Preface: The Transfiguration of the Lord** makes this reality known as a liturgical gesture: "For after he had told the disciples of his coming Death, / on the holy mountain he manifested to them his glory, / to show, even by the testimony of the law and the prophets, / that the Passion leads to the glory of the Resurrection."

The **Preface** recalls the essential paradox of the transfiguration and that God in the flesh transformed before our eyes to fulfill the Law and the Prophets is a prelude to the passion and resurrection. God himself is suffering, much like Abraham, to surrender his own Son. When the reading from Genesis is seen in the light of patristic interpreters who made God the one who emptied himself like an obedient servant, then we are able to lean into what this Second Sunday of Lent is all about: a record of a divine drama of love. The transfiguration of Christ becomes an icon of a promise of God's love fulfilled that longs for our hearing. The testimony of Moses and Elijah further reinforces the importance of listening to the Word that has been set on the mountain for his disciple.

Strategy for Preaching

Preachers will necessarily face one of the most difficult texts for preaching in the account of the "Binding of Isaac." Yet this strange and disturbing text's pairing with Mark's account of the transfiguration offers an opportunity to explore Lent and all its dimensions more deeply than we might expect.

The homily's core idea might invest the congregation in something like this: we may think that obedience is something for children, but the surrender to another is the highest act of love. The example of Abraham is a case in point. The story should shock us into a kind of horror at the demands God can make on a human being. But maybe underneath the test is a stunning reminder that "our father in faith" placed in God's hands absolutely everything he had. Abraham was not only willing to slaughter his son in sacrifice but to obey the seemingly insane inhalation of a promise of descendants that God made earlier. This act of "love" might seem like a complete act of betrayal on every level. That is meant to shock us, and it should.

Can we trust that deeply, even into the mystery of what we might think is absurd? Here, the preacher might enumerate the various ways in which we have seen the human condition in anguish over the last century: The Holocaust, nuclear destruction, racism that will not let go of us, abuse by trusted institutions; all of these represent the "Binding of Humanity." We are led like Isaac up the mountain to find ourselves at a complete loss and wonder at God's absence. No wonder people give up on faith.

But these horrific moments dissolve when we realize that God is being emptied along with us in these moments of grief and confusion and abandonment. Christ is bound and surrendered in God's own person and delivered and handed over to the powers. We might recall the various patristic readings deployed allegorically to indicate that it is God who, in the end, is the one who obeys out of love. It is God who has emptied himself of his own Son. So too does Jesus proclaim his own suffering at the transfiguration, recognizing that in his own surrender and kenosis he will deliver us into the kingdom, the hope of the resurrection that lies underneath the cross. How many situations have we faced where the difficulty before us cannot be explained away but that only faith, hope, and love can answer?

It is trust in God that will carry us through not only this Lent but beyond. Where we go, Christ has gone before us. Lent asks us to continue our journey toward both Calvary and the empty tomb. We can hide our faces like ostriches in the sand or awake from the mountain of Tabor and see that the glory of God is made perfect in complete surrender and gift of the self.

Third Sunday of Lent

Readings from the Ambo

Exod 20:1-17; Ps 19:8, 9, 10, 11; 1 Cor 1:22-25; John 2:13-25

The **First Reading** details the seminal moment when Moses gives human voice to the Decalogue (cf. the parallel text in Deuteronomy 5:6-21). The church's positioning of this reading on the Third Sunday of Lent favors a kind of communal self-inventory of the people of God during this season. As is well known, the first three commandments concern Israel's relationship with God, while the remaining seven regulate the social order and lay a foundation for human ethics and social responsibility. Some modern folks are apt to think of these laws as oppressive structures projected onto an ancient, nomadic people longing for a national and collective identity; as such, these codes carry little freight for our contemporary society. Yet St. Thomas Aquinas and a host of Judeo-Christian commentators throughout the ages have pointed to these commandments as the root of natural law, a kind of DNA-inscribed pattern into the human subject, which are the very constitution of human happiness, justice, and peace. The fact is that we will slip into some form of disordered idolatry unless we are redirected to do otherwise. And again, murder is not just a bad social act; it is an unnatural one as well. (Witness: God tells Cain that his brother's blood cries out to him in the book of Genesis.)

The Commandments dealing with God then set the tone and meaning for the subsequent precepts concerning relationships with our neighbor. The recognition that idolatry is narcissistic orders the social fabric so that the underlying cause for taking the life of another (the false gods of pride, anger, envy, and so on) will not be in jeopardy. Hence, the psalmist says today, "The law of the LORD is perfect, / refreshing the soul. . . . The precepts of the LORD are right, / rejoicing the heart." The commandments are not meant to please some overbearing authority but to regulate our lives into a right relationship with God and one another.

We might say that all the readings for today return us to the underlying basics of true worship; that is what drives Jesus' confrontation in the temple in Jerusalem and Paul's meditation on Christ crucified. Unlike the synoptic accounts of a similar episode (cf. Matt 21:17; Mark 11:15-19; Luke 9:45-48), which position Jesus' encounter in the temple at the end of his ministry, John deploys this episode as one of the early signs (it follows the first sign, the wedding at Cana) of his authority and the Father's glory. Indeed, John seems to be at pains to use the temple incident not as a provocation or excuse for the religious authorities to put Jesus to death, but precisely as a sign that stands alone. This sign is a return to basics, letting us know that even the temple will one day be destroyed and replaced by Jesus himself, who will be raised up.

In the end, Paul desires to return literally to foundations, Christ crucified, "a stumbling block to Jews and foolishness to Gentiles." In the Letter to the Ephesians, Paul will argue that Christ the cornerstone (*akrogoniaios lithos*) lays the foundation for the apostles and prophets. So Christ is a living temple built on the foolishness of the cross, but this cross calls all those who witness to its power to be fools for Christ. That may mean testifying in the marketplace, perhaps not as dramatically as Jesus does in Jerusalem, but owning the same zeal of Christ, which is a single-minded pursuit and devotion to God's interest and glory, even if it is over and against what others think of as valuable.

Connecting the Bible and the Liturgy

We know that the **Introductory Rites**, together with the **Penitential Act** at the beginning of the eucharistic liturgy, allow for the gathered assembly to acknowledge their sins along with God's merciful goodness and compassionate forgiveness. What is true throughout the year is even further emphasized during Lent. The **Entrance Antiphon**, for instance, says that God rescues our feet "from the snare." That entanglement is our sin. And so we say, "*Respice in me et miserere mei, quoniam inucus et pauper sum ego.*" Or: "Turn to me and have mercy on me, / for I am alone and poor," as it is translated in the *Roman Missal*. We might also translate *unicus* in this context—perhaps less elegantly—as "alienated." This word gives voice to the effect of sin and why we are asking God to turn and have mercy; there is deep and wounded poverty caused by the alienation of sin for which God's mercy is the only answer. *Unicus* is the state of humanity bereft of the commandments. Fittingly enough, such a plea occurs at the beginning of the Eucharist, where we are brought in precisely from a state of alienation due to sin and into the house of God and the table of the Word and sacrament.

The acknowledgment of our sins and its merciful remedy, then, surfaces in the **Collect**: "O God, author of every mercy and of all goodness, / who in fasting, prayer and almsgiving / have shown us a remedy for sin, / look graciously on this confession of our lowliness, / that we, who are bowed down by our conscience, / may always be lifted up by your mercy." The Collect shares an imploring heart similar to the **Entrance Antiphon**, begging God to witness to the collective penitence of those who have gathered into the house of God. The assembly, then, becomes united in its commonality by virtue of its acknowledgment of sinfulness and eagerness for mercy.

Of particular interest in regard to this **Collect** is the phrase "bowed down by our conscience." In other words, our guilt has followed us into this temple of the Lord, and we await a cleansing, healing touch. The First Reading allows the congregation to apply the very reality suggested in the Collect: for those of us who come with a heavy heart, we can confront ourselves by hearing the Word of the Lord. First among these checkpoints might be the very mercy and love of God that is being expressed in the law that establishes an ordered and just society. At the same time, though, the commandments properly lived provide a Lenten guide to righteous living. Such a road map to sanctity makes us the dwellers of the temple of Jesus himself. Our very act of participating in the Eucharist allows the Lord to cleanse us through his Word, and in sacrament to bring us closer to sanctification. We inhabit a house of prayer because those in it have made it holy by contrite hearts and allowed the living God to possess them and cast out what is not holy. The zeal of Christ has made us perfect vessels of worship at the Eucharist, a people have received "mercy down to the thousandth generation."

Strategy for Preaching

There is an old adage that used to be repeated to an older generation of those in the Benedictine tradition: "You keep the Holy Rule and the Rule will keep you." There is something rather wonderful about thinking of a law or code that is established not to make us slaves to its conformity but rather preserving us in love. Keeping the commandments establishes us in freedom to love one another and to love God.

That attitude does not come readily to most people who think of Lent and the Ten Commandments as highly restrictive precepts that, once violated, put us out of the world of God's love. Yet nothing could be further from the truth: the commandments are rejoinders to live a good and upright life for the sake of the Other, for a life of selfless behavior and moral rectitude; that is, freedom, not slavery.

The homiletic core idea for this Third Sunday in Lent might be a call to the congregation to consider how they need to realign themselves with God's love at the most basic level. This is a vocation examination into the very fundamental stance of our Christian baptism. As such, the language of Jesus in John's Gospel for today is a summons to rid ourselves of what we find that distracts us from orthodoxy—literally, right worship in the temple that is his Body.

We could start then with an allusion to the **Penitential Rite** and its act of acknowledging our sins; this is a communal "altar call," to use a modern evangelical term, asking the congregation to allow Christ to cleanse our own house of sin. We need to start from the ground up. Living witnesses to this refoundation are the RCIA folks, who will be sitting in the congregation at one of the celebrations of the Eucharist. Why have they begun to refound their lives? Can we do the same?

The **Gospel** is very visual and provides a nice format to ask the congregation to do some creative introspection on their *communal conversion*. Obviously, the liturgy makes this invitation quite evident, but the call to die to selfish interests and live for the sake of the community can never be emphasized enough. Along these lines, though, there might still be a companion summons to *individual conversion*. Both opportunities to renovate the self and build a new foundation on the Crucified Lord will involve naming the demons that one way or another make their way into our house; it is the love of Christ and his zeal, fortified with the commandments, that will help us build a temple with the Lord as a cornerstone.

Fourth Sunday of Lent

Readings from the Ambo

*2 Chr 36:14-16, 19-23; Ps 137:1-2, 3, 4-5, 6ab;
Eph 2:4-10; John 3:14-21*

The book of Chronicles may often strike us now living in the twenty-first century as an outdated catalogue of a long-forgotten world. What purpose would such a text serve, especially during Lent? How relevant is a seemingly irrelevant record of Israel's history for contemporary Christians?

The answer is simple: very relevant. The sweeping history set forth in 2 Chronicles shows us the pattern of Israel's forgetfulness of God, which eventually led to the exile by foreign powers. The parallel to this text is the book of the Prophet Jeremiah, crucial as a centerpiece for this penitential season. Chronicles and Jeremiah disclose God's attempt to send messengers "for he had compassion on his people and his dwelling place." Yet as both Jeremiah and Chronicles reveal, Israel not only ignored God but "despised his warnings, and scoffed at his prophets, / until the anger of the LORD against his people was so inflamed / that there was no remedy." It would seem that Israel passed a point of no return when it came to its relationship with God, and so exile became the inevitable consequence. In some sense, the long exile that Israel faced was self-inflicted: they were already in exile in sin and alienation from God; the next movement was the political embodiment of a collective spiritual crisis.

Yet the passage in the **First Reading** also discloses a surprising, even shocking, antidote of hope in the midst of despair and exile. Cyrus, a Gentile king of Persia, becomes God's instrument to liberate the nation and return Israel to Jerusalem. That a Gentile would be the cause of Judah's gathering and healing represents an astonishing reversal that only God could accomplish. That a foreigner would gather Israel into the house of God is not only an irony of history but the magisterial twist with which God has blessed the chosen people.

In some very real sense, the procession of Israel's troubled history must whisper to Paul when he engages his famous line quoted in the **Second Reading**. Oddly enough, even if the authorship of Ephesians is in doubt, the passage from that text in the Lectionary for today becomes a kind of descant to so much of Pauline theology available elsewhere: "For by grace you have been saved through faith, / and this is not from you; it is the gift of God; / it is not from works, so no one may boast." Indeed, Israel's liberation from exile was a purely gratuitous event, for which that nation can produce no self-credit at all. The Israelites' task after the exile is to only remember God's deeds and the work of grace, which Chronicles has done in such rich detail. That record of the works of the Lord and the communal remembrance of the salvific event certainly finds a place in the Christian community assembled at the eucharistic liturgy.

It is that the **Gospel** is well-positioned to show us God's final and definitive revelation to all during the exile of humanity's sin: Christ Jesus. This is how God so loved the world, by giving us his only Son so that all may be continually transformed by faith in the only Son of God. Once again, it is nothing that we did. As if to reinforce the continual reminder that is ours—a living remembrance that we ought not to forget those divine deeds—the Son of Man must be lifted up "so that everyone who believes in him may have eternal life." The cross of Christ is the definitive chronicle of God's mercy.

Connecting the Bible and the Liturgy

Laetare Sunday brings with it the joy of anticipating the Lord's resurrection, as we prepare to celebrate that solemnity of solemnities in all its mysterious splendor in the upcoming Triduum. The **Collect** reminds the congregation of the proximity of Easter when it asks God "that with prompt devotion and eager faith / the Christian people may hasten / toward the solemn celebrations to come." So it is not only a passive anticipation, but that we may do so as those who *festinare*, that is to say, are "in a hurry" or "making great speed." This hastening befits a people who have a *prompta devotione* and an *alacri fide* ("prompt devotion" and "eager faith"). This language suggests the interior disposition beneath the liturgy of *Laetare* Sunday, one that urges the assembly to claim a fundamental desire to celebrate the solemnity of our Lord's resurrection. Why the desire and the urgency? Because God, through the power of the Word has reconciled "the human race . . . in a wonderful way" (Collect). We know this to be true by faith and not by anything we have done. Faith is that cardinal virtue that gains its strength and impetus from holy desire. So, recognizing God's merciful reconciliation through Christ—as Paul reminds the Ephesians—becomes a tribute to God's own promptings—so that we may not boast. As St. Augustine would later famously say in the *Confessions*, "you called, you shouted and you shattered my deafness" (X.27).

Preface I for Lent (used this Sunday as an alternative when the Gospel for the "Man Born Blind" is not used) could not be more explicit when that text recalls for the faithful God's actions precisely as gifts—those unearned treasures. "For by your gracious gift each year / your faithful await the sacred paschal feasts / with the joy of minds made pure." We are, once again, urged to contemplate God's saving acts through the liturgy itself, a renewal that brings about our sanctification; that is the gift that only Christ can accomplish. Ours is but to be renewed this holy season through an urgent anticipation of what will be ours through grace. Further, we should be mindful of the work of the liturgy itself that "each year" makes the congregation "more eagerly intent on prayer / and on the works of charity, / and participating in the mysteries / by which they have been reborn, / they may be led to the fullness of grace / that you bestow on your sons and daughters." It is the liturgy, as the Preface suggests, which allows for our remembrance of the holy. It is the liturgy that continually keeps the church mindful of Christ lifted up on the cross as God's definitive act of gracious love.

So, *Laetare* Sunday is a day for rejoicing not only because we are moving toward Easter in a linear way but that we are participating in the saving act of God's merciful redemption even now; it is the present state of our redemption we celebrate as the mystery of the eucharistic Lord unfolds before our very eyes. The Lectionary for this Sunday reminds us of our forgetting and God's remembering, a rhythm that has taken place throughout salvation history. The anguished lament of Psalm 137 (**Responsorial Psalm**) shows us a recollection deeply felt in its urgency. The Eucharist carries us on from that world of despair to hope that has been promised the exiles:

"that we may always ponder / what is worthy and pleasing to your majesty / and love you in all sincerity."

Strategy for Preaching

The Johannine image of the Son of Man being lifted up should certainly be read by the Christian community (as it has been naturally enough over the years) as the lifting up of Christ on the cross so that all who believe in him may have eternal life. With faith comes the actualization of eternal life; the relationship with Christ begins our eternal life already present here and now. Jesus himself parallels the raising up of the Son of Man to Moses lifting up the serpent in the wilderness, the action of which in antiquity was thought to be a therapeutic cure: the very snake that bit the people becomes an instrument of healing. So too, the shameful cross is God's revelation of glory and salvation, the door that opens up a salvific relationship for all who believe.

But the preacher is in a bit of a predicament when delivering a homily on the cross of Christ crucified. It is not known when the crucifix became a fashionable accessory, but it remains so for lots of people. Even if a person does not choose to wear a crucifix as a piece of decorative jewelry, its place on others suggests that this once-saving symbol, an image of shame transformed, has lost its transformative power as a cultural religious icon for the devout Christian community. Not too long ago, we might recall, the cross was treated as a sacred instrument of power, even in secular literature and film (think of the vampire movies that have embedded the cross into a theology of good and evil). But the cross has been demystified in modern culture. That does not mean we become nostalgic creatures hammering away at the blasphemy of using the cross as an accessory, but we see the cross as an opportunity for the congregation to renew their faith.

How can we strategize about the cross as a living symbol of our redemption? The real visibility of the cross in the life of any Christian is the recognition we give to God's gracious gift of Christ (cf. the **Preface** as suggested above) and the mercy accorded us through the grace of redemption (**Collect**). There are plenty of people over the years who have a cross on the wall but fail to see its true power to save. The invitation is to get beyond the pedestrian use of the cross and see it lifted up high! If the cross were lifted high so that we truly saw Christ stretched forth, God emptying himself for the sake of love, what would that exultation be asking of us as a faith community? This invitation or question to the congregation might form the core homiletic idea, which is really the call to faith in action. The preacher might point out that the raising up of Christ on the cross will never allow us to forget God's love. But we have to look beyond the banal expressions of the cross represented by our own playthings and vanities and learn from the cross's own unique gift: God loving us personally and persistently, fully and relentlessly. Such wondrous love—to quote the popular spiritual—cannot be reduced to a commonplace but stands as an eternal remembrance. The cross, when accepted in faith, becomes etched in our hearts.

That sacred memory unfolds during the Pascal mystery that we eagerly await, indeed, what we speedily run toward. But that opportunity for faith, hope, and love in God's gift is already present in the gifts we bring to the altar on *Laetare* Sunday as an "eternal remedy" (**Prayer over the Offerings**). That present moment is lifted high enough to see and gives us every reason to rejoice.

Fifth Sunday of Lent

Readings from the Ambo

Jer 31:31-34; Ps 51:3-4, 12-13, 14-15; Heb 5:7-9; John 12:20-33

If last week's readings for the Fourth Sunday of Lent showed us a God who remembers his people, this subsequent Sunday discloses how that promise will be kept. Not missing a beat, Jeremiah, the prophet of Israel's exile, shows the house of Judah just how intensely the Lord intends to keep his promise: "I will place my law within them and write it upon their hearts; / I will be their God, and they shall be my people." God's expression of love is revealed in a new covenant, of course, which will be greater than anything Israel has known before. If the problem Jeremiah faced earlier was a people—particularly a religious and priestly hierarchy—who ignored God's deeds, this new covenant will be irresistible since it is not to be engraved in stone but in the hearts. As the Christian community prepares to approach the holiest times of the year and its culmination in the celebration of the Pascal mystery, we can only be reminded of the law etched in our hearts: this new covenant is Christ himself, the embodiment of God's love. He will be the Word written in the heart of the baptized, the covenant renewed in the church from age to age at the very heart of the church.

The **Responsorial Psalm** appropriately enough is taken from Psalm 51, perhaps the most famous of the seven so-called "Penitential Psalms." More to the point, the psalmist asks to be renewed and sanctified: "Create a clean heart in me, O God." The imagery of cleanliness is not about ritual purity, of course, but a determination to follow God's will. The clean of heart asks for "a steadfast spirit" to be renovated within him. God's Spirit becomes the great desire here and the eternal promise for finding a new heart when the author says, "Cast me not out from your presence, / and your Holy Spirit take not from me." This is a plea to be taken out of exile and to be brought into God's company. From a Christian perspective, then, the longing for the joy of salvation and the promise to witness to transgressors is an evangelical promise returned to the Giver of the gift; it is the response of the baptized in thanksgiving for the Spirit that will never be taken away.

This longing for cleansing is all well and good, but we must realize the "dangerous" implications of what we ask: there will be demands placed on those who desire purity of heart and conversion. Similarly, it is good for us to see the implication of what the Greeks are asking in John's Gospel when they say, "Sir, we would like to see Jesus." Really? Under what conditions? Are we ready to face that Son of Man glorified as a grain of wheat broken open when it falls to the ground and its body smashed apart? Jesus himself implicates us in his own questioning when he reminds us that those who hate their own life in this world will preserve it in the next. In the end, are we really ready to see the Son of Man draw all things to himself, lifted up high on the cross? Are we really ready for a suffering God?

These are a series of provocative questions, but they are appropriate for the life of Christian service and crucially need to be faced as we enter more deeply into this holy season. In the end, this life of service to our brothers and sisters is what it means to see God's glory. Service is exemplified in Christ's priestly intersession for us; it is Jesus' "prayers and supplication with loud cries and tears" according to the Letter to the Hebrews. Chapter 12 of John's Gospel, we know, is a prelude to the full revelation of God's glory, the grain of wheat fallen and broken, in the passion, death, and resurrection of the Lord that is to follow. Indeed, chapter 13 will demonstrate just how Christ the servant behaves when he washes the disciples' feet. The foot washing, the journey to the cross, and the passion and death of Christ all witness to how great a distance any disciple is willing to go with Christ. Asking to see Jesus, as the Greeks do, is dangerous enough, but gathering in the shadow of the cross as the true disciple is another example of a potentially difficult road less taken. Most will scatter like drifting grains and be left unbroken. And yet, as Jesus says, "Whoever serves me must follow me, / and where I am, there also will my servant be." Gathering around the cross is the only way out of exile.

Connecting the Bible and the Liturgy

Like many Sundays throughout the year, this Fifth Sunday in Lent puts a premium on owning our discipleship with the Lord. Our relationship with the living God is galvanized because God is the greatest of covenant keepers. The **Entrance Antiphon** for this Sunday could well be the refrain for the prophet Jeremiah's life work, a telling record of his dealings with the House of Judah. "Give me justice, O God, / and plead my cause against a nation that is faithless. / From the deceitful and cunning rescue me, / for you, O God, are my strength." Jeremiah and Christ Jesus himself are emblems of those who embody justice because they are exemplars of faithful witnesses who mirror God's own self. It is, after all, Christ's obedience unto death that allows him to hand himself over to the unjust.

We know that Christ is the concrete expression of God's faithfulness made incarnate, a living promise of God's love for his people. The Greeks may never see Jesus if they look for him only in a mythological expression of divine wisdom. The Letter to the Hebrews says that it was Christ's reverence, his *eulabeias*, that allowed him to be heard; it is his obedience that made his offering perfect. The implication is unavoidable here: obedience is an act of worship; it is never abstract but always incarnational. And so Christ's fidelity becomes foregrounded in a special way by his "supplications with loud cries and tears." With this in mind, **Preface I of the Passion of the Lord** makes an important connection to the readings, even though the recommended preface for this Fifth Sunday in Lent is Preface I or II of the Lenten prefaces. When those prefaces are used, Preface I of the Passion of the Lord forms an underlying catechesis for this homily and for the days to come and, in fact, is used at the liturgy beginning Monday of the Fifth Week of Lent. Notable among the connections between the Bible and the liturgy in this regard is the language of *catharsis*. The readings underline the place of the "clean heart" that is especially showcased for the congregation in the **Responsorial Psalm**, the language of Christ's sacrificial emptying in Hebrews and Jesus' analogy of the broken seed of wheat to discipleship: "For through the saving Passion of your Son / the whole world has received a heart / to confess the infinite power of your majesty" (Preface I of the Passion of the Lord). In other words, our corporate hearts have been replaced by newer, clean hearts, and the new covenant inscribed deep within that gift because of Christ's saving passion and death, which has sanctified all humanity. Indeed, the cross of Christ has been given jurisdiction and power, "since by the wondrous power of the Cross / your judgment on the world is now revealed / and the authority of Christ crucified." The might or *potestas* of Christ crucified reminds us that the cross receives its authority by the one who embraced it fully in obedience; it is obedience that, as the Letter to the Hebrews says, made Christ perfect. Therefore we can see that Christ's suffering accounts for the sacrifice for all and becomes the ultimate authority for all since Christ "became the source of eternal salvation for all who obey him." Our own obedience as disciples, then, becomes linked to Christ's own offering to God; our offering of our own fidelity in relationship with God is a participation in the work of Christ.

Strategy for Preaching

An old familiar adage says that we better be careful what we ask for, because we may get it. Consider, then, the **Prayer over the People** for this Sunday: "Bless, O Lord, your people, / who long for the gift of your mercy, / and grant that what, at your prompting, they desire / they may receive." If we are going to ask God for a clean heart through his infinite mercy, as the psalmist longs for, one that acts uprightly and justly and is faithful, then we better be able to fall to the earth and die to ourselves, like so many grains of wheat. Only then will we be able to be truly Christ's disciples, obedient to the Master crucified and risen.

John's Gospel typically portrays Jesus very much in charge of his own Messianic destiny. But this high Christology appears to be challenged in today's readings. Not only do we have the Letter to the Hebrews disclosing the suffering Christ, but Jesus is clearly in anguish in the **Gospel** as well when he tells his disciples, "I am troubled now. Yet what should I say? / 'Father save me from this hour'? / But it was for this purpose that I came to this hour." Christ seems to be revealing to us the very process of the obedient Son, a real christological drama that *Hebrews* makes lucid when that text says of Christ: "Son though he was, he learned obedience from what he suffered. . . ."

Can we lean into this aspect of Christ's relationship to the Father? Certainly not completely on our own, but through grace and with the aid of the biblical and liturgical texts we are able to sense that the early stages of Christ's passionate surrender begin here, with a theological explanation of his own death and resurrection. So, with some reference to **Preface I of the Passion of the Lord**, the homiletic core idea might be to invite the assembly to ask to see Jesus as he really is—the one who has come to serve and be obedient and who asks us to do the same.

The congregation could be challenged to face Jesus as he is—not how we wish he would be. There are all sorts of super-friendly Savior representations in Hollywood film history, greeting cards, even graffiti in the New York Subway. Nobody wants to knock God's kindness in the way these representations of Jesus depict the Son of God, but the call to serve is less a matter of being comforted than comforting others. After all, Christ's obedience is an act of worship. The grain of wheat dies so it can feed the flock. The liturgy itself causes us to think about how we will die to our own self-absorption and to be made perfect in God's own offering at the altar: "Hear us, almighty God, / and, having instilled in your servants / the teachings of the Christian faith, / graciously purify them / by the working of this sacrifice" (**Prayer over the Offerings**). This is, in a word, Psalm 51 as a liturgical expression, to "Give me back the joy of your salvation, / and a willing spirit sustain in me." If we allow word and sacrament to work deep in our hearts, then we will be sanctified and ready to become servants, our worship made perfect. The well-plotted homily will guide the congregation to accept their role as disciples, purified through Christ's work and an assent to a difficult desire.

HOLY WEEK

Palm Sunday of the Passion of the Lord

Readings from the Ambo

Mark 11:1-10 or John 12:12-16; Isa 50:4-7;
Ps 22:8-9, 17-18; 19-20; 23-24; Phil 2:6-11; Mark 14:1—15:47

The richness of the day that begins Holy Week is surely sensed in the number of readings on which we might reflect today, some of which will be determined by the particular focus on one of the three forms of The Commemoration of the Lord's Entrance into Jerusalem. The First Form, for which the Messianic Procession includes an extended oration, the blessing of palms, and one of the three synoptic Gospels appropriate for the Liturgical Years A, B, and C, is also the most complex. There are also three antiphons used as strophes for psalms in honor of Christ the King. These readings focus our attention on the one who comes in the name of the Lord. We participate as a congregation in the people's acclamation of "Hosanna to the Son of David." The Johannine reading (an option for Year B) brings a sobering, prophetic reminder (quoting Zechariah 9:9) that this king comes seated not on a great white steed, carrying in a messianic insignia and ready to level his enemies, but humble and *"seated upon an ass's colt."* If we have been closely following the readings in the last few weeks of Lent in the B cycle (i.e., the Fifth Sunday: "Whoever loves his life loses it . . ."), then we will know that this is the messiah who comes as a servant king. The disciples themselves receive such an insight only after his entrance into Jerusalem, "when Jesus had been glorified / [then] they remembered that these things were written about him / and that they had done this for him."

The Second Form is the **Solemn Entrance** while the Third is the **Simple Entrance**. Like the First Form, we should observe the way in which the biblical texts are used in collaboration with movement in the assembly. The Second Form requires that the Gospel be read after which there is a procession to the altar. The Simple Procession does not require a collective procession of the faithful or a proclamation of the Gospel before Mass begins as usual but lays special emphasis on the **Entrance Antiphon**, by which the presider introduces the historical reenactment of Passion Sunday, indicating its proximity to the Passover and its welcoming of the Messiah into Jerusalem.

The readings are going to hold a variety of meanings depending on the Form chosen for the day, and preachers should be aware of the way in which the Scriptures will be shaped by the liturgy and the texts that accompany these sacred rites. I will touch on the aspect of biblical and liturgical readings more substantially in the next section, but the unusual character of the liturgy today has already begun to inflect its own hermeneutic on the congregation, now brought into the biblical scene, as it were, as living witnesses to the Messianic King entering Jerusalem. Moreover, the welcome provided by the acclamation in the assembly can only strike us as ambivalent, since the readings are overwhelmingly poised to greet not power but humility. The servant model that Jesus has made known so clearly during Lent in Year B will follow the Servant Son of Isaiah (50:4-7) in the **First Reading** in a special way. Indeed, the faith of Christ disclosed to the disciples in John 12:20-33 ("Yet what should I say? 'Father, save me from this hour'?") finds a point of interface with the Suffering Servant who says, "The Lord GOD is my help, / therefore I am not disgraced; / I have set my face like flint, / knowing that I shall not be put to shame." Then again, the Philippians hymn also calls attention to the servant God who "emptied himself, / taking the form of a slave."

If we use the servanthood of Christ, then, as a lens with which to view Mark's passion narrative, the text becomes a record of the suffering servant who has remained faithful to God's covenant unto death. On the level of symbol, the breaking of the alabaster jar of perfumed oil by the woman at the house of Simon the leper at the beginning of the **Gospel** is an image of Christ himself being broken and poured out as the servant. This servant portrait not only echoes Isaiah but also Psalm 22 and Paul's vision of the humble Christ in the Philippian's hymn as well. The breaking of the alabaster jar sets the symbolic tone for what is to come; it explains Jesus' service at the table, the surrender at Gethsemane, the passivity during his trial (uncharacteristic of his Galilean ministry) and ultimately his death on the cross as sacrificial victim. For this final act on the cross, Christ will be poured out for the sake of many, emptying himself utterly and completely.

Connecting the Bible and the Liturgy

Perhaps the most obvious feature of the liturgy today is its overwhelmingly public character. Even if the First Form is not used for the Procession, the congregation in most parish settings plays the role of the people as actors in the **Gospel**, reenacting Jesus' entry into Jerusalem. The waving of palms, the collective voices in the antiphons, and the singing of hymns showcase the public nature of religion and underline its witness value; this solemnity is a model for "full and active participation" in the liturgy. The celebrant in all three Forms names the reality of the gathered assembly as those who welcome Jesus and reminds the assembly of the Holy Week that is to follow. In the First Form we hear: "Today we gather together to herald with the whole Church / the beginning of the celebration / of our Lord's Paschal Mystery, / that is to say, of his Passion and Resurrection." Further, the presider underscores the important role of the assembly in making the celebration of the paschal mystery a witness of faith, an active participation in the reality of Christ's passion, death, and resurrection. "For it was to accomplish this mystery / that he entered his own city of Jerusalem. / Therefore, with all faith and devotion, / let us commemorate / the Lord's entry into the city for our salvation, / following his footsteps, / so that, being made by his grace partakers of the Cross, / we may have a share also in his Resurrection and in his life" (First Form).

I can think of no other moment during the church year when the baptized assembly is invited to participate so actively in the physical and corporate work of the Scripture through the liturgy. The collective nature of the celebration for Passion Sunday is an opportunity to absorb the theological refrain voiced by the congregation at every eucharistic celebration: "Blessed is he who comes in the name of the Lord. Hosanna in the highest!" We spread the branches of our welcome, our faith, hope, and love as we receive the Messiah into our midst during this most holy of weeks: it is the entrance of the suffering Servant of Isaiah sitting on the ass's colt; it is the confession of the baptized to ask God to "graciously grant that we may heed his lesson of patient suffering / and so merit a share in his Resurrection" (**Collect**). Ultimately, it is in our recognition of Christ's "taking the form of a slave" that we know that "the pride of the ancient foe is vanquished / and the mystery of our redemption in Christ is celebrated" (**Preface II of the Passion of the Lord**).

Finally, the liturgical celebration of the passion on Palm Sunday emphasizes the exciting and rich theological meaning of our redemption being near at hand—so near that we are witnesses. Easter is a week away, to be sure, but the public entry of Jesus into Jerusalem and his welcome into those gates announcing that the kingdom of God is near at hand is the eschatological victory present on this day in symbol, into which the congregation itself has entered.

Strategy for Preaching

It should go without saying that this day above all others ought to be a time for Christocentric preaching, reminding the congregation that the mysteries that are unfolding in the Scriptures and the liturgy today and throughout Holy Week are drawing them ever deeper into the paschal mystery of Christ, whom they are welcoming as servant King, God's self-gift to his people. Along these lines, this day presents itself as an opportunity for challenging the hearers to walk the path the Lord himself trod, a road that has already begun in the procession of the current celebration. In a sense, the Christian faithful are asked to surrender themselves to the Word, even as they are participating in the active role of the Scriptures and the liturgy for today; they are to participate in the very emptying of the self and to live into the experience of the Word in Christ's passion, death, and resurrection.

The **Procession** has made a move in the homiletic already: what must it have been like to view Jesus as both Messiah and Servant entering Jerusalem, only for him to be rejected later by these same people? To ask this is to enter into the experience of Christ himself, poured out and emptied and handed over. Can we follow him throughout this week to the cross and then to the empty tomb? These questions hint at the homiletic core idea that is certainly theologically mandated by the Scriptures for today. The preacher will find abundant catechetical help for structuring a homily in the patristic and contemporary writings on Christology and the large section dealing with the same in the *Catechism of the Catholic Church* (571-637). This may be a homily that more folks than usual will hear, if past experience in attendance is any indication. The return of those with less than sporadic attendance is an even greater reason to craft the homily as a rearticulation of the Creed and its Christocentric mystery of faith. One tactic in realizing the homiletic core idea is to use Isaiah's Suffering Servant and Paul's Philippians hymn as touchstones into an understanding of God's humility. That particular mystery accentuates a virtue to which every Christian ought to aspire; it is also a quality that will claim the mixed congregants, since humility is a kind of universal symbol of honesty and authenticity.

One of the first liturgical acts of the newly elected Pope Francis was to celebrate the Mass of the Lord's Supper in a prison for youth, washing the feet of men and women, Christian and Muslims. Young people, in particular, yearn for these qualities in their schools, governments, churches—and church leaders. But Jesus is the first of witnesses to humility, emptying himself of divinity for our sake. Additionally, the preacher ought to be mindful of the peculiarly Markan christological perspective and fold this synoptic Gospel's point of view into the tactics in order to express the homiletic core. We will get a very different portrait of Jesus on Good Friday, of course, with John's account of the passion. For now, though, Mark's passion narrative is fascinating in its economy and uncompromising in its disclosure of the Jesus who emptied himself for the sake of the Father's will and our salvation.

Thursday of the Lord's Supper
(Years ABC)

Readings from the Ambo

Exod 12:1-8, 11-14; Ps 116:12-13, 15-16bc, 17-18;
1 Cor 11:23-26; John 13:1-15

The first half of chapter 12 in the book of Exodus deals with the Lord's instructions to Moses on the specifics of celebrating the Passover and the feast of Unleavened Bread. There is a little shift beginning in verse 21 when Moses tells the elders how to carry out these divine instructions. Although our passage is concerned only with what God says to Moses, the section in which Moses transmits God's orders to the elders suggests the emerging institutionalization of Passover: not as a private revelation to Moses, who was unique among men, but as a liturgical feast with which the elders were charged to carry out and repeat through *zikaron*, memory.

The keeping of Passover as a memorial of the passage out of Egypt cannot be emphasized enough, since its celebration clearly represents a moment of life and death for Israel. Later generations would recall God's deliverance from the tenth plague and the meal that ushered in the Exodus from Egypt as a renewal of God's promise to the people of the covenant. Among the many noteworthy features of the Lord's instructions to Moses is a divine reordering of the calendar: "This month shall stand at the head of your calendar; / you shall reckon it the first month of the year." This would be Nisan, the first of months in which the Passover meal would commemorate the great work of God for Israel.

In a certain sense, Paul's first letter to the Corinthians recalls the very dynamic divine presence with Moses in the book of Exodus concerning divine instruction and its institutional transmission. "I received (*parelabon*) from the Lord what I also handed on to you." The verb that Paul uses for "handed on" is *paredoka*, which can also mean "passed on," even "passed over or delivered to." I am not suggesting that Paul had this in mind, but there is a kind of "passover" going on when he *paredoka* ("or handed on") to the Corinthians the tradition of the Lord's Supper. Furthermore, the connection of the Passover in Egypt is further established by a meal commemorated through memory. "For as often as you eat this bread and drink the cup, you proclaim the death of the Lord until he comes." This is the *anamnesis*, the remembrance of the saving event of Christ, his Passover, when he was handed over for us.

Jesus' final meal with his disciples is both a Passover and a Passing-on in John's gospel; it is a transmission of how to treat one another. As is well known, John does not include the institution of the Eucharist on the night before Jesus' passion as the Synoptics do. For a variety of reasons, the eucharistic theology of the Fourth Gospel would extend into the symbolic reaches of the whole gospel (such as the "Bread of Life Discourse") and not be limited to the night the Lord was handed over. Nevertheless, there is a *paredoka* going on between Jesus and his disciples. The act of love is replicated by a footwashing, which in first-century Palestine was the province of a slave or servant to offer guests upon entering a household. The tradition of footwashing was probably ubiquitous in many cultures and was recorded in the Hebrew Scriptures prominently in the book of Genesis and elsewhere. Christ was taking on the role of the servant at the meal, then, and demonstrates this behavior *sui generis*, having received no instruction: the Lord's service emerges directly from him, and he passes it, like his farewell Passover with the disciples in the Synoptics, with the instruction for *anamnesis*. "If I, therefore, the master and teacher, have washed your feet, you ought to wash one another's feet." Humility and hospitality, then, are "institutionalized" as ritual actions, as virtues to be observed in the Christian community. Modeling divine hospitality and humility, all take on the role of a servant in service to one another in a kind of passing over from the selfishness of this world to the light of God's grace. Humility and hospitality are integrally related to the celebration of the Passover of the Lord and are virtues upon which the Johannine community, the community of the Beloved Disciple, built its eucharistic theology of table fellowship.

Connecting the Bible and the Liturgy

It is significant that the church has chosen chapter 13 of John's gospel for Holy Thursday, which has as a fulcrum the footwashing scene. The emphasis on the Servant Christ who handed himself over to death for the sake of many is replicated symbolically by the church's own reenactment of the footwashing at the Liturgy of the Lord's Supper after the homily. In addition, the readings, the presidential prayers, and **Preface** for the day speak poignantly of the way that Jesus' great act of love was institutionalized in the Eucharist.

Consider the **Collect**, which not only draws an emphasis on Christ's being handed over but on delivering *himself* unto death. *Morti se traditurus* is a reflexive action, translated by *The Roman Missal* as "when he was about to hand himself over"; the implication here is that Jesus freely gave himself in love (the lavish footwashing scene in John shows this divine hospitality) and "entrusted to the Church a sacrifice new for all eternity, the banquet of his love." But there is more. We know that this is a night of being handed over as well, "for he knew who would betray him; for this reason, he said, 'Not all of you are clean.'" So we are dealing with Christ's freely giving himself but also a human agency acting to betray him. The Roman Canon (**Eucharistic Prayer I**) picks up the double meaning of the verb *tradere* by simply leaving it ambiguous: "Celebrating the most sacred day (*quo Dominius noster Iesus Christus pro nobis est traditus*) on which our Lord Jesus Christ was handed over for our sake." The word "Canon" accurately captures the Johannine Jesus: the one who was betrayed but who also freely handed over himself.

For our sake: that is the other, necessary half of Christ's eucharistic offering of love, the self-surrender in service unto death. We are drawn into this Eucharist by the God who has called us to participate in this most sacred Supper "that we may draw from so great a mystery the fullness of charity and of life" (Collect). The eucharistic meal then is a purifying one, granting the assembly *plenitudinem caritatis* in this work of redemption. As the **Prayer over the Offerings** makes clear, our very active participation in the Eucharist becomes a memorial of the sacrifice itself and "*opus nostrae redemptionis exercetur*" (the work of our redemption is accomplished). That liberation occurs in the sacrifice of Christ's blood on the cross, an *anamnesis* repeated and institutionalized in the Eucharist. If Jesus named the betrayer as not clean, we hope to find our sins washed away in Christ's blood. As the **Preface: The Sacrifice and the Sacrament of Christ** says, "As we eat his flesh that was sacrificed for us, we are made strong, and as we drink his Blood that was poured out for us, we are washed clean."

Strategy for Preaching

The homily for Holy Thursday may emerge from a number of different fonts, flowing from the same source: divine service, freely given. The institution of the Eucharist, the call to serve in priestly ministry, the community of the beloved, all stream from the initiative of Christ's hospitality and mandate to keep his memory in love. The challenge for the preacher will be to center the homily on *one* homiletic core and to develop an idiom that speaks to contemporary culture about a mystery that appears so difficult to comprehend. Jesus' service to his disciples appears clear enough in John's gospel and so is his commandment to do likewise. But do table service and footwashing speak to a fast-food culture with very little sense of hospitality and driven by individualism?

A core homiletic idea will allow the congregation to explore their experience of hospitality and encourage them to serve the community in grateful response. These expressions of welcome and selfless giving mediate God's own surrender of himself for our sake. By naming this grace, the preacher anticipates Jesus' own gospel injunction to serve.

Here is an organizational structure naming some tactics to engage the assembly along the lines of hospitality that might open a window into an understanding of Christ's own self-sacrifice.

I. Who opened a door for us in our life's journey? Was it a parent or a teacher or a friend? Where would we be today without that gesture of love?

   A. A telling example of service that opened a door for countless poor is Dorothy Day and the Catholic Worker. There are Catholic Workers in cities all over that extend the eucharistic table Jesus began this night. The altar of sacrifice becomes our table of service for the poor as we hand ourselves over to them and all those in need in service.

II. Christ was handed over as the Paschal Lamb for our Passover from sin and death to new life. Exodus illustrates the lamb that saved the people; our exodus from sin comes from the Paschal Lamb.

   A. Christ offered himself for our sins and at the Last Supper anticipated the free offering of his life (cf. *The Catechism of the Catholic Church*, 606–11).

III. There is no service without a surrender of power: that is true humility and hospitality. As we partake of the memorial of this sacrifice, we remember Christ as he remembered us. "The work of our redemption is accomplished."

   A. We are mindful of our mission to love, having been loved ourselves and remembered. Name the particular instances in which grace will unfold in my life in the future. Whose feet will I wash in grateful service?

Friday of the Passion of the Lord (Years ABC)

Readings from the Ambo

Isa 52:13–53:12; Ps 31:2, 6, 12-13, 15-16, 17, 25;
Heb 4:14-16; 5:7-9; John 18:1–19:42

The selection from Second Isaiah is the fourth and longest of the Servant Songs, and arguably the most powerful; it is a fitting icon for Good Friday of the Lord's Passion. The Song is a description of vicarious suffering: "[I]t was our infirmities that he bore, / our sufferings that he endured." The reading places itself at the center of the community as a highly relational text, offering the Suffering Servant as one who purifies the people from their sins. In the experience of the exile, Second Isaiah is well in the tradition of attributing mediated sacrifice of the one for the sake of the many. Indeed, the scapegoat was part of Israel's cultic ritual, and the prophets Jeremiah and Ezekiel also endured pain for the sake of the community's redemption. Moreover, the Suffering Servant is not only an individual but the community of Israel itself, the suffering people in Israel who endure sorrow and loss for the sake of the future revealed by prophetic oracle.

The passage in this **First Reading** is framed by a haunting presence that opens and closes the Servant Song: "my servant shall prosper" the passage begins; and "I will give him his portion among the great," near its closing. This is the language of the Lord guaranteeing his presence to his Beloved, even in the midst of anguish. Moreover, the last portion of the passage in particular offers hope by way of fruitfulness and new life for the many: "If he gives his life as an offering for sin, / he shall see his descendants in a long life, / and the will of the LORD shall be accomplished through him . . . / through his suffering, my servant shall justify many, / and their guilt he shall bear." The promise from God is that his chosen people remain close to him and find expiation through exile.

The imagery alone would guarantee this fourth Servant Song a place on Good Friday, with its language associated with a servant of God being "raised high" and a man "of suffering," "pierced," "like a lamb led to the slaughter," he "opened not his mouth." The Passion narratives will find their own narrative interpretation of this fourth Servant Song in the Person of Jesus, of course, as does the letter to the Hebrews, which is a kind of theological, christological gloss on the work of Christ the Servant and his priestly sacrifice for the sake of many. Some might claim that the passage here is a bit tough to absorb, but when juxtaposed with Second Isaiah's Servant, the letter to the Hebrews unfolds its riches for the Christian community. The author wraps the mystery of the incarnation (one who is able "to sympathize with our weaknesses") around a cultic expression of priestly atonement: "In the days when Christ was in the flesh, / he offered prayers and supplications with loud cries and tears / to the one who was able to save him from death." In so doing, Hebrews helps us to understand how Christ's suffering became redemptive, a purifying offering because "Son though he was, he learned obedience from what he suffered; / and when he was made perfect, / he became the source of eternal salvation for all who obey him." The writer of this very rich text's last observation allows the community to participate in the offering of Christ through their own obedience.

The first two readings provide a crucial antechamber for our passage into John's passion narrative, with its rejection of the Servant, his being led to the slaughter like a lamb, but also his glorification. The high Christology present in the text contrasts to varying degrees with the Synoptic texts proclaimed on Passion Sunday: John's account of the passion repeatedly alludes to a Jesus aware of his fate, as when the Lord says to Peter, "Shall I not drink the cup that the Father gave me?" That Christ is brought to slaughter and pierced at precisely the moment of the day of preparation for the Passover links Jesus to the Lamb brought to sacrifice for the sake of liberation for the community. The numerous allusions to the Hebrew Scriptures during John's passion narrative also remind us of the fulfillment of a plot greater than the one that is transpiring before us, with God as the author and the one who will vindicate his Son and raise him to glory, even as "he shall be raised high and greatly exalted."

Connecting the Bible and the Liturgy

The striking entrance of the celebrant and his assistants with a full prostration at the beginning of the liturgy suggests that this is one day that the church is without words, all the more to underline the letter to the Hebrews in which Jesus himself "offered prayers and supplications with loud cries and tears." The silence that troubles this day acknowledges the Lamb that is dumb before the slaughter. The opening prayer breaks the silence with a plea from the whole church that this assembly of the presanctified enters the protection of God's mercy to "sanctify" his servants, "for whom Christ your Son, by the shedding of his Blood, established the Paschal Mystery." The use of the word *famulos* (servants) aligns the congregation with the role of Christ himself as Suffering Servant, who was obedient unto death. As servants of God, we find our "source of eternal salvation" precisely as servants—"for all who obey him," as the letter to the Hebrews suggests. Moreover, as servants, we are helpless before God, urgently begging his mercy.

The unusual ritual that accompanies this day highlights the work of Christ's passion like no other, and the readings climax to the moment when the Suffering Servant is offered up on the cross. The crucified Christ has an exalted place in the Fourth Gospel as a disclosure of God's glory. And the **Solemn Intercessions** place a special emphasis on the mediation of the cross for the sake of all human kind, from the church itself to those of every nation and religion, from the faithful to the unbeliever. Each of the prayers that follow the orations have specific allusions proper to the intention, but the first one, "For the Holy Church," seems to set the tone for the rest of these supplications when it says, "Almighty ever-living God, who in Christ revealed your glory to all the nations, watch over the works of your mercy." The reach of Christ's intercession is as unfathomable as God's mercy and so we can only adore the one in gratitude who pleads for us by the wood of the cross, the instrument of our salvation and redemption.

Strategy for Preaching

The advantages of preaching on Good Friday are many, since the assembly will be comprised of the devout members of the congregation seeking to understand the mystery of the Lord's passion and death in a deep and meaningful way. The liturgy itself is a kind of homily, with the cross as its center, and so the preaching forms something of a companion piece to a mysterious disclosure, giving voice to the profound articulation of the Word voicing its "loud cries and tears." Along these lines, a theological explanation of the sacrifice of the cross is certainly in order, but it would be useful if it occurred in a way that allowed the listening assembly to feel and experience the event in an immediate, rather than abstract, way. After all, the sacrifice of Christ on this day is a purifying event, and so the closer the homily approaches a catharsis for the congregation, the more the preaching approximates the liturgical action of which it is a part.

One creative way of approaching a homily on Good Friday is by way of an indirect theological expression through a monologue, in this instance an eyewitness report of the events surrounding the passion. The monologue is something along the lines of a dramatic retelling of an event from one person's perspective. A monologue on Good Friday would pull out a character from the passion narrative in John's gospel and relate the events from the perspective of that character. What would the garden in the Kidron valley and the events of the betrayal look like from the point of view of one of the participants, say Malchus, the high priest's slave? Or how about the gatekeeper who had an encounter with Peter in the courtyard? Mary, the mother of Jesus, or the Beloved Disciple at the foot of the cross? We already have a popular gospel song suggesting witness: "Were you there when they crucified my Lord?"

Here are some of the advantages of the monologue homily:

1. A subjective point of view allows the hearer to participate in a very affective way the events of the Gospel, from which he or she might be otherwise separated by a cultural distance. This separation might be particularly true when we consider the events of the cross.

2. Holy Week should offer a variety of modes of preaching, and the monologue homily for Good Friday allows for an intimate, vivid expression of an interior witness that is particularly suitable to the Johannine Gospel.

3. There is a chance to problematize the way we view and judge characters. If we are quick to assign blame to Peter or even

Judas, granting them a "hearing" fills the picture out a bit more on this day when God's compassion is boundless.

4. This style of homily could also lead the congregation to further meditation on the passion of the Lord, particularly imagistic prayer of the kind Ignatius Loyola encourages his retreatants to engage in in the *Spiritual Exercises*.

Easter Sunday
of the Resurrection of the Lord

The Easter Vigil in the Holy Night
(Years ABC)

Readings from the Ambo

Gen 1:1–2:2 (First Reading); Ps 104:1-2, 5-6, 10, 12, 13-14, 24, 35
or Ps 33:4-5, 6-7, 12-13, 20 and 22

Genesis's first (Priestly writer's) account of creation is a story of origins, a fitting initiation to the Liturgy of the Word for the Easter Vigil. The Liturgy of the Word begins with a familiar text, underneath which is a brave and simple faith: *"Bereshit bara Elohim et hashamayim ve'et ha'arets"* (In the beginning, when God created the heavens and the earth). The root of the first word of the Hebrew Bible, *bereshit*, is from *rosh*, meaning head or chief, underlining this story of origins. In contrast to the second (Yahwist writer's) reckoning of creation, this passage reveals a lofty and mysterious maker of the cosmos whose *ruah* or spirit hovers over the waters and permeates the corners of all created things, breathing into the nostrils of humankind the breath of life. The story climaxes with the creation of human beings, made in the image of God. This *imago Dei* becomes a key theological term that will underlie Christian anthropology for centuries and continue into the present day. With the proclamation of this reading at the celebration of the passion, death, and resurrection of the Lord, the recognition of the human subject as *imago Dei*, crystallizes the gift of our redemption purchased for us in Christ, now restored.

Gen 22:1-18; Ps 16:5, 8, 9-10, 11

The story of Abraham and the *Akedah*, or Binding of Isaac, is a heart-wrenching moment in salvation history, which the patristic

97

fathers would seize as an allegorical representation of God's surrender of his own Son unto death. Needless to say, the violence of a text in which God asks the first patriarch of Israel to sacrifice a child can only strike the hearer as barbaric. Yet, as some have argued, this may be a story that rails against human sacrifice, since God prohibits Abraham's actions and finds a ram in his stead. Still, the violence is hard to ignore. Benjamin Britten's *War Requiem* (1962) renders the ferocity of the sacrifice of Isaac palpable when he retells the story: Abraham ignores the angel's intervention and slays his son anyway. The story as Britten refashions it locates the violence to kill in the heart of the human subject, stretching back to antiquity. That iconoclastic reading notwithstanding, the raw emotion present in the text as we have it here points us to an emblematic example of unflinching obedience to God's command, even at the expense of one's dearest love. It is that white-knuckled emotion that is meant to wash over us, singling Abraham out as the father of our faith.

Exod 14:15–15:1; Exod 15:1-6, 17-18

The selection from the book of Exodus catches the chosen people at a climactic moment on their journey from Egypt to the Promised Land, when a definitive boundary has been crossed and their ruthless pursuer has been eradicated. With the crossing of the Red Sea, as with many key moments in the Hebrew Scriptures, the patristic authors would find a christianized allegorical reading. Origen, for instance, would discover a profound symbolic connection between the crossing of the Red Sea and Christian baptism, which allegorizes Pharaoh as the power of Satan drowned in the waters of new life in Christ. Therefore the response of the people of Israel and the newly baptized is the same: "I will sing to the LORD, for he is gloriously triumphant." This text, then, gathers the community of Israel and the Christian faithful on the side of the same sea, all of us waiting to cross into the Promised Land of our redemption. In addition to an allegorical interpretation informing Christian baptism, this passage has been a hermeneutical blueprint for those kept in bondage awaiting freedom from the 1960s civil rights movement to apartheid in South Africa.

Isa 54:5-14; Ps 30:2, 4, 5-6, 11-12, 13

In the last of the Zion oracles, Second Isaiah speaks to the exiles of a God who will never give up on the chosen people: the promise will endure forever. Beginning in verse 1, Isaiah uses a series of spousal images that vividly bring to light God's covenantal love. At the same time, the immanent presence of the Lord contrasts strikingly with the transcendent God of the universe: "[t]he One who has become your husband is your Maker; / his name is the LORD of hosts." Like some powerful images in the Bible, these metaphors can be somewhat troubling and patriarchal for contemporary hearers. Are we to take the Lord, calling back Israel during the exile, as "a wife married in youth and then cast off" or in a "brief moment . . ." "abandoned" and "[i]n an outburst of wrath" faced a God who hid his face? To understand the "enduring love" expressed by the biblical author we may have to suspend modern sensibility for a moment and lean into the historical presence of the text that desires to convey a God of mercy and pity. Interestingly, there is another side to this God, infinitely more complex than we imagine. The portrait of the Lord given by Second Isaiah is of a repentant God, who likens these days of exile to the time when he renewed a covenant with Noah, which became an eternal promise. The passage's overriding intention asks us to see a God of unconditional love, remembering with some sentiment, a covenant of peace.

Isa 55:1-11; Isa 12:2-3, 4, 5-6

One way of understanding this passage is to see the text precisely as a kind of rejoinder or companion piece to the previous reading. Having testified to a steadfast covenant in which justice and peace will be established in foundations and battlements of precious stones, God now prepares a banquet for his people. This festive meal is extended to everyone without cost, a fitting celebration from the God who loves unconditionally. Yet alongside this promise of water to the thirsty and grain for the hungry, there is also the plea for conversion, to heed God and eat well, to "Seek the LORD while he may be found, / call him while he is near." Once again, we face a God who is both merciful and powerful. These two seemingly irreconcilable characteristics converge in God's *dabar*, the word that, like "seed to the one who sows / and bread to the one who eats," achieves its proper end and does not return to God "void." God's power is accomplished in the very act of intending goodness, which is mercy and abundance—watering the earth and making it both fertile and fruitful. From a Christian perspective, the baptismal imagery and invitation to conversion and renunciation is clear enough: all are invited to renew themselves in God's saving waters and at the table of God's endless mercy. The Lord's banquet gathers the lost, even as God's memory of the covenant assured to David identifies his descendants as precious. In the response that follows, taken from First Isaiah, that promise is reified: "You will draw water joyfully from the springs of salvation."

Bar 3:9-15; 3:2–4:4; Ps 19:8, 9, 10, 11

Speaking to Israel in a time of captivity, Baruch presents God's wisdom and commandments as the anchor of salvation. Although Israel has rejected "the fountain of wisdom," Baruch offers a return to prudence as a pathway back to the Lord. "Turn, O Jacob, and receive her; / walk by her light toward splendor." The underlying virtue embedded in Baruch's admonition to Israel is hope, since when we know where prudence, strength, and understanding abide, then we will also know "where are length of days, and life, / where light of the eyes, and peace." The advice Baruch has for Israel is echoed in the psalm response: "Lord, you have the words of everlasting life." The word of God and the precepts of the law are the building blocks for faithful and virtuous living in the land of exile. In a sense, Baruch has to rearticulate a whole tradition to a people who have lost everything, including their sense of direction, as it were. Which way is home? He speaks to Israel of a wisdom tradition in order to refound a people in the midst of exile and darkness. It is the Lord God who has found these precious people and gives them direction. In Baruch's hands, wisdom becomes the arbitrator of life, a handmaid of the Most High, the law that can be returned to over and over again: "She is the book of the precepts of God, / the law that endures forever." This rebuilding for Israel will be a pathway lit by the splendor of wisdom, a light that will never go out, even in the midst of the diaspora.

Ezek 36:16-17a, 18-28; Ps 42:3, 5; 43:3, 4 or,
either Isa 12:2-3, 4bcd, 5-6 or Ps 51:12-13, 14-15, 18-19

Ezekiel's utterance is both a rebuke and a promise. The Lord recalls the reality of Israel's transgressions and the penalty they paid—scattering and dispersion among the nations. Most of all, it is for the sake of God's holy name, which has been profaned in exile, that the Lord has relented and will redeem his people by sprinkling clean water upon them to cleanse them from their impurities and idols. A central image that focuses on this redemption is a promise of transformation: "I will give you a new heart and place a new spirit within you, / taking from your bodies your stony hearts / and giving you natural hearts." The spirit of the Lord will also inhabit this new Israel, even as that same spirit will give life to the "dry bones" in the valley the prophet encounters and records in chapter 37:1-14. God guarantees new life to those in exile, since those who have been lost will be gathered. Like Second Isaiah, the water imagery is a baptismal mystic bath when seen from a Christian perspective. When the catechumen dies to sin in baptism it is then that that new life begins in Christ: that is the coming of the spirit that animates the hearts of those who have traded their stony hearts for ones made of flesh. Christians have been gathered in from sin, that place of reckless and unruly exile, and have been brought under God's re-creative vision.

Rom 6:3-11; Ps 118:1-2, 16-17, 22-23

Paul finds himself in the company of Isaiah and Ezekiel as he also promises newness of life, once we are dead to the power of sin and alive in Christ Jesus. In a certain sense, Paul's theological discourse on baptism and its connection to the death and resurrection of Christ forms something of a commentary for all those who have listened to Isaiah and "come to the waters" and have found "new life." This newness of life has been purchased by Christ's own death and resurrection, freeing us from being "in slavery to sin." Paul makes it abundantly lucid that all those who are baptized participate in Christ's work, since they are "dead to sin / and living for God in Christ Jesus." The liturgical context of this reading of the epistle from Paul shifts the tone of the vigil rather dramatically, since after the last reading from Ezekiel the presider will intone the *Gloria in excelsis Deo* and then acknowledge that the Lord has made holy "this most sacred night with the glory of the Lord's Resurrection." Paul's words to the Romans, then, are blooming with the reality of new life brought by Christ and the place baptism holds for Christians, since "We were indeed buried with him through baptism into death, / so that, just as Christ was raised from the dead / by the glory of the Father, / we too might live in newness of life."

Mark 16:1-7 (Year B)

There are few passages in scripture as momentous and jarring as Mark 16:1-7. Unlike the other three parallels to Jesus' resurrection

(Matt 28:1-8; Luke 24:1-12; John 20:1-10), Mark's epilogue disclosing the aftermath of the resurrection is far from comforting. In fact, these first witnesses to the resurrection of the Lord—Mary Magdalene; Mary, the Mother of James; and Salome—do exactly what the young man dressed in white tell them not to do. He tells them not to be alarmed, but they are *tromos* or "trembling." He tells them to go ahead in the direction of Peter and the other disciples where they will see the Risen One, but instead they *ephugon*, or "flee" from the tomb. And he tells them to *eiphate*, or "tell" what they have seen, but instead they say nothing to anyone.

Such details are in verse 8, however, which is not part of the reading. Instead, the Lectionary ends on an upbeat—not a bad thing, to be sure. But why not face the congregation with the reality of the whole scene, which seems to be much closer to what we know of human emotions and, more important, the demands of faith. Preaching Mark 16:1-7 and omitting verse 8 seems incomplete. Faith is provoked by the awesome reality of God's transforming power, which will cause us to move into the "dark faith" of trust and hope, as St. John of the Cross put it. Indeed, this faith often comes in retrospect through the power of God's grace, having seen in hindsight the wonders the Lord has done. Along these lines the congregation is placed precisely in the point of view of these first witnesses to the resurrection, if we allow them also to respond in faith to the mystery of the Risen Lord. Who would not be slack-jawed at the sight of an empty tomb with a witness to the resurrection telling us to preach what we had just seen? In the end, however, this young man—with his white robes, perhaps a symbol of the newly baptized, as some have argued—becomes a very contemporary guide to God's saving power and to the liturgical assembly, having just heard record of God's salvation history this night of nights.

An empty tomb, a baptismal witness, and the mission to preach what we have seen—could there be a better invitation to mission on this Easter Vigil? It is our turn to proclaim fearlessly and to run toward the crucified and risen Lord who waits for us.

Connecting the Bible and the Liturgy

The opportunities to make connections with the Scriptures and the liturgy for the Easter Vigil are almost too many to enumerate, to say nothing of doing so in such a short space. But from the perspective of unique opportunities, the *Exultet*, that ecstatic announcement like no other, certainly presents a panorama of salvation history filled with emotion that will find its echo in the sweep of the scriptural readings. Indeed, the bringing of the light of Easter to the earth echoes with the excitement of Prometheus unbound as the fire radiates, "ablaze with light from her eternal King." The Genesis text will bring to our horizon the Creator who first created that light that now finds its benediction as Easter fire. Indeed, the coming of the light is also the brightness brought to the exiles, led out of Egypt and given the good news of hope by Isaiah and Ezekiel. When it comes to the **Blessing of the Baptismal Water**, this text rehearses the primal waters fashioned by the Creator from the beginning and now made new in Christ. The freedom from bondage, "set free from slavery to Pharaoh," expressed in Exodus now celebrates the gift of living water offered in gratuitous largesse from the God who invites all to "come to the waters" that have no price.

Additionally, there is a wonderful opportunity to connect the Scriptures with the liturgy at the Easter Vigil in the **Prayers after the Readings**. The global reach of the readings to all people is highlighted in the prayer after Genesis 22:1-18, for instance, when the presider begs God to pour out "the grace of adoption throughout the whole world . . . [and] through the Paschal Mystery make your servant Abraham father of nations." The prayer makes the obedience of Abraham so astonishingly vivid in the Scriptures that there ensues an immediate invitation to the liturgical assembly to do likewise in their own (sometimes painful) call to do God's will: "Grant, we pray, that your peoples may enter worthily into the grace to which you call them." Similarly, after the reading concerning Israel's passage through the Red Sea, the parallel with the congregation is once again established between the two worlds: "grant, we pray, that the whole world may become children of Abraham and inherit the dignity of Israel's birthright." In fact, the prayer makes it clear that the Lord has not ceased from doing such wonders, since this is a God, *"cuius antiqua miracula etiam nostris temporibus coruscare sentimus"* (whose ancient wonders remain undimmed in splendor even in our day). Needless to say, asking God that in *Abraehae filos et in Israeliticam dignitatem totius mundi transeat plenitudo* in the current political climate is a bold claim, but the connection between the people of

Israel and the Christian community ought not to be overlooked, or its interfaith relations go underappreciated—especially during the Easter Vigil. With the catechumens crossing the Red Sea into baptism and the Christian community renewing their baptism by renouncing the slavery to the pharaoh of Satan, the liturgical assembly and the people of Israel are deeply united, and, in this very recognition, God's promise of liberation becomes clear from age to age, even as Abraham has become the father of faith and of many nations.

Strategy for Preaching

The lavish richness and the deep breadth of the readings and the liturgy for the Easter Vigil present the preacher with a formidable task: how to capture the incredible panoply of texts, scriptural and liturgical, which encompass this night in a homily that is less than ten minutes in length. We have just watched salvation history being retold before our eyes. That makes the Easter Vigil a unique preaching experience. Indeed, the homilist should not make the mistake of thinking that preaching for the vigil is identical with that which will be proclaimed at the liturgy during Easter Day. The character of the Easter Vigil will mark a homily that understands the sweep of salvation history, the gift of baptism, and the place of the resurrection in the life of the Christian community.

Below are three practical tactics for preaching on this night of nights, all of which may be expanded or diminished as needed.

The arc of the homily can first be sketched by attending to all of the readings and identifying *one* characteristic in each of them during a session of *lectio divina*. I am recommending one characteristic so that these features might be resources when the homily is shaped: First Reading: Gift; Second Reading: Obedience; Third Reading: Liberation; Fourth Reading: Covenant; Fifth Reading: Rebirth; Sixth Reading: Hope; Seventh Reading: Redemption; Eighth Reading: New Life; Ninth Reading: Faith.

1. After the characteristics are identified, use the orations following the readings to enter into a prayerful dialogue with how you understand the text. What do you want to ask of these texts based on the liturgy that responds to each of the scriptural selections?

2. After this process, see what homiletic core emerges. This core might look like the following: This is the night when God has brought us out of the darkness of sin and death and liberated us in the waters of redemption. Given the multiple combinations of readings and liturgical texts, there are any number of core homiletic sentences that might surface in the course of a prayerful encounter before the homily is preached.

3. After the core homiletic idea is established, introduce the variety of dialogue partners to start organizing the homily. There are the scriptural texts that will broaden the core homiletic idea. In the case of the core just recommended, the readings from the vigil such as Exodus, Isaiah, Ezekiel, Paul, and Mark all help to establish credibility to the focus or core homiletic sentence. Lastly, the liturgy for the vigil provides further text to establish a dialogue such as the *Exultet*, the Baptismal Liturgy, the Preface I of Easter, and the proper Presidential Prayers for the Eucharistic Liturgy.

Based on this strategy, a possible outline for the homily could be organized in this fashion:

I. Introduction (leading into the homiletic core sentence).

II. This is the night when God has brought us out of the darkness of sin and liberated us in the waters of redemption.
    A. Exodus 14:15–15:1
    B. Prayer following this reading.
    C. *Exultet.*
    D. Blessing of Baptismal Water.

III. But we tend to live in exile, away from God, unaware of the covenant that has endured forever.
    A. Ezekiel 36:16-17a, 18-28.
    B. Isaiah 54:5-14; 55:1-11.
    C. Prayer following the reading.
    D. Preface.

IV. So it will take faith to live the experience of the resurrection.
    A. Mark 16:1-7.

    B. Romans 6:3-11.

    C. Baptismal promises.

    D. A story (short) illustrating a discovery of new life. This may be a secular story or a religious one illustrating making alive what once was dead.

  V. Conclusion (closing off the core idea). We are united this night with the children of Abraham as we are freed from our bondage, even as the earth shakes us loose into God's kingdom of his Christ.

Easter Sunday
of the Resurrection of the Lord
At the Mass during the Day (Years ABC)

Readings from the Ambo

Acts 10:34a, 37-43; Ps 118:1-2,16-17, 22-23;
Col 3:1-4 or 1 Cor 5:6b-8; John 20:1-9

The **First Reading** from Acts is a fitting summary leading up to the moment of Jesus' resurrection. Peter's address to the centurion Cornelius and his household recapitulates the life, ministry, death, and resurrection of the Lord for the Gentiles. The rising of Christ from the dead is a message that is meant for all. As Peter begins his speech (not included in the selection from Acts here), "In truth, I see that God shows no partiality" (10:34b NAB), or more graphically in the Greek text, *prosopolomptes*, meaning to lift up someone's face, showing favorites. As Paul would say in 1 Corinthians, this message of the resurrection is the good news that allows us to celebrate the feast of the paschal lamb with a little yeast that "leavens all the dough." Therefore Jesus himself showed no partiality but "went about doing good and healing all those oppressed by the devil, for God was with him." After Peter's speech, Acts 10 will conclude with the Holy Spirit falling upon all who heard the Word in the house of Cornelius. The Spirit falls without partiality as well but comes to those who hear the Word.

While the Good News is meant for all, Jew and Gentile alike, there are certain demands placed on the receivers of the Word. Like Peter, Christians proclaim and witness to the life, death, and resurrection of Jesus. Like Cornelius and his household, the invitation is to hear and believe. Hearing the Word opens those present to the eschatological moment of the coming of the Holy Spirit; that is as true for those who hear Peter's preaching as it is for the assembly of the baptized gathered for Eucharist on this first day of the week on Easter morning in the twenty-first century.

In a very different context than Acts, Paul writes to the Colossians in prison encouraging them to be hearers of the Good News of the resurrection of the Lord. Throughout the letter to the Colossians, Paul stresses the authority granted to Christ through the power of the resurrection, which has rescued them from death and pagan practices and *metestesen* or transferred, us into the kingdom of his beloved Son. Paul, himself in chains, is conscious of being transported by "what is above, not of what is on earth," longing for Christ to appear with him in glory. So the source of Paul's encouragement is abiding in Christ, which is accomplished in baptism because the Christian's "life is hidden with Christ in God."

The selection from John's gospel brings about closure in so many ways. Having run to the tomb where Jesus once lay, the Beloved Disciple "saw and believed." The story of the resurrection is something like the last piece of a puzzle that has gone unsolved until the final ecstatic moment. In John's gospel, Jesus has performed signs from the wedding at Cana to the cleansing of the temple, until he himself became the definitive sign of God's glory on the cross. Now, at last, the disciples who were closest to Jesus put the missing and jagged piece into its place to complete the picture. The astonishment of the resurrection now begins a new age and a new *kairos* of creation: the first day of the week. The site of the empty tomb yields to an acknowledgement of profound understanding of the Scriptures and Jesus' teaching concerning his place in salvation history. In Luke, two other disciples will have a similar moment of faith, but its revelation comes not from the empty tomb, but from Jesus himself in the Scriptures, the breaking of the bread, and the prayers.

Connecting the Bible and the Liturgy

With the dramatic events in John's gospel close at hand, a poignant phrase in the **Collect** to recall is this: "O God, who on this day, through your Only Begotten Son, have conquered death and unlocked for us the path of eternity." As described by the author of John's gospel, the tomb is locked, and then Mary Magdala came there and "saw the stone removed from the tomb." She at once proclaimed to the disciples, as the **Sequence** says, "The tomb of Christ who is living, the glory of Jesus' resurrection." Moreover, the writer is at pains to describe a race on the path to see if what Mary said was true, as Peter and "the other disciple" ran and made their way to Jesus' empty tomb. They arrive, breathless, to a new discovery of life and resurrection. Therefore God has literally helped us to beat a pathway to the gates of eternity, or *aeternitatis nobis aditum*. The image of the disciples running at the proclamation of Mary Magdalene is also the remarkable beginning of the transmission of this Good News of eternal life: the Word has begotten the Word, which leads quite literally to the *resurgens* of new life. Additionally, Paul's situation in writing to the Colossians is a memorable connection here as well. As we pray in gratitude to God who has "unlocked" the gates of eternity, so too does Paul urge the Colossians to seek the Christ who is above, now glorified at the right hand of God. It is Christ who has trod that pathway to eternity and made it clear for all those who have died in him; they now have a life that is hidden or *kekruptai* in God.

Depending on whether or not the presider chooses to ask the congregation to renew their baptismal promises after the homily, the **Collect** provides a fitting prelude to these prayers when it prays that as we keep the Solemnity of the Lord's Resurrection we may, "through the renewal brought by your spirit rise up to the light of life." With the baptismal renewal, a catechetical moment for the assembly awaits them, as the assembly recognizes the presence of the risen Christ's spirit in their own renewal; it is an invitation to remind the assembly that "we have been buried with Christ in Baptism, so that we may walk with him in newness of life."

Finally, if the Roman Canon (**EP I**) is used, there are the proper forms of the *communicantes* that harken back to the readings and provide yet another catechetical moment, as it begins, "Celebrating the most sacred night (day) of the Resurrection of our Lord Jesus Christ in the flesh." This doctrinal moment concerning the resurrection should not be passed through lightly, since the resurrection of the body is a seminal article of faith and, appropriately enough, is part of the **Gospel** narrative and its clues. When Peter sees the empty tomb, the burial clothes are in separate places, an important indication that Jesus' rising was not based on a hysterical vision or some kind of a spiritual rising, but a corporeal one. The very bodily resurrection of

Jesus will be taken up again in next week's Gospel as John recounts Thomas's encounter with the risen Lord and his wounds.

Strategy for Preaching

Who would disbelieve the sight of the risen Lord? As hinted to earlier, the popular imagination has cultivated any number of episodes concerning the resurrection that are not entirely biblical in their origin and representation. This first day of the week when it is still dark, Mary Magdalene, Peter, and "the other disciple" Jesus loved face a far more existential encounter than a vision of the Lord; they face the empty tomb and must interpret its consequences. We know that in John's gospel, Jesus will make himself known as a risen body in a variety of ways after this initial moment—appearing to Mary Magdalene in the garden, revealing himself to the disciples in the locked room and by the Sea of Tiberius. But this Easter Sunday faces the Christian assembly with deep questions of faith, baptismal renewal, and the search for Christ amid the darkness of despair. The homiletic core idea is literally a matter of life and death. The question for this Easter morning for the Sunday assembly might be shaped around this: how do we understand the empty tomb as a call to believe God's promise for eternal life?

A good preaching plan for developing this question is to help the congregation to come to the same conclusion as the Beloved Disciple. "He saw and believed" should be the goal toward which the homiletic arc is moving. To this end, the preacher might consider a kind of "retelling" of Jesus' life and ministry, death, and resurrection along the lines that Peter proclaims in the house of Cornelius. According to John's gospel, the site of the empty tomb triggered in the Beloved Disciple is an insight, *pisteuein*, "he believed." If we are to take the Beloved Disciple as the first witness of the resurrection, we might consider his witness value to the works or signs of Jesus as a way into understanding and believing. That strategy does not mean a repetition of the whole gospel, but helping the hearer to unlock the mystery of God's gift of eternal life.

To consider one such sign early in John's gospel: the cleansing of the temple (2:13-25). That is an important episode in the life of Jesus and the disciples precisely because verse 22 makes a specific reference to the activity at the temple and the recollection the disciples have after Jesus rises from the dead. "Destroy this temple and in three days I will raise it up. . . . Therefore, when he was raised from the dead, his disciples remembered that he had said this, and they came to believe the Scripture and the word Jesus had spoken" (2:19b; 22). The preacher might begin by asking the assembly to ponder what it would be like if the very building in which they were worshiping might vanish. What would they have? The Johannine community faced the destruction of the temple and Jesus himself seems to peel off the layers of external temple practices early in John's gospel, seemingly to replace it with himself as the new temple that is raised up. When all is taken away from us—even the security of institutional religion—and we stare only at an empty tomb in the dawn of the morning, do we see the Lord before us?

A courageous story of faith is the episode immediately following this passage (John 10-18) in which Mary meets Jesus in person. She was with him to the end—right up to the cross and came to the (empty) tomb to care for him. That is the faith that begins with love. The homily could build on this premise and use other contemporary stories of the strong relationship between love and faith. It is probably not an accident that the Beloved Disciple reached the tomb first because of this love and was also the first to believe in the resurrection as its first witness. Stories that show love as the gateway to faith and trust will underline the devotion of the Beloved Disciple to love and believe: standing at the foot of the cross and racing to the tomb has born the fruit of testimony—the gospel itself.

In the end, the buildings we come to adorn with our Easter lilies and spring flowers are wonderful places, but nothing substitutes for the temple of the risen Lord. Like the disciples we come to the Lord, running with all we have and find ourselves witnessing to his rising from the dead. The Eucharist allows us once again to recognize him in the garden that the church has invited us all to dwell in on this fragrant Easter morning.

EASTER TIME

Second Sunday of Easter

Readings from the Ambo

Acts 4:32-35; Ps 118:2-4, 13-15, 22-24;
1 John 5:1-6; John 20:19-31

The Second Sunday of Easter—and subsequent Sundays in Paschaltide, for that matter—will most obviously foreground the spiritual and eschatological consequences of the resurrection of the Lord. The Gospel of John's account of the disciples in the locked room, riddled with fear and dread (occurring in all Years in Cycles A, B, and C), contrasts sharply with the First and Second Readings in the Lectionary.

The **First Reading** from Acts in Year B shows us the aftermath of that singular, Pentecost moment in the life of the disciples and the early church when "[w]ith great power the apostles bore witness / to the resurrection of the Lord Jesus, / and great favor was accorded them all." Is it possible that these disciples could possibly be the same men who cowered in fear in that hideaway before Jesus encountered them? The first thing that Jesus gives to the halting disciples is peace: "Peace be with you," he tells them. It would seem that the **Gospel** is pointing out that the event of the resurrection itself is not sufficient to embolden the apostles. Far from it. All week long, the readings during the Octave of Easter have shown us how terrified the disciples have been after Jesus was taken from them. Only his very person can give them what they truly need. Further, Christ's presence not only grants these followers his peace but strengthens them for service: "As the Father has sent me, so I send you." In a real sense, when Jesus breathes on the disciples, he is already anticipating Pentecost: "Receive the Holy Spirit. / Whose sins you forgive are forgiven them, / and whose sins you retain are retained."

The reconciliatory features of Christ's presence are obvious enough in this scene, and Thomas plays an important role in revealing just how crucial the unity of the faith community is in being "of one heart and mind," a gift that is also present in Acts. Why was Thomas not with the disciples when Jesus came the first time? His absence may suggest that his faith witness was not strong enough to stand with the rest of the disciples, even in their terror. When it comes to unity of purpose, faith, hope, and love are strengthened by the presence of other witnesses, something that the disciples would learn more fully at the Pentecost event. The loner will be all the more doubtful until he is in the presence of authentic community. We are strengthened when we see others who believe, as John tells us in the **Second Reading** that "Jesus is the Christ [and] is begotten by God. . . . In this way we know that we love the children of God / when we love God and obey his commandments." In other words, Thomas has been shown not only the wounds of Christ's person but the marks on the Body of Christ of those gathered waiting to be healed. In placing his hands in Jesus' hands and side, Thomas makes not only a personal affirmation of his relationship with the Lord but a kind of refrain that could be repeated by the whole church, filled with the Spirit of the Lord and faith in the resurrection: "My Lord and my God!"

Connecting the Bible and the Liturgy

Although this day has been recently named "Divine Mercy Sunday," it is hard to imagine that every Sunday could not be called an invocation of God's mercy. Indeed, it is fitting that the **Collect** for today begins with an address to "*Deus misericordiae sempiternae.*" As the Gospel will show, this is a God who, in his Christ, has penetrated the sin of our locked doors and set us free from death. Death is what shuts us into rooms from which there is no escape unless Christ enters these walls. Overall, the Collect itself is highly charged with energetic language that celebrates the liturgical and historical reality of the paschal mystery. Indeed, the Collect makes a theological case for the liturgy as a site where faith grows stronger, like the disciples at the appearance of the risen Lord, since God, "in the very recurrence of the paschal feast / kindle[s] the faith of the people you have made your own," becomes the one to "increase . . . the grace . . . bestowed, / that all may grasp and rightly understand" those mysteries. Special rhetorical emphasis has been laid on the reception of this grace for the assembly: "*quo lavacro abluti, quo spiritu regenerati, quo sanguine sunt redempti.*" The *Missal* translates this nicely into a triple clause in English, which has a similar effect of assigning the origins of these mysteries: "in what font they have been washed, / by whose Spirit they have been reborn, / by whose Blood they have been redeemed." In the end, the Collect makes it clear that the assembly has celebrated the paschal mystery and that we are now closing the Octave of Easter.

One gets the sense of witness pervading the church's voice in the Collect, a legacy of the gift of the Spirit in Acts: "With great power the apostles bore witness / to the resurrection of the Lord Jesus." With the petition to increase the grace God has already bestowed, there is a profound sense of hope not only for those few gathered behind a locked room, fearful and helpless until the Lord appears in their midst and says, "Peace be with you." Those who have celebrated "the very recurrence of the paschal feast" contrast with Thomas who asks for proof rather than the grace of belief. Graced belief makes all things possible, since "[e]veryone who believes that Jesus is the Christ is begotten by God, / and everyone who loves the Father / loves also the one begotten by him." Small wonder why Jesus himself says, "Blessed are those who have not seen and have believed."

The Second Sunday of Easter asks us a blunt question: does the celebration of the passion, death, and resurrection of the Son of God make any difference in our lives? Or is it business as usual until next year? If we acknowledge that we have been "renewed by confession of your name and by Baptism" (**Prayer over the Offerings**), then "our reception of this paschal Sacrament / may have a continuing effect / in our minds and hearts" (**Prayer after Communion**). After exploring the wounds of the risen Lord, the question above would have been answered differently by Thomas. So too, the sanctified community, washed in the Blood of the Lamb, allows its celebration of Easter to be a time for God to renew our faith, hope, and love. That the liturgy changes us is clear, since we too have gathered in order to hear the voice of Christ say to us: "Peace be with you."

Strategy for Preaching

Here we will pick up on something observed in the previous section and allow the question to form a homiletic core. How does the resurrection make a difference in my life? Clearly, the readings and the liturgy suggest that the resurrection, while a doctrine and a creedal backbone of the church, is not only about life after death; it is about a way of living in the world because God has changed all things in Christ: we are living in a resurrected time, where Christ is truly present and living in our midst.

Of this resurrection Scripture attests, but so do we and the voiced tradition of the church in the liturgy. Despite their fears, the disciples are transformed by the risen Lord. The First Letter of John allows that we testify to the love of God—real and active in our lives—by our faith. So, belief in Christ's resurrection—what Thomas comes to acknowledge eventually, through God's mercy—and a recognition of his divine presence are closely entwined. The final outcome of the resurrection is the healed community established by the Spirit of reconciliation of Christ's work on earth. "With great power the apostles bore witness / to the resurrection." We are inheritors of that witness.

It is the role of the preacher to get the congregation to claim this very role of witness to the resurrection, allowing the baptized to answer the question: how does the resurrection make a difference in my life? All week the Gospel readings have shown different ways in which Jesus revealed himself to his disciples. In the closing of the church's Easter Octave, or Divine Mercy Sunday, we might say that the revelation of Christ has been poured upon the whole church in order to say, "My Lord and my God." That is a devout prayer about the awe of God's mercy. The flowing may serve as a conduit for the hearer at the assembly, an avenue to allow the congregation to voice this prayer as individual subjects but also as a community. The outline moves on a trajectory from question to recognition, much like Thomas himself.

    I. Does the resurrection make a difference? There is violence, poverty, and sin still present in our world.

   II. But the clear sign of Christ's power of the resurrection is reconciliation, or the peace we extend to others—even those who perpetuate violence and sin in the world.

     A. The Gospel shows us Jesus extending peace to the disciples.

     B. There is forgiveness.

     C. Thomas explores Jesus' wounds.

III. We must often look at the difficult side of the resurrection—
how it was purchased—only through suffering, dying, and
death. That is how the world is given peace. (Illustration: story
of witness)

A. So resurrection makes a difference if we live and die the way
Jesus did and continue to explore the wounds of division
and apply the healing balm of reconciliation.

Third Sunday of Easter

Readings from the Ambo

Acts 3:13-15, 17-19; Ps 4:2, 4, 7-8, 9;
1 John 2:1-5a; Luke 24:35-48

The **Gospel** for Year B proclaimed this Sunday is the identical text for Year A, although the present selection is a shortened version of the Emmaus narrative. The whole story builds persuasively to the final disclosure of Jesus on the scene: from confusion and desolation, the wandering disciples finally discover that the "stranger" is really the Lord. We are aware from the first verse of our present reading that Jesus was made known to them in the breaking of the bread—"*hos egnosthe autois en te klasei tou artou.*" From a literary perspective, the reader is allowed to share knowledge of the outcome of the story before the disciples themselves, granting us a kind of privileged status or knowledge. Additionally, our focus becomes invariably associated with food and its eucharistic language, linking Jesus' presence with the word spoken and the bread broken.

As with the appearance to Thomas in the locked room, Jesus' presence is concretized in his wounds ("he showed them his hands and his feet"), as if to equate the suffering Christ with his real presence all the more. So it is not just that Jesus has returned; he has also been revealed as one who has endured the pains of death. For what end? "Then he opened their minds to understand the Scriptures. / And he said to them, / 'Thus it is written that the Christ would suffer / and rise from the dead on the third day.'" There is an important aspect of the Lukan Jesus here precisely as an *interpreter of his own history,* an identity he has claimed from the moment he entered the synagogue in his hometown of Nazareth, in Luke 4:16ff., when he told the congregation that the Scriptures would be fulfilled in their hearing. Here, once again, Jesus announces himself in the context of salvation history, this time as the Christ who suffers and dies. But the contrast with the earlier scene in chapter 4 could not be more different. The minds of the disciples are opened on the way to Emmaus, and they are comforted by his presence. Clearly, we are meant to see that the risen Jesus comes even in the midst of those who are troubled and doubtful, and those who make their journey outside Jerusalem are no exception. That Jesus comes to comfort but also interpret tradition gives authority to those who gather in his name, who become witnesses to the afterglow of the resurrection. Undoubtedly, the breaking of bread becomes linked to the memory of Christ's interpretation of his own history, which then becomes passed on to these disciples at Emmaus.

Peter testifies to the same Lord in Acts, saying that Jesus was once put to death, "but God raised him from the dead; of this we are witnesses." Like Jesus, Peter puts the death and resurrection of the Messiah in context, since "God has thus brought to fulfillment / what he had announced beforehand / through the mouth of all the prophets, / that his Christ would suffer." To be sure, Peter's words to the Jews have been used to justify anti-Semitism over the years, as late as debates occurring at the Second Vatican Council during the formulation of what would become *Nostra Aetate* (1965), the Declaration on the Relation of the Church to Non-Christian Religions. Yet Peter himself fairly absolves any religious group of guilt and moral responsibility and recognizes that these leaders "acted out of ignorance." The point is not to blame—still less to imbue on future generations some kind of guilt for Christ's death, which is both an outrageous and preposterous act of anti-Semitism—but to witness for the sake of the name. This proclamation of Christ is the effect of the resurrection, which has cast reconciliation and peace on believers and nonbelievers alike. As the First Letter of John says, "He is expiation for our sins, / and not for our sins only but for those of the whole world." Any division based on malice, social injustice, or what was once absurdly called "deicide" should be seen for what it is: a grave sin against God's chosen people. The risen Lord has made it clear that "the love of God is truly perfected" in those who keep the commandments of love. The historical role that Israel plays in salvation history cannot be exaggerated, and Jesus himself reckons his fulfillment of God's plan by virtue of the prophets who bore him witness.

Connecting the Bible and the Liturgy

What are the fruits of the resurrection? At first glance, it would appear that the disciples have a hard time grasping that there are any fruits at all. But then Jesus discloses himself in various ways, significantly in the word and in the breaking of the bread. The result of these divine revelations in the most ordinary of circumstances—and often in the midst of fear, pain, and desolation—is peace. Not a worldly peace, but peace brought about by reconciliation with God. So, the travelers on their way to Emmaus, like the fearful disciples in the locked room, have the resurrection interpreted for them by Jesus himself, a verification that Christ is not an illusion but a reality.

The church's response to the gift of the resurrection can also be expressed in a word: exultation. That is the rejoinder given to the assembly from the deacon at the Easter Vigil. We witness the same joy from the astonished travelers when they find Jesus in the breaking of the bread. So, the **Collect** encourages the congregation to lean into a prayer of hope and endless praise: "May your people exult for ever, O God, / in renewed youthfulness of spirit, / so that, rejoicing now in the restored glory of our adoption, / we may look forward in confident hope / to the rejoicing of the day of resurrection."

We should not miss a crucial point here: our resurrection has already begun by virtue of Christ's redemption in the paschal mystery. The Collect allows us to see the continuance of the resurrection now and on that final day by emphasizing the continuity of our rejoicing. Our "youthfulness of spirit . . . in the restored glory of our adoption" in baptism will be echoed again in a life that will never die; our exultation will be like the joy we experience when we too break the bread and find there the risen Lord present among us. So it is that Jesus comes to bring peace to the church at every age, to all those who are troubled or in any way afflicted. He is the first fruit of the resurrection. Therefore the church is joyful beyond words. The **Prayer over the Offerings** also claims our attention for the joyful response owed to Christ's defeat of sin and death: "Receive, O Lord, we pray, / these offerings of your exultant Church, / and, as you have given her cause for such great gladness, / grant also that the gifts we bring / may bear fruit in perpetual happiness." These gifts have a poignant echo this particular week, since, like the disciples on the road to Emmaus, we offer the Lord a simple repast and find ourselves in his risen presence. Like Peter in Acts, the church is gathered in witness to this same risen Lord. This is the church whose joy has been renewed in the breaking of the bread with the hope in the risen Christ that they "may attain in their flesh / the incorruptible glory of the resurrection" (**Prayer after Communion**).

Strategy for Preaching

The readings and the liturgy are instructive concerning the understanding of the fruits of the resurrection, but these are lessons that are hard to come by for a fast-paced culture that tends to delight in fleeting pleasures. The patristic authors, like St. Augustine, imagined the kind of exultation experienced by the church at the resurrection stretched out for all eternity for the blessed. But what does such a moment look like for a world filled with anxiety? In a word, the congregation may find it more than difficult to get past conventional notions of the resurrection as "living on after you die," instead of the call to see the breaking of the bread as an invitation to see the risen Lord in an eschatological moment, present for all the ages.

Nevertheless, the core homiletic idea might be this: to allow the congregation to recognize that the joy of Jesus' presence in the Eucharist is a foretaste of the resurrection. That along with the disciples on the way to Emmaus, they too might leave the worshiping assembly with hearts on fire, that Jesus *"hos egnosthe autois en te klasei tou artou."* The assembly ought to allow their feelings—those moments of exultation that the Presidential Prayers speak so consistently of this day—to inform their belief. It is clear that the disciples are won over by their strange visitor on the road to Emmaus, having shared fellowship with him. Their hearts were burning within them as the Lord spoke of his place in salvation history. Indeed, Jesus' very presence leads the travelers to consolation on their way, and from there they come to belief and proclamation. So it is with all Jesus' appearances to his disciples, beginning with Mary Magdalene. It is the Lord's own person who fosters proclamation and witness; that is the power of the Spirit at work in Peter in Acts as well.

Fortunately, the congregation is on familiar and holy ground here. As far as the initial foray into the homily, what about initiating something regarding the capacity of the human subject to recognize and rejoice in the presence of a loved one? This is an ability that could be drawn out in a homily for the congregation by illustrations from novels or films or news events (often reuniting loved ones separated after a long absence). Charles Dickens and other great nineteenth-century novelists were famous for allowing the plot at the end of their long tomes to be closed by the coincidence of recognition. Such reunions are extremely powerful. When we are ourselves part of such a reunion, maybe seeing a friend from high school after long years of separation, there is a kind of joy that cannot be duplicated. We cannot but witness this reality and speak of its joys to our family and friends.

We can find that recognition unfolding in the liturgy, most obviously in the breaking of the bread. The homily might encourage the congregation to seek the Lord in the context of the journey of the liturgy, even in times of discouragement or desolation. We will be given the grace to find him in the midst of the assembly and in the breaking of bread. It is certainly key to emphasize that they recognized him: it is not a personal eucharistic moment of piety but a corporate act recalling the Beloved. Nevertheless, the challenge for the congregation is how persistent that search for the risen Lord with this assembly will be week after week. Is the Eucharist something we take for granted, or is it a new experience, opening us up for another vision of time and place, an awareness of God among us?

Fourth Sunday of Easter

Readings from the Ambo

Acts 4:8-12; Ps 118:1, 8-9, 21-23, 26, 28, 29;
1 John 3:1-2; John 10:11-18

The book of Acts testifies to the boldness of the apostles after the resurrection of Jesus from the dead and the subsequent coming of the Holy Spirit. Chapter 4, from which the **First Reading** is taken, reminds us of the consequences of Christian preaching: there will be a strange alchemy of both believers and persecutors (and the greatest of persecutors will become the greatest believer), despite God's victory over death and the outpouring of the Spirit on the church.

In the post-Pentecost setting in Acts (although the liturgical year positions Pentecost, of course, as yet weeks away), Peter and John find themselves facing religious authorities, not unlike the Master himself, coincidental with some of the same cast of unlikeable characters who were principles in Jesus' passion and death, such as Annas the high priest and Caiaphas. This group also includes the Sadducees, particularly notable because of their strict observance of the Law and their denial of the resurrection of the dead. It is precisely the resurrection of the dead that is at issue, of course, together with the disciples' power to cure the disabled man and extend their influence among the people that causes these men to be placed in custody.

With the convergence of the past events surrounding the death of Jesus, this passage in Acts and all of chapter 4, in fact, is an interesting study in the charismatic at war with the institutional. The contemporary Jewish religious establishment clearly senses the jeopardy that the apostles' preaching places on their own authority, even as they were similarly alarmed at Jesus' own authority in their midst. Peter's speech reverses the conventional religious power structure by placing Jesus' name as the foundation upon which a new power—God's reign—will be made. Jesus' name forms the core, then, of this early Christian preaching, even as it evokes his presence by its utterance. The metaphor of the building is deployed quite usefully, implicating the religious establishment in a loss they cannot foresee: the destruction of the temple. Jesus is *"the stone rejected by you, the builders, / which has become the cornerstone. / There is no salvation through anyone else, / nor is there any other name under heaven / given to the human race by which we are to be saved."* Finally, the religious leaders pretty much repeat their ossified roles they played out with Jesus, but Peter stands as redeemed: where once he denied the Master, he now helps to build this living temple, laying the cornerstone by his preaching the name.

In contemporary Christianity we might say that the saving name is Jesus the Good Shepherd, the subject of today's **Gospel**. It is true that few folks in the West have any sense of the dynamics at work between shepherd and sheep, but we know enough to realize that the shepherd functions as a saving foundation for the flock; without such a leader, the sheep are lost and scattered. Moreover, this is no anonymous shepherd who names himself *"ho poimen ho kalos,"* the Good Shepherd, who lays down his life for his sheep. These sheep know the shepherd and he knows them. Once again, the power of the name and the sacred intimacy it invokes to befriend, heal, and save becomes the gateway to the living Lord. The identity of the shepherd forms the literal basis for the "pastoral" care that Peter and John access in Acts. We cannot know for sure where we are being led, but we trust the Shepherd. We can look forward to being more fully united with the Shepherd and knowing him ever deeper, ever more fully. As 1 John reminds us, "we are God's children now; / what we shall be has not yet been revealed."

Connecting the Bible and the Liturgy

The Gospel for Years A, B, and C lays textual claim to various sections of John 10:1-30, a discourse on "the Good Shepherd." Year B finds itself within the middle of this section, perhaps the most intimate disclosure of Jesus in the chapter and, arguably, one of the most poignantly rendered in John's entire Gospel. The **Collect** identifies the congregation as the humble flock and asks God to "lead us to a share in the joys of heaven." The implication here is much like the

First Letter of John in the **Second Reading**—"what we shall be has not yet been revealed." It is the Shepherd who guides us. This Collect calls the Shepherd *fortitude pastoris*, or "brave Shepherd," as the *Missal* translates that phrase. This expression undoubtedly reflects the church's pondering of John 10:1-30: the Good Shepherd, the brave shepherd, who lays down his life for his sheep. Christ has laid down his life so that we might see what has not yet been revealed. This brave shepherd contrasts mightily with the hired man, *ho misthotos*. This term is really neutral because the Greek just implies a wage earner, not one who necessarily is a profiteer. But because he is just a wage earner and employed as a manager of the sheep rather than one who loves them, he "runs away." By contrast, the true pastor speaks the truth to the powers and cares for those who are in need. Chapter 4 in Acts discloses the apostles-as-shepherds who are steadfast. A text that is worth reflection in this regard (but obviously not used on Sunday) is **Preface II of the Apostles**, which alludes to the faithful pastor, the shepherd, who is the polar opposite of the hired man: "For you, eternal Shepherd, do not desert your flock, / but through the blessed Apostles / watch over it and protect it always, / so that it may be governed / by those you have appointed shepherds / to lead it in the name of your Son." Once again, the name by which the new temple is built leads shepherds and sheep.

Perhaps a more salient text for Paschaltide in the celebration of this day is **Preface III of Easter**, which also expresses the courage of the Shepherd, although not explicitly alluding to that metaphor in John 10. "He never ceases to offer himself for us / but defends us and ever pleads our cause before you: / he is the sacrificial Victim who dies no more, / the Lamb, once slain, who lives for ever." The role of the Shepherd, then, becomes expanded as sacrificial, the one who surrenders his life for the sheepfold.

An interesting feature of today's Gospel text and its connection with the liturgy can be found in the **Prayer after Communion**, which strikes me as a bit unusual: God is addressed as the Shepherd when it says, "Look upon your flock, kind Shepherd, / and be pleased to settle in eternal pastures / the sheep you have redeemed / by the Precious Blood of your Son." This is a marvelously complex way of understanding the Trinity, particularly the relationship between the Father and the Son in the context of the Shepherd; it is God who is Pastor leading and guiding by his will to eternal life. The prayer seems to want to bend the ears of the assembly into an expansive Trinitarian thinking that acknowledges that to Almighty God belongs the Shepherd, the Redeemer of the sheep; all belongs to him, now redeemed by his Son, who never leaves the flock untended. Here, we meet the suffering God, who can never be far away from his people, the true shepherd who never deserts his sheep. As Pope Francis reminds the church, "the Shepherd must smell like the sheep."

Strategy for Preaching

We can sometimes make religion altogether too complicated. It is really all about the name of Jesus, the foundation of the new temple. It is well known that the Greek and Russian Orthodox traditions have had a rich history of the "Jesus Prayer" for centuries, echoing a cry from the flock in sometimes desperate pastures for the need to be saved and led to greener fields: "Lord Jesus Christ, Son of God, Savior, have mercy on me, a sinner." In addition, contemplative traditions in both the East and the West hold to a practice of centering prayer that often focuses on a single word like "Jesus" to find a simple pasture of rest and recline with God.

Peter's preaching runs through Acts not with a lot of masterful rhetoric but with the power of the name of Jesus (that he denied, of course, during the passion of the Lord), the essence of any Christian evangelization. No, it is never about us. Coming to terms with the power of the name of Jesus in our relationship with the true Shepherd hints at the dynamics between sheep and shepherd, between ecclesial pastor and eternal Pastor. The core homiletic idea for today might simply be a challenge for the assembly to live out the name of Jesus, posed in a single question: how well do we know Jesus and allow his power to act through us day by day?

To strategize this homily, take a few steps backward to contemplate the reality of God's knowledge of his flock, his people. Try to sense God's knowledge of me as a preacher and what is being asked of me to shepherd his people in proclamation of the Gospel of Good News? The Presidential Prayers, such as the **Prayer after Communion** for this day, remind us of the deeply personal way God has owned the sheep: "Look upon your flock, kind Shepherd." This is an invitation to imagine God looking at his sheep. How do you think God sees you? God may see in us the disabled man in Acts, whom Peter encounters; or the psalmist rejoicing in God's goodness portrayed in the **Responsorial Psalm**; or the contemplative John writing the letter to the early church: "See what love the Father has bestowed on us."

The second section of the homily or rejoinder to the initial section is to consider how God sees his flock as a mirror to the first. How do we see God? How do we know the Shepherd, Jesus? Do we work at knowing him in the Scriptures and sacraments of the church? We come to know the Shepherd in our personal and communal prayer, in our encounters with one another.in the course of the day. Sometimes we encounter God within the sheepfold; sometimes we find him outside the gates, knowing that he is running after us when we are lost and cannot find our way back.

For reasons known only to God, the Shepherd has gathered this particular group of people, this baptized assembly into this Eucharist—disabled, rejoicing, grateful. I can learn from the rest of the flock even more about the shepherd as I respond in faith at the eucharistic liturgy—that is, the gathering pasture of God's love.

Fifth Sunday of Easter

Readings from the Ambo

Acts 9:26-31; Ps 22:26-27, 28, 30, 31-31;
1 John 3:18-24; John 15:1-8

The **First Reading** is taken from chapter 9 of the Acts of the Apostles, recording one of the great milestones in biblical and church history: Saul of Tarsus, once the greatest persecutor of the Way, has seen the risen Lord and become, in an astonishing moment, an apostle. In fact, church history will reckon him *the* apostle, even though he was not historically present to Jesus of Nazareth. It is this very moment from which Paul himself will reckon his own identity precisely as an apostle—transfixed and converted by the risen Lord from persecutor to missionary. The selection here details some of the fallout from that remarkable conversion that would change the face of Christianity. Having recovered from his blindness and been baptized, Paul preaches in Damascus that Jesus is "the Son of God." Once again, the scene is filled with irony from this erstwhile tormentor of the early church. Paul was originally on his own way to Damascus to capture some Jewish/Christian converts to the Way with letters of extradition. Now he confuses everyone by proving that Jesus is the Messiah.

What is the result of all this? Paul himself is now persecuted and suspect by the people he hunted down when he comes to Jerusalem. This is a telling human moment when the new witness to the risen Lord attempts to become a disciple and finds resistance: they were *"pantes ephobounto auton"*—all afraid of him—"not believing that he was a disciple." This interesting connection between fear and belief is remedied by another disciple. When Barnabas testifies on Paul's behalf to the other disciples, we are able to see the importance of community building based on goodwill, witness, and the dispelling of fear that lies underneath doubt. Paul still faced difficulties with the Hellenists (they would try to kill him) so he disappears from the scene in Acts until chapter 11:18. Meanwhile, Peter will become the ideal spokesman for the Lord (a corrective to his denial during the passion), fortifying the disciples and bringing the Good News to the Gentiles like Cornelius (in chapter 10). For his part, Paul will head off to his hometown of Tarsus, the events of which he will relate later to the church in Galatia (Gal 1:21-23).

On a symbolic level, the **Gospel** illustrates God's part in the story of Paul, who was once a wild vine but has been pruned to bear much fruit. Jesus deploys one of the greatest and best-known images in the Hebrew Scriptures to express the interconnection between the Lord and the living community who takes its life from him. Arguably the most forceful part of this analogy discloses the intimate relationship the Father holds with the Son and the rest of the members: Christ says that the Father "takes away every branch in me that does not bear fruit. . . . You are already pruned." The Greek word that is translated "pruned" here is *katharizo*, which in its classical usage has to do with cleansing, especially in regard to ritual purity. In the sense of *katharizo*, Paul has been purified from his sinful past in order to do acts of love and obey the new commandments, a drama that has unfolded in Acts and that will benefit the whole vineyard. Indeed, Paul proves his love for the risen Lord by obeying his commandments, despite persecutions and rejection by the disciples. He follows the one who is the True Vine, knowing that, as the First Letter of John says, "God is greater than our hearts and knows everything."

Connecting the Bible and the Liturgy

From a contemporary point of view, if the initial joy and enthusiasm of the Easter event has dimmed somewhat for the congregation by the time the Fifth Week of Easter comes around, the readings and liturgical texts for today should enkindle a new fire, sparked from the ambers of the great fire of the Easter Vigil. In fact, the **Collect** not only recalls those who were made new in baptism at Easter but asks God to continue this saving event in our lives to "constantly accomplish the Paschal Mystery within us." This prayer echoes another petition, often used at religious profession, begging God who began this work within the one about to pronounce vows to "bring it to completion." In the Prologue to his Holy Rule, St. Benedict echoes Philippians 1:3-13 when he urges his monks to pray every time they start a good work that God will bring it to completion.

That God plants and tends his vineyard is really the story of salvation history, an allusion Jesus makes more vivid in his own role as the vine and his disciples as branches. Paul's conversion on the way to Damascus and subsequent activity in Jerusalem in Acts 9 lets us know that God is always involved in shaping and pruning the vineyard of his people. Why? Jesus tells us, "By this is my Father glorified, / that you bear much fruit and become my disciples." Therefore the **Collect** reinforces the hope of the congregation, letting the assembly know that the Master of the Vineyard is intimately involved in their lives: "that, those you were pleased to make new in Holy Baptism / may, under your protective care, bear much fruit / and come to the joys of life eternal." Like Paul, those who have been baptized have undergone *katharizo* and begun anew, having been cleansed in a mystic bath.

The overall impulse of the readings for today allows for a dynamic that shows God tending to the members of the vine, but that these branches are able to sense their unity with Christ as well as their connection with one another. Barnabus comes to Paul's aid in Acts by reporting to the other disciples how the former persecutor had seen the Lord and had "spoken out boldly in the name of Jesus." All are focused on the vine because they sense their origins. Their one desire becomes the belief in the name of God's Son and, as 1 John puts it, to "love one another just as he commanded us." This is how the branches stay firmly attached to the vine: "Those who keep his commandments remain in him, and he in them, / and the way we know that he remains in us / is from the Spirit he gave us." The **Prayer over the Offerings** concretizes this unique relationship among the disciples of the Son and the Father when the prayer reminds the congregation of the "exchange" about to occur in the Eucharist, the renewal of the branches with the vine about to bear abundant fruit, the pruning of the congregational vine for the wine of the kingdom: "O God, who by the wonderful exchange effected in this sacrifice / have made us partakers of the one supreme Godhead, / grant, we pray, / that, as we have come to know your truth, / we may make it ours by a worthy way of life."

Strategy for Preaching

It is an important vocational question to ask what the preacher bears in relationship to Christ and the other members or branches of the vine in God's vineyard. On the one hand, the homilist helps to nourish the branches at the Eucharist and make these parts of the True Vine bear fruit by deepening the faith of the baptized. At the same time, though, the preacher is also one of the branches and, as such, becomes the first among the listeners, commissioned and sent to others in the vineyard. In this regard, the Master Preacher, Paul, who was himself first pruned and then sent to preach among the Gentiles (thereby pruning them as well), urged his fellow disciples to cooperate with the Vinedresser in cultivating the vineyard.

We know that not everyone has had a dramatic Pauline conversion, but it is vital to reflect on the ways we have grown closer or more distant to the Vine, been pruned, and then called to live as fruitful members. These three components, then, form a core homiletic idea around which to organize the homily.

Introduction: A good introduction might be to briefly rehearse the life of Saul as we see him portrayed in Acts, before his conversion on the way to Damascus, and then go on to detail the events leading up to a change so dramatic that its implications are still felt to this very day.

I. That is the experience of conversion: it affects us and other members of God's vineyard. Something or someone is going to change us and our relationship with Christ either for the good or not.

   A. Contemporary story of change with its movement toward transformation.

II. But we have to be open to being pruned. As branches of the True Vine, are we open to meeting the risen Christ even when we set out on our own way?

   A. The measure of our willingness to be trimmed occurs in how we receive and carry out the commandments to love. The degree to which we own the commandments Christ gave his disciples is the power with which we will embrace our neighbors, the occasionally annoying other branch often in our way.

III. That is what the Prayer over the Offerings means by asking us to come to the truth by "a worthy way of life." The truth of Christ will prune us.

    A. The risen Lord has initiated a new way of relating to him and to others.

    B. Ongoing conversion is part of living out our baptism.

    C. Prayer after Communion invites us to receive the Eucharist as a way of partaking of conversion, "to pass from former ways to newness of life."

Sixth Sunday of Easter

Readings from the Ambo

*Acts 10:25-26, 34-35, 44-48; Ps 98:1, 2-3, 3-4;
1 John 4:7-10; John 15:9-17*

The **First Reading** encompasses one of the great moments in Acts—one among many—that announces an outpouring of the Spirit in an unexpected way. The encounter of Peter with Cornelius remains a testimony to an all-inclusive God, a Spirit that mysteriously penetrates both Jews and Gentiles alike. That unified embrace of the Holy Spirit should not surprise us, since the Pentecost event itself was a dismantling of the Tower of Babel in which an understanding of nations was initiated by common understanding in language. In the contemporary global age, we are apt to understand the God that has seized Peter with such rapturous attention: "In truth, I see that God shows no partiality. / Rather, in every nation whoever fears him and acts uprightly is acceptable to him." The historical context of Peter's comprehension of this moment is indeed astonishing, since this witness is a far cry from the God of the chosen people who, in their reading, *did* show partiality according to the way that Hebrew Scriptures understood the Holy One. Even Paul will bow to Jewish pressure in Acts 16 when he has Timothy circumcised, seemingly because the young man's father was a Greek. At the same time, with the conversion and baptism of the (uncircumcised) Gentile Cornelius, are we to see the loss of the Jewish nation as God's chosen ones?

By no means: the circle of God's love has always been unfathomably wide; it is our hearts that are so tiny and need to grow to understand the mysterious depths of that divine compassion that seeks to embrace, like the Father in Jesus' parable in Luke 15, both sons. What we cannot grasp—and never will—is that God loves all people as his chosen ones. The people of Israel are first among his children and the first to be called his own, but they have not lost their place in the Ark of God's heart. Like Paul, Peter still thinks of himself as a Jew, albeit one who has come to a new understanding of his identity in the light of the Christ. Hence this moment in Acts 10 gives him a new understanding of the Hebraic God. Now Peter brings that astonishing news to others. So the conversion in Acts 10 is as much Peter's turn toward a divine largesse as it is anything else. Peter's gratitude and humility in his encounter with Cornelius knows that the love of the Spirit must be shared.

In a certain sense, Peter has come to terms precisely here with Jesus' love commandment in John 15 by recognizing God's impartiality and love for all. This love, in the end, yields an inclusive vision of all humanity—indeed all creation—the kind that allowed saints such as Francis of Assisi to praise "brother sun and sister moon." The text convicts its readers of the necessity of a moral conversion that allows for what Jesus refers to as the greatest of love. "No one has greater love than this, / to lay down one's life for one's friends." We become friends of God and not slaves because of our recognition that, as 1 John says, "love is of God; / everyone who loves is *begotten by God and knows God*" (emphasis added). The Greek text has marvelous alliterative force: *gegennetai kai ginoskei ton theon*, as if to strengthen the connection between these two realities of being begotten and knowing. Clearly, Peter recognizes the love of God in Cornelius and has been active in ways unrecognizable before the resurrection of Christ and the outpouring of the Spirit. Christ has been raised, having freely given his life for all humanity. This free gift from God and born of God's own self-emptying recalls, once again, the all-inclusive power of divine love: if Christ died for all humanity, then we are all brothers and sisters to him, friends of God and one to the other, "so that we might have life through him." The superabundance, the *magis* of the Spirit in baptism awaits these Gentiles, who will now be begotten by God.

Connecting the Bible and the Liturgy

When the **Entrance Antiphon** asks the assembly at the beginning of the liturgy to *"annuntiate usque ad extremum terrae"* ("proclaim to the ends of the earth"), it is articulating the sound of liberation made possible by the resurrection of Christ. With the defeat of sin and death, "The Lord has freed his people, alleluia." That means *all* people, as implied in Acts, where Peter recognizes that "God shows no partiality." Further, we are enjoined—indeed, commanded—by the Risen One to love one another, even as we enjoy the fruits of the resurrection, the liberation purchased for us. The way to keep the commandments of love is to abide in the love of Christ. So the **Collect** prays that "we may celebrate with heartfelt devotion these days of joy . . . and that what we relive in remembrance / we may always hold to in what we do." The implication here is that the eucharistic liturgy will keep our feet to the fire when it comes to the love commandment.

These are strong words, powerful language to keep the faithful, well, faithful. "Heartfelt devotion" (a nice translation of the Latin expression *affectu sedulo,* or a kind of "sincere feeling") may appear to be filled with emotional freight, but the religious connotations are from fleeting feelings. On the contrary, celebrating this "heartfelt devotion" demands a certain commitment on the part of the congregation, not as a group of slavish robots but of devoted sons and daughters of those begotten by God. This response of the baptized comes from the God "who loves us first" and is sustained by how we remember that love in the eucharistic liturgy. This last expression to remember is a poignant and vital communal recognition of the *anamnesis* at the liturgy, with the assembly acting in love for the sake of recalling the love of the Savior. Indeed, the Eucharist itself is an act of abiding in Christ's love, the very exchange of friendship that is the act of *recordatio.*

Like Paul, who will account his graced transformation for work with the Gentiles in Galatians 2ff. and elsewhere, Peter himself comes to a remembrance not unlike the congregation assembled for worship. We are all one in Christ Jesus, remembering the God who embraces all and calls us to do the same. **Preface IV of Easter** speaks eloquently about the replacement of the old with the new, initiating a new time, a resurrected time. It is in "this time above all" that newness occurs on every level, cosmic and personal. "For, with the old order destroyed, / a universe cast down is renewed / and integrity of life is restored to us in Christ." Like Peter, we marvel at the work of the spirit, to reveal God's wonders, to labor to bring about in us a conversion and understanding of the love commandments so that we show no partiality in loving but respect all humanity as brothers and sisters in Christ. That is the old order that has been destroyed, the order of sin and death, of separation and prejudice. That conversion will require us to see the world in a new way, redefining us so that, in the words of Gerard Manley Hopkins, Christ may "Easter in us."

Strategy for Preaching

We have an enormous capacity for keeping God's greatest wonder, the paschal mystery, something distant, allusive, and strange—of keeping the mystery of God's redemption in Christ just a bit less than a "heartfelt devotion." The resurrection, for many, happened to Jesus once upon a time, maybe; it is like a fairy tale: it is nice to believe in and when it happens after death. The resurrection remains a sort of Christian fable or bonus for hanging in there all those years and going to church. Yet the life, death, and resurrection of Christ is a mystery of our very life in God; not about a dead body walking around, but the in-breaking of new life, Christ himself: he has risen in historical time and defeated sin and death forever. Yes, the implications of the resurrection have a direct claim on me now, especially insofar as I am capable of conversion and keeping the love commandment as I remember the Lord in the great assembly together with my brothers and sisters.

Those claims relate directly to how we relate to our brother and sister. Indeed, God's kingdom disclosed in Christ reveals a life where there is no partiality. As baptized members of the Body, we are, like the master, called to lay down our lives in love. Therefore the core homiletic idea could be this: if Jesus' resurrection has changed the way we live for God and one another, how far are we willing to go to give our love away?

The preacher ought to note the "if . . . then" rhetorical organization here. The congregation will be placed in a position of pondering the reality of the resurrection as a divine event that has direct implication on how they view their lives. This proposal asks the hearers to consider ways that they might consider reshaping their lives because of God's revelation in this new time, resurrection time. Peter's encounter with Cornelius in Acts illustrates one in the process of forming and reforming (although Paul will give a very different account of Peter in Galatians). Peter's transformation comes from an unlikely source—an uncircumcised Gentile—yet driven by the Spirit that shows no partiality. Where does the assembly find such moments throughout the course of the day, sites to discover this all-inclusive God?

The point of departure to answer this question is the eucharistic liturgy, which reveals the God of no partiality in the context of a diverse assembly. The Body is assembled and drawn together as the Body is broken and Blood poured out. Is there anything else on earth like the Eucharist that dismantles the walls that separate one another? The Eucharist is indeed the place where the "universe cast down is renewed, / and integrity of life is restored to us in Christ" (**Preface IV of Easter**). Gentile and Jew have no distinction; neither does friend nor enemy.

So the resurrection invites us to conversion now, ushering us into the new life of grace. We can keep Christ at arm's length or fully embrace him in a stunning new awareness of who we are, to whom we belong, and where we are called to live this new life of grace.

The Ascension of the Lord

Readings from the Ambo

Acts 1:1-11; Ps 47:2-3, 6-7, 8-9; Eph 4:1-13; Mark 16:15-20

There are a few variants in the Lectionary that will shape the preaching for this festival day. The readings for the Solemnity of the Ascension of the Lord are identical for the Vigil Mass and the Mass during the day. Within Year B, the First Reading is identical to Years A and C. There are optional selections (all from Ephesians) for the Second Reading. The Gospel is taken from Mark for this Year.

The end of Mark's Gospel presents us with something like closure for a story that, paradoxically, is never ending. On the one hand, Jesus returns to the Father and "was taken up into heaven / and took his seat at the right hand of God." Here, we may sense that Christ has accomplished the work he was sent to do. From his baptism in the Jordan to the angelic young man's announcement at the empty tomb, the Lord has performed the work of redemption and returned to the Father. At the same time, however, Christ is still working in his disciples and accomplishing the mystery that is ongoing: "the Lord worked with them / and confirmed the word through accompanying signs." In this regard, we might say that a chapter has ended, but the story of salvation history has yet to be concluded, when God will draw the curtain on history. That said, this material for today taken from Mark 16:15-20 appears to be missing in the most reliable of Greek manuscripts and only known beginning in the late second-century BC. It is probably true to say that this version of the ascension of the Lord has been gathered from other New Testament witnesses. Nevertheless, we are still left in awe and wonder and, yes, proclamation after Mary Magdalene testifies to the risen Lord in 16:14, that immediately precedes the Gospel for today. The ascension account, though added here, mixes assurance of the Lord's abiding presence with the jaw-dropping account of God's deeds.

The underlying question for the readings for this Solemnity, then, is this: now that Jesus has been raised and returned to the Father, will he come again and when? The angels in Acts encourage the disciples to remember that "[t]his Jesus who has been taken up from you into heaven / will return in the same way as you have seen him going into heaven." This promise of Christ's Second Coming, his return to his beloved, is the gift of hope "resulting in knowledge of him," according to Paul's Letter to the Ephesians (**Second Reading**, First Option), praying that they may "know what is the hope that belongs to his call." Indeed, Christ's work was to bestow on humanity the gift of grace through the unity of the Spirit as we were called to the "one hope" the "one Lord, one faith, one baptism; / one God and Father of all, / who is over all and through all and in all" (Second Option). We do not have to long for anything except the Spirit of Christ, and to long for his coming. Like the disciples, we go out to perform signs and wonders through Christ by "building up the body of Christ, / until we all attain to the unity of faith / and knowledge of the Son of God, to mature manhood, / to the extent of the full stature of Christ."

Connecting the Bible and the Liturgy

"He ascended into heaven and is seated at the right hand of God, the Father the Almighty." These familiar words professed by the congregation in the Nicene-Constantinopolitan Creed at the Eucharist echo the realities of this Solemnity: that Jesus has ascended and even now sits at God's right hand interceding for the sake of the church, which continues his mission on earth. The **Collect** for the Vigil Mass for today aptly expresses the double-pronged intention of the Solemnity set forth at the end of Mark's Gospel. Jesus has ascended into glory as the apostles look on, but that experience is the occasion for rejoicing at his continued, abiding presence; we live by God's promise. "O God, whose Son today ascended to the heavens / as the Apostles looked on, / grant, we pray, that, in accordance with his promise, / we may be worthy for him to live with us always on earth, / and we with him in heaven."

The creedal statement of Jesus' ascension discloses for us in mystery the God who is both transcendent and immanent: it reaches back to the God Moses experienced in the burning bush as an encounter with the Holy Other on sacred ground, yet so close that this God has come for the very purpose of liberation of his people. Therefore Jesus sits now at the right hand of God with his wounds of victory from the cross he endured, making continual intercession for all of humanity for the remission of sins. It is an intercession made especially clear, when we "Behold the Lamb of God," the one who takes away the sins of the world, yet hidden in simple bread and wine. The **Prayer over the Offerings** delivers the congregation's prayers to God through Christ raised to his ascended glory, but mediator for the church and the world. "O God, whose Only Begotten Son, our High Priest, / is seated ever-living at your right hand to intercede for us, / grant that we may approach with confidence the throne of grace / and there obtain your mercy." Additionally, the **Preface I of the Ascension of the Lord** clearly expresses Christ's intimate role as High Priest, now that he has ascended: "Mediator between God and man, / judge of the world and Lord of hosts, / he ascended, not to distance himself from our lowly state / but that we, his members, might be confident of following / where he, our Head and Founder, has gone before." We can sense a marvelous reverberation in this language with Mark's Gospel account of the ascension's closing words, "while the Lord worked with them / and confirmed the word through accompanying signs." Put another way, the Mediator lives among his people so, unlike the men of Galilee, we do not have to stand looking up to heaven. Rather, we see his power interceding for us on earth because he now sits at God's right hand.

As always, a meditation on one mystery leads us to contemplate additionally the wonders of Christ's person as both God and Man. The incarnation did not end with the ascension of the Lord because Jesus united himself with us for all eternity and prays for us to the Father in the unity of the Holy Spirit. Therefore, as the Proper Form of the *communicantes* has it in **Eucharistic Prayer I** (*The Roman Canon*) for this Solemnity, we celebrate "the most sacred day / on which your Only Begotten Son, our Lord, / placed at the right hand of your glory / our weak human nature, / which he had united to himself . . ."

Strategy for Preaching

The ascension of the Lord prepares the Christian faithful for the coming of the Spirit and reinforces Christ's promise to abide always with his people. That may sound all well and good to some members of the congregation, but how does this mystery play itself out in the lives of men and women who work and love? To ask this question is really to ponder how Christians live the creed they profess or embody Christ and his mysteries. The underlying feature of the Solemnity before us—perhaps, from the point of preaching, the most neglected of all the great feasts that celebrate our Lord's mysteries—is the way the ascension writes our hope for the future. To instill hope as a motivational force empowered by Christ's intercessory love should guide the homily today. Hope is the great answer to that ubiquitous homiletic question lurking on the edges of every pew in every church: so what? In a sense, the homiletic task here is to transform religious spectacle ("why are you looking up at the sky?") into virtue, passivity into uncompromising faith in the Lord's intercession and promise of return. Preachers should imagine the two men dressed in white garments in Acts saying to their own congregation, "This Jesus who has been taken up from you into heaven / will return in the same way as you have seen him going into heaven."

The **Collect** for the Vigil Mass then allows the preacher to structure the homiletic text in a way that answers a provocative homiletic core idea, complementary to our creedal profession of the ascension itself: if we believe that Jesus ascended into heaven and sits at God's right hand, then where is he now? The Collect celebrates Jesus' ascension but also lays claim to a singular desire that "we may be worthy for him to live with us always on earth."

So we might envision this homily in three parts:

I. The reality of Christ as ascended to God the Father.
   A. Creed.
   B. *Catechism of the Catholic Church* (659-667).
   C. The power of Christ's intercession because he is the Incarnate Word.
   D. Illustration of a contemporary "intercessor" for peace, etc.
II. Christ works in us also here on earth.
   A. Can we name the ways in which Christ is here among us as "word made flesh?"
   B. Sacramental realities, especially baptism and Eucharist.

III. This awareness allows us to abide in hope.

    A. A short story or illustration of someone who continues to abide in hope and keeps vigil for the coming of God.

    B. The church keeps vigil for the Spirit, soon to be upon us.

Seventh Sunday of Easter

Readings from the Ambo

Acts 1:15-17, 20a, 20c-26; Ps 103:1-2, 11-12, 19-20;
1 John 4:11-16; John 17:11b-19

The Gospel for today is taken from a larger section in the Johannine text, often referred to as the Prayer of Jesus (17:1-26) or the Priestly Prayer of Jesus, which accentuates a Trinitarian unity among Father, Son, and Spirit. From this monologue, it is clear that Jesus intends to involve his disciples or the Christian community as participants in this very intimate relationship occurring in the Son's relationship with the Father and in which the Spirit will play a crucial role: "protect them in your name that you have given me, so that they may be one, as we are one. . . . Sanctify them in the truth; your word is truth" (NRSV). Together with the disciples gathered around Jesus, we can anticipate a coming "sanctification" by the Spirit in the word, which is truth. As the disciples prepare to go out into the world, they are sent forth even as Jesus has been *apesteilas*, that is, "sent" by the Father. "And for their sakes I sanctify myself, so that they also may be sanctified in truth" (NRSV). Christ will sanctify himself by glorifying the Father on the cross, which will also sanctify his disciples.

We have a less poetic example in the Acts of the Apostles of what it means to be sent forth. This episode used in the **First Reading** in which the apostles are recalled into Twelve as the "new Israel" allows for the symbolic assembly of the church at the coming of the Spirit in chapter 2. Much like the contemporary church awaiting the Solemnity of Pentecost, this reconstitution of the apostles prepares for the Spirit. Therefore we should see the choice of Matthias as an example of collegial election in the early church (of which this deliberation is an excellent and marvelous example of dialogical governance), but also as a gathering in of history, as it were, salvation history ready to be sanctified anew as the new order in the church at Pentecost unfolds in a strong wind and tongues of fire. In some sense, the Twelve play their most important role here, as they await the coming of the Spirit in chapter 2. Since they will vanish from the narrative early in chapter 6, we see discipleship re-forming itself after Jesus' ascension until they gather into one place fifty days after the Passover in the most important event in the lives of the disciples and the early church since the resurrection of the Lord from the dead.

The Spirit will strengthen and sanctify those gathered for their reassembly into Twelve even before his coming on Pentecost. It is the witness to the resurrection itself that bestows the Spirit on the apostles. Their witness coincides with the gift of the Spirit. As 1 John says, "This is how we know that we remain in him and he in us, / that he has given us of his Spirit." We partake of Christ's Spirit by our love, which draws us together into unity. The same Spirit that will topple the Tower of Babel at Pentecost has already been at work in the hearts of believers, witnesses to the resurrection.

Connecting the Bible and the Liturgy

Both the **Entrance Antiphon** and the **Collect** for today claim God's ear. *"Exaudi, Domine, vocem meam, qua clamari ad te"* or "O Lord, hear my voice, for I have called to you." Similarly, the Collect begins, "Graciously hear our supplications, O Lord." This language articulates the heart of the assembly, the Body of Christ, expressing itself in love to the Father in full confidence that we will be heard, "so that we, who believe that the Savior of the human race / is with you in your glory, / may experience, as he promised, / until the end of the world, / his abiding presence." This translation appears to read somewhat awkwardly because of its excessive punctuation, among other choices. Be that as it may, the final clause is suspended until the end of the sentence and finally makes clear the desire of the Christian community: "his abiding presence among us."

Jesus guarantees that enduring presence in his Prayer to the Father. "Holy Father, keep them in your name that you have given me, / so that they may be one just as we are one." We have become participants in the divine life of the Trinity as Jesus asks the Father to consecrate us "in truth." The ascension reveals plainly enough that Christ has both returned to the Father but still abides: he shares his own self with the disciples, a full expression of which will occur in the Pentecost event. As **Preface II of the Ascension of the Lord** says, "after his Resurrection / he plainly appeared to all his disciples / and was taken up to heaven in their sight, / that he might make us sharers in his divinity." *"Ut nos divinitatis suae tribueret esse participes"*: as sharers in his divinity we literally remain in Christ as members of his body because of the gift of the Spirit, a coming we will soon celebrate as a body, the church. That divine gift grants the faithful life in Christ: "This is how we know that we remain in him and he in us, / that he has given us of his Spirit," says 1 John.

No wonder that the church expresses a real and sure faith at the Eucharist, in which the body acts in and through Christ. As the **Prayer after Communion** says, "Hear us, O God our Savior, / and grant us confidence, / that through these sacred mysteries / there will be accomplished in the body of the whole Church / what has already come to pass in Christ her Head." We might note that as we began the liturgy with a cry to be heard, so also we conclude with another plea to the Father to attend to the voice of the church at prayer. The emphasis on hearing can only remind us of our need for intercession, a divine mystery that Christ as Ascended Lord continues to do, as he sits at God's right hand for our good. So the Gospel reminds us as well that Christ's work of sanctification is ongoing, even as we lift up our hearts to the Lord. "And I consecrate myself for them, / so that they also may be consecrated in truth."

Strategy for Preaching

As we anticipate the great Solemnity of Pentecost, while still very much in the shadow of the Lord's ascension, today's readings invite the preacher to focus on the Spirit-filled sense of collegiality and its link to re-formation, unity, and the abiding love of the Trinity indwelling in the faithful. Depending on where the preacher prefers to locate the center of gravity for this Seventh Sunday after Easter, the text could be shaped in at least three different ways, with three distinct core ideas. At the same time, the preaching may also be guided so that these three ideas function as a kind of triad of components for one homily, each of which move the homily forward toward a conclusion.

So what is offered below are the sketchy outlines for four separate homilies for this day, all of them with an eye toward Pentecost.

If there are three separate homiletic core ideas:

A. I. Core: The early church was driven by a trust in God's ability to enable the work of Jesus to continue after the resurrection, and it is true for us as well.

   A. Witnesses to resurrection (Gospel accounts).

   B. Acts 1:15-26 (reconstitution of the Twelve).

   C. The disciples keep vigil for Pentecost as a sign of their faith.

  II. Can we allow the Lord to gather us together and rebuild as a result of the risen Lord?

   A. Eucharist reforms us as we cry out to be heard.

   B. Collect.

   C. A contemporary story about rebuilding after a disaster like Hurricane Katrina or Super Storm Sandy.

  III. That is how we meet Pentecost: waiting and reassembled in witness.

   A. Pastoral example, such as a recent parish clustering or RCIA membership after Easter.

B. I. Core: The only way into unity is love.

   A. Marriage is the sacramental sign of unity.

   B. 1 John (Second Reading).

   C. Belief in God draws us together in unity.

  II. But we continue to resist. Why?

   A. Selfishness and preoccupation.

   B. Power and conquest militates against the peace of unity.

   C. Where is the invitation to go beyond these human inclinations that show that we are caved in on ourselves?

  III. The Creed we profess is a rallying point for reassembling ourselves each week and recommitting our lives to Christ and the church.

   A. Acts 1:15ff.

   B. John 17ff. "[T]hat they may be one just as we are one."

C. I. Core: God longs to take up residence in our dwelling place.

   A. Baptism.

   B. Pentecost.

   C. Jesus consecrates us in truth (John 17ff. Preface II of Ascension).

   II. We open our hearts here at the Eucharist but also as we go forth to mission.

   A. Prayer after Communion: "pass from former ways to newness of life."

   B. God living in us allows us to abide in the Trinity.

   III. We carry Christ with us wherever we go.

   A. Communion Antiphon for Year B: "I will not leave you orphans, says the Lord; / I will come to you again, and your heart will rejoice."

   B. Illustration: a story about a rescue, perhaps a firefighter saving someone from a burning building.

D. If the homily is one text (that is to say, all the above ideas are conflated into a single homily), the major coordinates might be as follows and could use the suggestions above to fill out the three sections included here:

   I. We are called to build one another up as a church.

   II. And we enlarge the circumference of our unity through our diversity and acceptance of one another.

   III. So we always carry the love of God in Christ as the Lord abides in us with his constant presence.

Pentecost Sunday

Mass during the Day

Readings from the Ambo

Acts 2:1-11; Ps 104:1, 24, 29-30, 31, 34; Gal 5:16-25
(1 Cor 12:3b-7, 12-13) Seq., Veni, Sancte Spiritus;
John 15:26-27; 16:12-15 (John 20:19-23)

The First Reading from Acts, chapter 2, which details the famous episode of the Spirit's descent on the early church, functions as a visual template for this Solemnity and is, of course, obligatory for Years A, B, and C. But how that Spirit is parsed by Paul in the Letter to the Galatians or 1 Corinthians (optional choice for Year B), together with the two choices available for the Gospel in John, will determine the particular biblical character of this extraordinary Solemnity today.

The coming of the Holy Spirit in the Acts of the Apostles portrays a fulfillment of a promise made by Jesus in John 15:26-27; 16:12-15. On a basic level, Jesus not only predicts the future coming of the Spirit but expresses the life of the Trinity when he tells the disciples, "When the Advocate comes whom I will send you from the Father, / the Spirit of truth that proceeds from the Father, / he will testify to me." In some sense, then, the coming of the Spirit in Acts only makes complete sense when that episode becomes framed by the Gospel. Indeed, I would like to think of both **Gospel** passages that may be used today as necessary partners to the coming of the Spirit in Luke-Acts. The other Johannine text, 20:19-23 (used for Year A) is a kind of double for Acts 2. The disciples are gathered in one place, but this time the driving wind that comes among them is Jesus himself: "'As the Father has sent me, so I send you.' / And when he had said this, he breathed on them and said to them, / 'Receive the Holy Spirit. / Whose sins you forgive are forgiven them, / and whose

149

sins you retain are retained.'" The common feature of both the scene with the Lord and the disciples in *John* and the descent of the Spirit in Acts is not only the presence of the one Lord empowering his disciples but the call to be reconciled with one another: Acts 2 signals a unity among diversity, the fall of the Tower of Babel, even as the Johannine Jesus commissions his chosen ones to forgive and reconcile. The church was founded on the foundation of forgiveness, understanding, and reconciliation.

This "same God" Paul emphasizes to the Corinthians as drawing all the diversity together into one *soma*, Body, and one *pneumatos* Spirit. "There are different kinds of spiritual gifts but the same Spirit; / there are different forms of service but the same Lord; / there are different workings but the same God / who produces all of them in everyone." Undoubtedly, the manifestation of God's presence in the Holy Spirit partakes of the kind of peace and reconciliation Jesus himself has purchased for our redemption. Paul wants the Galatians to know that there is a behavior change in regard to the Spirit's activity in their lives, since "the fruit of the Spirit is love, joy, peace, / patience, kindness, generosity, / faithfulness, gentleness, self-control" (Gal 5:22). These are the gifts of the same Lord who has given peace to his disciples in a small locked room and set them free because "[a]gainst such there is no law. / Now those who belong to Christ Jesus have crucified their flesh / with its passions and desires." Mindful of the call in 1 Corinthians to become One Body, the call for all Christians is to put away the things that gnarl at the flesh and to become one with Christ Jesus. That is the foundation upon which the church has been built that we also celebrate today, when all together we "hear them speaking in our own tongues / of the mighty acts of God."

Connecting the Bible and the Liturgy

"For, bringing your Paschal Mystery to completion, / you bestowed the Holy Spirit today." So begins the **Preface for the Solemnity of Pentecost**, rendering a marvelous sense of closure to a process the church has engaged in since Ash Wednesday. Jesus himself draws the curtain on the work he has done by sending the Holy Spirit to the disciples in the locked room: the breath of the Lord, which once swept upon the waters of creation at the dawn of creation, is now the final gift of the Paschal Lamb on those he has made "adopted children / by uniting them" to the "Only Begotten Son."

The gifts of the Spirit, as Paul tells us, are many in its diversity, but Jesus' Spirit is one and allows for the power of love; it is peace that he brings to the disciples, and it is reconciliation that he asks them to transmit to the world. The implication here is that the church is born of peace, compassionate understanding, and unity. As the **Preface** continues, "This same Spirit, as the Church came to birth, / opened to all peoples the knowledge of God / and brought together the many languages of the earth / in profession of the one faith."

The Spirit articulates for us, then, the single utterance, "Jesus is Lord," as Paul tells the Corinthians; the Spirit witnesses for all Christians born of baptism. Moreover, we ask the Spirit to labor continuously in the church to disclose the hidden mysteries of God. The **Sequence** for today is really all about labor—the Spirit's labor, visible and invisible. "Heal our wounds, our strength renew; / On our dryness pour your dew; / Wash the stains of guilt away." That Spirit will come down once more "like the dewfall" (**Eucharistic Prayer II**). Indeed, in the context of the Eucharist, the celebration of the Spirit is especially poignant, for the church begs that "the Holy Spirit may reveal to us more abundantly / the hidden mystery of this sacrifice / and graciously lead us into all truth" (**Prayer over the Offerings**). The ongoing revelation of the mysteries of the kingdom, a grace poured out on the whole church this day, unfolds before us the birth of hope. This day is only the beginning, not only of the church's mission but of our understanding of how we lean into God's future and the astonishing work of evangelization that has yet to be done. Although Christ is the definitive expression of God's revelation, the Spirit of the Lord has come upon us once again, even as it took hold of the disciples in a locked room. As the psalmist says in our liturgy today, "When you send forth your spirit, they are created, / and you renew the face of the earth."

Strategy for Preaching

The homily for the Solemnity of Pentecost can be something of a challenge for preaching. On the one hand, the biblical readings and the liturgical texts all point to newness, driven by the Spirit, freedom from fear and reconciliation. At the same time, however, the hearer in the assembly expects to encounter these very themes in a homily that can be, unfortunately, fairly predictable. So how can the preaching for Pentecost "make it new" as the American modernist writers living in the early part of the twentieth century used to say? Is there a way of positioning the listener so that he or she hears the coming of the Spirit as a strong wind of surprise, infused by the breath of the living God?

If the preacher rises to this challenge of making Pentecost speak as it did when the Gospel was first preached, then the assembly takes on the character of those disciples in the locked room, waiting to be set free. So the homiletic core idea might be to face the congregation with the following question: what are the fears that are trapping you in your world and how can you invite the Lord's Spirit to free you from these terrors? If the assembly can grab hold of a liberation from fear based on Christ's promise of peace and reconciliation, there will be a birth—not only into freedom but into proclamation to tell the Good News as a church community.

As suggested in the previous section, the **Sequence** has an important role to play in underlining the role of the Spirit as a laborer. A good introduction might access the opening lines that deal with the desperate need for peace and reconciliation. The congregation implores the Spirit to come and "[h]eal our wounds, our strength renew; / On our dryness pour your dew." The use of the Sequence as part of the Introduction to the homily also sets the stage for the desire for the Spirit, a collective zeal that often goes unmentioned on this feast.

But we have to make room for the spirit by acknowledging our fears: they tend to crowd out God's liberating presence. So the **Communion Rite** prays that we be "safe from all distress." At this point in the homily, a description of a pastoral encounter might be worth recollecting for the congregation in which the preacher remembers a movement from sin to grace, fear to freedom.

Finally, the last movement in the text is to suggest that the Spirit is laboring to free us, which is evident in the readings for today and recalled in the **Preface**; the Spirit of Christ motivates us continually to tell the Good News of peace and reconciliation. This liberation is how we understand the people of God gathered in gratitude to worship the Father through Christ in the unity of the Holy Spirit. In the end, the Eucharist allows us to utter a single sentence throughout the course of our life: "Jesus is Lord." That proclamation only comes with the help of the Spirit, as Paul tells the Corinthians. It is also the phrase that knits us together as brothers and sisters, members of the same body in Christ. It is the Spirit that continues to animate the church, renewed at the Eucharist, so we pray that "we may always be aflame with the same Spirit / whom you wondrously poured out on your Apostles" (**Prayer after Communion**).

 # ORDINARY TIME

Second Sunday in Ordinary Time

Readings from the Ambo

1 Sam 3:3b-10, 19; Ps 40:2, 4, 7-8, 8-9, 10;
1 Cor 6:13c-15a, 17-20; John 1:35-42

The **First Reading** involves us in the call of Samuel whom God calls as a child during the service of the unfortunate priest, Eli. The vocation story of the young man and his nocturnal interlocutions and vision of a God appears to be shifting the weight of the prophetic charism in the early portions of the book of Samuel. The priestly activity of Eli's sons, Hophni and Phineas, is severely critiqued because of their greed and rebellion. The Ark of the Covenant is captured by the Philistines, thirty thousand men fall in Israel, including Hophni and Phineas. Eli himself dies when he hears the news. But God intervenes with an encounter that appears to prioritize the mystical over the cultic.

The dynamic between Samuel and Eli is very telling: the older man appears out of touch with God's voice—much like the priest's own culture—while the Lord speaks to the very young. To this end, 1 Samuel concerns itself with the contours of vocation. Samuel was called in the context of a priest's service but would become a judge and a prophet as well. Kingship emerges first with Saul, of course, and then David, with Samuel functioning as an intermediary presence all along. In the wave of this vocational activity, God acts—sometimes even seems coerced to act—when the people of Israel demand a king. But so much of Scripture deals with God's breaking into scenes just like those occurring between Eli and Samuel; the question becomes: who is listening? With God's breaking into the collective and personal history of humanity, the call of Samuel is something of a template for the way in which the Lord calls—unbidden and in surprising ways—amid the circumstances we could not predict.

The same character of vocational call is at work in today's **Gospel**. Here, however, the prophetic voice of John the Baptist names God's presence already established in our midst. Where our glimpse of God's activity in 1 Samuel in the First Reading allows for the infrequent revelatory character of the Holy, the Gospel for today is at pains to point out an acclamation: "Behold, the Lamb of God." Vocation comes in the most ordinary ways and illuminated by the working of human instruments. "It was about four in the afternoon," when Jesus the rabbi invites not prophets like Samuel but disciples to follow him. Interestingly, these men, though ordinary, will have their lives altered in extraordinary and radical ways. Simon receives a new name to mark the occasion, and his name would be changed to Cephas or the "Rock."

Perhaps Simon's name change in the Gospel is something of a ratification of Paul's text in the **Second Reading** when he tells the Corinthians that "you are not your own." Christ has purchased all the disciples at a price. So our own discipleship is a very reminder that our "bodies are members of Christ." Vocation in this context is the acknowledgment not only of who we are and what we are called to become, but whose we really are and before whom we listen, saying, "Here am I, Lord; I come to do your will."

Connecting the Bible and the Liturgy

The Scriptures for today point us steadfastly in the direction of the mystery of vocation. Appropriately enough, the Second Sunday in Ordinary Time finds us on the heels of the Baptism of the Lord, where Christ's own call from the Father was affirmed at the waters of the Jordan. That said, the liturgy for today—particularly the Presidential Prayers—gently urges us to claim our own vocation as Christians in a wider global and ecclesial context. In order to understand this calling, though, we will have to grasp whose we are and to whom we belong.

From the perspective of today's **Collect**, the vocation of those gathered to worship is praise and thanksgiving, much as we might expect: "Almighty ever-living God, / who govern all things, / both in heaven and on earth . . ." With this invocation, we are assenting to the God who interrupted Samuel's sleep—indeed the sleep of all Israel; the God who animated John the Baptist to proclaim the presence of the Lamb in the midst of the crowd; the God Paul advised the

Corinthians to "glorify . . . in your body" (*"doxasate de ton theon en to somati humon"*). It is this same God that we, like these newly chosen disciples of Jesus, have found in the Messiah, the Lamb of God.

At the same time, however, the vocation of Christians is also to pray on behalf of others who share our vocation in the Mystical Body of Christ. In a sense, we arrive at our own prophetic stance through prayer for the members of the Body. We daily linger on the question Paul puts to the community in Corinth: "Do you not know that your bodies are members of Christ?" The Second Vatican Council's magnificent Constitution on the Church in the Modern World (*Gaudium et Spes*) makes the church's own vocation clear when in the first paragraphs of the document the church is reminded that it is to be in dialogue with the world. Echoing this reality, the Collect continues: "Mercifully hear the pleading of your people / and bestow your peace on our times." This petition readily acknowledges very early in the secular calendar (we are only weeks after the New Year, after all), that the world is desperately in need of peace and that the living Body of Christ is called to intercede for the sake of the suffering world. The Lamb is in our midst offering himself up for the good of the church and the world, even as John the Baptist made his presence known to the disciples.

That same Body standing before the Lamb at the altar of the Eucharist asks that "we may participate worthily in these mysteries" (**Prayer over the Offerings**). We repeat Christ's enduring offering of himself in a memorial for all God's people, "for whenever the memorial of this sacrifice is celebrated / the work of our redemption is accomplished." The congregation as the very Body of Christ (and Paul means this literally) offers praise and intercession for the living and the dead. Therefore we acknowledge with John the Baptist the presence of God in this worship-filled assembly at the **Communion Rite** when the presider says, "Behold the Lamb of God / behold him who takes away the sins of the world. / Blessed are those called to the supper of the Lamb."

Strategy for Preaching

Christian vocation is more than occasionally left to the solitary confines of an empty house—as if the individual needs no dialogue to discern the deepening of our baptismal witness. If we are all someone like Samuel discerning a voice, then finding another human being to companion us along the way in understanding that vocation is critical. It is easy to forget that baptism is an immersion into the waters of the church, the Body of Christ, the beginning of a lifelong conversation with Christ who stands as the Head of this community of members. Vocation, the call to witness to the Lamb more fully in Christian discipleship, is a mediated experience through the human family. The biblical testimony in today's readings support that discipleship occurs in the context of community. Samuel verifies his interlocutions during the night with Eli, who becomes a kind of mediator or spiritual midwife for the young boy's encounter with the mysterious God. The disciples are called as part of a cohort. Jesus asks them a seminal question that begins the dialogue. "What are you looking for?" Andrew implicitly answers this query when he turns to his brother and tells him, "We have found the Messiah." That is how Peter comes to Jesus—because someone else disclosed his own faith witness.

The preaching for today might focus on a kind of mystagogical testimony on the sacrament of baptism, something of a bookend to last week's celebration of the Lord's baptism. The core homiletic idea could be: our baptism called us to put on Christ as a garment very literally, and as we continue our vocation to seek him in the context of community, we will need to check the condition of our white robe to renew that covenant.

I. Introduction: might center on the image of our white garment sandwiched beside our everyday wardrobe—what we put away in storage, not used anymore.

II. That storage cannot be the case with our white garment given to us at our baptism; it is a vocation that asks us to wear it day after day.

    A. Rite of Baptism.

    B. Candle that is given as image.

    C. **Second Reading**.

III. We need the lamp to search for Christ; that is why we were given this light at baptism—to deepen our witness and of the other members of the Body. That is vocation.

    A. Story about guiding another on a journey, perhaps taken from literature, or a real story about mentoring.

      B. Gospel text of Andrew inviting Peter to see that he found the Messiah.

      C. John's revelation of the Lamb.

IV. Baptismal witness will always be our true and lasting vocation.

      A. *Ephphata*—be opened: how do we do this?

      B. Examples of Samuel, John the Baptist, Paul as those who have been opened by God.

      C. Discover the disclosure of the Eucharist opening up the presence of Christ as the Lamb of God.

      D. The revelation of the Christian community in our midst.

Third Sunday in Ordinary Time

Readings from the Ambo

Jon 2:1-5, 10; Ps 25:4-5, 6-7, 8-9; 1 Cor 7:29-31; Mark 1:14-20

The three readings for this Sunday all focus in their various ways on repentance. The psalmist sets the tone in the **Responsorial** refrain: "Teach me your ways, O Lord." From a Christian perspective, we cannot doubt the hope embedded in conversion: that there is a loving God who, in asking us to change, remains present, living, and active in our lives and who longs to bring us into the kingdom that Jesus announces.

The book of Jonah concerns itself with the prophetic utterances of repentance to Nineveh, the capital of Assyria. But this intriguing little book peels layers of multiple conversions—the people and beasts of Nineveh, Jonah, and, finally, God. The book of Jonah also deals with God's pursuit of Jonah, the prophet who delivers the message of conversion. That said, it is next to impossible to grasp the dynamics, the force, and the humor in the book of Jonah without reading the text in its entirety. Fortunately, the weekday Lectionary cycle parses the book so that we can understand that God's once-fearful judgment against a whole people can be abated, even while well-intentioned prophets still hold on to the old ideals. Even the animals are willing to put on sackcloth and ashes in Nineveh, so how can the Almighty resist a people "who do not know their right hand from their left" (4:11, NRSV)? There is a gentle God in these pages who makes himself known, who appoints big fish, worms, and plants to teach the reluctant prophet among us the lessons of compassion and diversity.

In the context of conversion, Jesus comes across like a force to be reckoned with. We are still quite early in the Markan text with none of the birth narratives to gradually coax us into the Messianic presence. That is all for the good, because we sense that there is something quite urgent about this particular **Gospel** account. In a sense, Mark is echoing Luke 4:16ff. when he portrays Jesus as claiming that this is a time of fulfillment, *peplerotai o kairos*. Another way of saying this might be that the time has arrived, so to speak, because the time is full and bursting forth into witness of the truth of that fulfillment. The time is at hand because Jesus is on the scene to announce the kingdom for which he is not only a spokesman or prophet but its very embodiment, which is to say its *peplerotai*. "Repent, and believe in the gospel" will occur not only because of the message but because of the messenger. If Jonah and Jesus share a unique allegorical connection (the former spent three days in a whale, while our Lord was swallowed up by the earth for the same amount of time), their association ends there: Jesus needs no conversion, but his very purpose is to bring others to the truth as he chooses his disciples and announces the Good News of the kingdom of God and its fulfillment.

Time and its very fulfillment is very much a part of Paul's message to the Corinthians in the **Second Reading**. So the apostle, who will reckon his own identity precisely as an "apostle," as one born outside of time, posits a reversal of the usual way of doing business in time—marriage, grieving, rejoicing, burying, selling. Why? From the perspective of one who has encountered the risen Lord, there can be only one perspective: "For the world in its present form is passing away." Yes, the kingdom of God is at hand.

Connecting the Bible and the Liturgy

We tend to imagine repentance as an individual turning away from sin and setting a source toward righteousness. And indeed, when it comes to conversion, our Lord's encounters in the Gospels are directed as challenges to particular individuals to "go and sin no more." But we ought not to let the emphasis on personal responsibility eclipse the corporate challenge to conversion as well. All three readings this Sunday ask the faith community to deepen their awareness of sin as part of the human experience. Jesus comes to Galilee not just for the few but for all who will hear; that is a "fulfillment" that cannot be contained even by time itself. We purchase that Messianic time by our own conversion to sin no more and to believe in the Gospel. Paul addresses the Corinthians and tells them that they ought not to be preoccupied because "the world in its present form is passing away," while the prophet Jonah went to Nineveh to preach to a people to repent not on his time, but God's.

The Eucharist invites the congregation into a corporate admission of sin at the beginning of each celebration, perhaps an aspect of the liturgy that gets overlooked by the assembly from a communal perspective. The **Confiteor**, as part of the **Penitential Act**, asks for individual accountability (hence "I Confess") amid the worshiping community. It is good to note that this prayer of contrition addresses its intention not only to God but also to "my brothers and sisters." The triple *mea culpa* serves to underline the need for repentance and the desire on the part of the whole assembly for Christ's intercession. This public, communal expression of guilt is unique in our culture, and timely, since this corporate admission of sin serves as a witness to humility and humanity. The baptized assembly may not be as notorious as the Assyrians in Nineveh, but the collective admission of guilt relives those early moments of Mark's Gospel when Jesus walked along the shores of the Sea of Galilee.

We prepare for the kingdom at hand and its fulfillment by anticipating the eschatological meal of the Eucharist, which is not bound by time but present to us as a fulfillment of Christ's memorial. Thus we gladly confess or guilt before the Eucharist as we open up to hear the Good News, even as Andrew and James and John become disciples after hearing the proclamation that the kingdom is at hand. Christ enjoys a special room in our heart so that he might enter and enlarge our house, so that he might come "under our roof." The time is at hand because we have chosen to open the door and let him in, despite our sin and shortcomings.

Strategy for Preaching

Jesus sets the gold standard for preaching and getting right to the point, especially visible in this early moment in Mark's Gospel. It is hard to miss the urgency of Christ's call to conversion, directly on the heels of John's arrest. And the messenger matches the message: the kingdom of God is at hand; and indeed he is, as God is made present among his people. The challenge for preaching will inevitably involve proclaiming this "fulfillment," which is to say the now of the kingdom on Sunday in Ordinary Time. How can preaching make the Good News fresh to the people of God who long for a saving word, indeed, to be converted to that very Gospel.

Needless to say, some kind of diatribe on conversion will do very little to cultivate the sense that the time has come, that the fulfillment of the kingdom is at hand; that comes from a sense of the holy presence in our midst and a longing to be part of that reign of God. Angry rampages about pet peeves are not only inappropriate in preaching, but they are ineffective for mature adult conversion, which so obviously must come from the heart of the congregation and not the doleful waxing of a doomsday "preacher." The key to unlocking the language of the kingdom is relationship: how do I imagine my friendship with the living God and his Anointed One? This imagining crosses the threshold of the kingdom, awaiting fulfillment now. Is it coincidental that Jesus announces the kingdom and the conversion needed to apprehend its presence at the very moment he chooses his disciples? It will be necessary to examine our lives and reform them while entering into a reinvigorated discipleship with the Lord. So the core homiletic idea for this Sunday might look something like this: if God's kingdom is at hand, what does that time of fulfillment look like for me? This strategy is a kind of wake-up call to the assembly, asking them to envision the call Jesus has given to his disciples to follow his path and reform our lives along with the contours of the Gospel. The relationship that grows will need to change, to be converted, and to believe. A possible structure might look this way:

I. Introduction: When we think of kingdoms, what comes to mind? (Camelot, knights, movies like *The Lord of the Rings Trilogy*.)

II. But Jesus' declaration is not a fantasy of the past but an unleashing of God's power now.

   A. Time of fulfillment (Gospel and Second Reading).

   B. Relationship of disciples; they are invited to come nearer.

   C. Image: A mother giving birth begins a new relationship with a living being and with her husband as a fellow parent.

III. So that requires that we reimagine ourselves into this kingdom, a kind of rebirth.

   A. That means conversion (Jonah's story).

   B. Not only individual change but corporate change as well.

   C. The Confiteor is a way of understanding a corporate responsibility for change.

   D. The Eucharist is the now of the kingdom for which we are preparing.

   E. We have moved into a new relationship with God and one another just by being present in this worship of thanks and praise.

Fourth Sunday in Ordinary Time

Readings from the Ambo

Deut 18:15-20; Ps 95:1-2, 6-7, 7-9; 1 Cor 7:32-35; Mark 1:21-28

The **First Reading** occurs within a large web within the book of Deuteronomy, beginning in chapter 12 and running through 26:19. This text deals primarily with the code of laws in ancient Israel. In fact, immediately preceding the passage for today is a prescription against child sacrifice, magic, and the occult (18:9-14). In this regard, Deuteronomy 18:15-22 seems more than slightly out of place, since this portion of the text speaks of God's promise to raise up a new prophet like Moses. "I will put my words in the mouth of the prophet, who shall speak to them everything that I command" (NRSV). At the same time, though, there is a codification here against "any prophet who speaks in the name of other gods, or who presumes to speak in my name a word that I have not commanded the prophet to speak—that prophet shall die" (NRSV). The overriding concern of the passage is *authenticity*: from where does the true prophet get his genuine witness? From God, of course, because that prophet is like Moses. Speaking in the name of the Lord by one who has not listened to that voice will result in that person being held accountable. The concern with false prophets occupies no little space in the Hebrew Scriptures and became an arena for battle for those called by the true God, such as Elijah. Even Paul would be on guard against prophecy that really was not genuine when he tells the Corinthians to be wary of those who speak in meaningless tongues in 1 Corinthians (14:1-25).

It is this prophetic authenticity that also surrounds the ministry of Jesus. When Jesus comes to Capernaum, he amazes the crowds by casting out a man possessed by an unclean spirit. The result is a ratification of Jesus' prophetic identity: "'What is this? / A new teaching with authority. / He commands even the unclean spirits and they obey him.'" This authority gives Jesus power over unclean spirits and, indeed, unclean tongues. It is one of the many Markan ironies that the unclean spirit is in awe of Jesus' power and acknowledges his divine identity while the disciples are mute on that crucial utterance: "'I know who you are—the Holy One of God!'" Jesus' rebuke of the unclean spirit perhaps has as much to do with keeping the so-called "Messianic secret" in Mark as anything else. Therefore, even the unclean spirit may speak the truth.

This passage occurs early in Mark's Gospel as Jesus shows himself extremely focused and energetic. Mark uses the Greek word *euthus* to describe the immediacy and urgency with which Jesus has come to Capernaum, yet another indicator of prophetic zeal as the Lord begins to establish the restoration of God's people and the proclamation of the kingdom. We tend to see Paul's letter to the Corinthians as a signature piece of pastoral concern for those in ministry, and rightly so. But writ large, the advice Paul has for those engaged in the Lord's work "to be free of anxieties" suggests that it is necessary to will the one thing necessary—to have the *euthus* of the authentic prophet. Once again, we are reminded of Deuteronomy's concern for establishing teaching with authority, in the line of Moses. Jesus passes on to his new disciples an exemplary quality of the prophetic that has jurisdiction over unclean spirits, while healing and making whole. We can easily see, then, that the prophetic becomes linked to establishing the kingdom. The true prophet with authority to teach is one with God's will, because he speaks in God's voice and through his holy Word.

Connecting the Bible and the Liturgy

False prophets: the Scriptures rally against them. Elijah fought them. Moses said they would meet a bad end. In the biblical tradition of God's covenant with his people, speaking the truth is a non-negotiable. The voice that is deep within must come from the heart, and that exclamation, in the end, is the sound of the true prophet.

The **Collect** gathers together the faithful people of God with the call to righteous living, much like the voice of Moses in the book of Deuteronomy we heard in the First Reading. The first sentence of the Collect, though brief, sums up the two greatest commandments: "Grant us, Lord our God, / that we may honor you with all our mind, / and love everyone in truth of heart." Clearly, Jesus' *euthus* throughout Mark's Gospel, his single-minded drive toward preaching repentance and the kingdom of God and sanctifying—emblematically typified in the person of a broken and possessed man in the Gospel for today—finds its way in the Hebrew Scripture's command to love God above all things. The conflict Jesus faces with the demons in the Gospel remains a purification from all that is not holy, all the idolatry that divides us from our loving intention toward God. The man's exorcism is a call to freedom of worship with a complete and integral and authentic sensibility: to love God and neighbor "in truth of heart."

The liturgy seizes the congregation, then, with the demands of authentic worship, embeds us in the Great Commandments to love God and our neighbor. In a sense, we have been called to recognize the authority of the Body of Christ as teacher, sanctifier, and preacher. As the **Entrance Antiphon** reminds us, "Save us, O Lord our God! / And gather us from the nations, / to give thanks to your holy name, / and make it our glory to praise you." To this end, the eucharistic liturgy, as always, becomes the wellspring of our sanctification with which our own false idols may be cast out, and we might be made new in complete freedom. This action occurs through God's own self-gift in Christ, even as we offer ourselves as an oblation at the liturgy. As Paul tells the Corinthians in his discussion of the call to service, an action that draws them into holiness, the worshiping assembly also comes to the holy table offering our very lives, without anxiety or the need to please anyone except the Father of all blessings: "O Lord, we bring to your altar / these offerings of our service: / be pleased to receive them, we pray, / and transform them / into the Sacrament of our redemption" (**Prayer over the Offerings**). The true heart is made so by the authority of God's Son and the perfect offering "that through this help to eternal salvation / true faith may ever increase."

Strategy for Preaching

It is hard to imagine that in these days when everyone seemingly wants to be famous for at least fifteen minutes, on either *American Idol* or let's call it the "Next New Thing" where people get to air their personal agenda or living space on either cable or network television or YouTube, that a common phobia still remains: public speaking. What is it about getting up in front of a crowd of fellow human beings that terrorizes us to near distraction? Personal experience with teaching homiletics over the years has confirmed that even those who feel called to preach face fundamental problems with nervousness and insecurity when they face the assembly on Sunday morning, especially at the beginning of their ministry. From all that we've been able to tell from surveys and sociological data, our fear lies in being somehow detected by the crowd as a fraud—that what we say does not match who we are and how we live. That is the question of authenticity.

Believe it or not, this is a good thing; a healthy fear (as long as it does not cripple us) can be helpful because this emotion drives us toward transparency and authenticity and to live, as the **Collect** suggests, "in truth of heart." If preachers are true witnesses in this regard, then they are the litmus test for authenticity; those who bring the Word are the inheritors of the prophets God intends to raise up like Moses to speak the truth with love. The foundational identity of the preacher that has its roots in this prophetic role is the *herald*, long revered in the Scriptures beginning with angels coming from heaven as messengers, to Moses and John the Baptist challenging the people of Israel. The preacher in the liturgical assembly gathers the congregation together in honesty to love God and neighbor. That preaching will only be effective to the degree that this modern herald honestly claims the mantle of authority in teaching from Jesus himself.

As in several Sundays of the church year, the readings and the liturgy call for an explicit self-examination of the preacher. Needless to say, the preacher ought to be practicing daily a self-examination in the light of Scripture, but sometimes the task is more obvious when we ask others to deal with their own sense of authentic living before the Lord. When the preacher faces the humble self, the congregation will sense an authentic witness of the Good News by the preacher's joy and transparent pastoral love in the course of only a few homilies. So the core homiletic idea might be to consider how we might deepen our honesty with God so as to serve him as a herald in freedom and love for the sake of others more completely. In this way, the preacher is claiming a right of succession from Moses through Jesus, the latter of whom grants the grace of his abiding presence in the pulpit and elsewhere.

Here is a brief suggestion for an outline:

  I. What exactly does honesty mean to me?

   A. Where is the call to authenticity that faces us today and how does it reveal itself?

   1. Government, church, local leadership, relationships.

   2. Do we sense our own inauthenticity at times?

 II. Moses and prophetic tradition call the nation to live according to righteousness.

   A. Jesus as the sanctifying presence of God in the world.

   B. Gospel text: Jesus sanctifies the possessed man who then moves into the world of community.

   C. Sacraments as restoration of the whole person to community of love. (Examples: baptism, Eucharist, reconciliation, sacrament of the sick.)

III. Liturgy as a gate of sanctification here at this very moment, where God calls us to authenticity through the authority of Christ's memorial meal.

   A. Collect.

   B. Eucharist calls us to surrender ourselves to others and God and all our concerns for our own ego.

   C. Paul's example of pastoral service.

   D. The summons to "Go and announce the Gospel of the Lord" is the invitation to live in authentic witness by God's authority and not the world's.

Fifth Sunday in Ordinary Time

Readings from the Ambo

Job 7:1-4, 6-7; Ps 147:1-2, 3-4, 5-6;
1 Cor 9:16-19, 22-23; Mark 1:29-39

The book of Job raises some of the most difficult and complex questions in the Wisdom literature of Israel. The whole text is not widely studied even by preachers but functions somewhat anecdotally in popular culture as the trope, "She or he has the patience of Job." The narrative acts as a Hebrew short story or tale, showcasing a man who, through no fault of his own, suffers the victimization of Satan's wiles. Key to understanding the text is God's role, that is, passive in the face of devastating loss of property, family, and health. Additionally, Job must also answer the questions posed to him by his friends Bildad, Elphaz, and Zophor, who surface traditional responses to evil and divine injustice, in order to make excuses for God through rational order and just punishment. Job maintains his innocence through it all, and in the passage we see excerpted for the **First Reading**, the unfortunate man tells God of his misery, "My days are swifter than a weaver's shuttle; / they come to an end without hope. / Remember that my life is like the wind; / I shall not see happiness again." With such an outcry of the human heart, the book of Job is a crucial piece in the life of the Judeo-Christian community because it names the struggle we all face in the context of seemingly unanswered prayers, human suffering, and innocent victimization. There is no putting a pretty face on the book of Job (although scholars have concluded that the end of the text was, in fact, a kind of redaction of "restoration" that was not part of the original piece).

171

It may seem peculiar, then, why this **Responsorial Psalm** was chosen as a rejoinder to the book of Job. Why deploy a song of praise in the midst of terrible suffering? This Responsorial is probably not so much putting a brave face on a difficult situation, but more responding to the entire book of Job. In some sense, the psalm (147) replicates the response of the faithful witness who, like Job, refuses to give up faith even in the midst of difficult suffering. At the same time, the Responsorial holds out hope for the afflicted: "He heals the brokenhearted / and binds up their wounds." And indeed, Job's stalwart behavior, humbled by God's revelation of omniscience and grandeur, becomes the model for the psalmist, who will echo Job's lament throughout the Hebrew Psalter in various places.

In this regard, the **Gospel** text exhibits Jesus as God's instrument in how he heals and "sustains the lowly." The driving out of demons that engaged Jesus in last week's Gospel text is now joined to healing ministry. Additionally, we see one of the early signs of the repressing of Jesus' identity when "he drove out many demons, / not permitting them to speak because they knew him." The disciples, like Job, will have to work at understanding the wisdom of God as it is revealed in mystery through Christ. Despite the wonders Jesus accomplishes, including "preaching and driving out demons throughout the whole of Galilee," Christ himself remains a mystery. The disciples will flee at the last, of course, because only some outsiders—the demons and a Gentile centurion—acknowledge that Christ is "the Son of God." Jesus will also be interpreted by later traditions as a mirror of Job— the faithful witness, who continues his mission, despite the lack of trust on the part of his disciples and being besieged and taunted. Paul's words to the Corinthians are applicable here: "I have become all things to all, to save at least some. / All this I do for the sake of the gospel, / so that I too may have a share in it." It is faithfulness that accorded Jesus and Paul and Job the opportunity to disclose a faith so strong that it even conquers death.

Connecting the Bible and the Liturgy

The biblical readings for this week explore the difficult side of humanity: the loneliness, frustration, and anger of Job, the demands of the Gospel, and the stewardship of Paul in the face of a diverse ministry. As Paul says, "To the weak I became weak, to win over the weak." And finally, the Gospel brings to the fore the torments of illness and evil to which all of us are subject, albeit not in so dramatic a fashion. Jesus himself has to withdraw "to a deserted place" to pray, apparently in order to gather himself up to the Father before continuing to preach the Good News.

That we are all weak and in need of God's transforming love is the centerpiece of Jesus' healing ministry, an episode of which is disclosed in the Lord's curing of Simon Peter's mother-in-law. The liturgy positions the congregation before the altar of God as needy and awaiting heavenly gifts of food to help sustain us on our journey in the wilderness. Like Jesus himself, we have come to a place for refreshment. "O Lord our God, / who once established these created things / to sustain us in our frailty, / grant, we pray, / that they may become for us now / the Sacrament of eternal life." The **Prayer over the Offerings** acknowledges God's blessings, as it prepares us for Christ's living-giving memorial meal that sustains us.

But there is more here. We will note that after Simon's mother-in-law is cured, she waits on Jesus and the others. We are indeed needy people, but our salvation in Christ draws us into a generous response to serving one another, to become, as Paul says, "all things to all, to save at least some." Our own lives are transformed, together with the bread and the wine, into a unified Body at the service of the rest of the members. In the end, it is all about gift—and the Giver of the gifts we bring, which we return in gratitude in the *Orate Fratres*: "Pray, brethren (brothers and sisters), / that my sacrifice and yours / may be acceptable to God, / the almighty Father." Why? *"Ad utilitatem quoque nostrum totiusque Ecclesiae suae sanctae"* ("for our good / and the good of all his holy Church"). This is our service at the table of the Lord, together with Simon Peter's mother-in-law, who also serves, having been cured.

After we have felt the Lord's healing power, we can only offer back what we have: our very lives. So the **Prayer after Communion** acts as something like a coda on a majestic hymn to these biblical and liturgical connections when it says "O God, who have willed that we be partakers / in the one Bread and the one Chalice, / grant us, we pray, so to live / that, made one in Christ, / we may joyfully bear fruit / for the salvation of the world." That "fruit" is nothing less than Paul's clarion call to spread the Good News, despite the weakness of our human condition: "All this I do for the sake of the gospel, / so that I too may have a share in it."

Strategy for Preaching

This may seem like an obvious point, but it always bears repeating: preachers must exegete the assembly so that these evangelizers may "become all things to all, to save at least some." The awareness of the pastoral needs of the congregation grants dignity and honor to the gathered baptized who have come in Christ's name in praise and thanksgiving. As the biblical and liturgical texts are preached, these become living entities of the Word for the hearer in which *cor ad cor loquitur*.

There are despairing Jobs, sick mothers-in-law, and a host of other needy folks in the eucharistic assembly, waiting and hoping for a saving word from the homily. They are weak, like the preacher himself; but the people long for the salvation of the Word, even as they pressed Jesus for healing in Mark's Gospel. We need the Lord to "sustain us in our frailty." As we can intuit from the Pauline text today, the evangelizer must be able to access a certain amount of flexibility in order to meet the people of God where they are and, together with the faithful, offer a sacrifice of gratitude for the service of God and one another.

There are no rhetorical points of beginning to prepare the homily at its earliest stages except an encounter with the Lord in silence, a withdrawal into a deserted place so that this contemplative union might bring the Word into the service of love in mission. So the core homiletic idea might be a contemplative one, directed at both the preacher and the assembly: how might we encounter more deeply the word of salvation in the Scriptures and the liturgy in order to help others hear a saving word?

The challenge for the preacher seems clear enough, but what about the congregation? The connection the preacher establishes in solitude and prayer will already be an incalculable link with the people of God. Listening to the joys and sorrows at the heart of the world, to paraphrase *Gaudium et Spes*, is the foundation of the healing mission of Christ. Can the preacher make that visible for the assembly? The preacher has the resources of music, literature, and the arts that articulate the same kinds of expressions articulated in the Scripture and the liturgy; these make the pains of Job, Simon Peter's mother-in-law, and the church at Corinth very real to the hearer. Consider for instance the thousands and thousands of characters available as testimonies to human suffering and what they did with their pain, which includes many who were not as accepting as Job—such as Ahab in Herman Melville's *Moby Dick*. The preacher can then help others in worship to see the living text proclaimed and the healing power of Christ among us.

Sixth Sunday in Ordinary Time

Readings from the Ambo

Lev 13:1-2, 44-46; Ps 32:1-2, 5, 11;
1 Cor 10:31–11:1; Mark 1:40-45

There is a clear and obvious connection between the First Reading and the Gospel, since both texts deal with a condition thought to be leprosy. Actually, the word used in the book of Leviticus is more general, *tsara'at*, which could mean several skin diseases and undoubtedly does not refer exclusively in the strict sense to what we now call Hansen's Disease. The more salient point, however, is that the larger context of the Levitical text from which the **First Reading** has been taken (13:1–14:47) deals with being unclean and, in a particular way, the Levitical priest's function regarding the purification of *tsara'at*: the priest was supposed to verify whether or not the person was unclean.

It may seem cruel to banish a person to the margins of a society, "making his abode outside the camp," but the restrictions and the ritual surrounding the restoration carry with it some commonsense precautions regarding contagious diseases and infection in the community. For one thing, anyone who touches a leper becomes polluted or unclean. As is often the case, there is an obvious alliance here between ritual and health. This Code of the Law makes Jesus' action in the **Gospel** not only radical but also dangerous: "Moved with pity, he stretched out his hand, / touched him, and said to him, / 'I do will it. Be made clean.'" Bafflingly, after this transgression of religious custom, Jesus follows the Law to the letter, telling the man to show himself to the priests; it is a puzzling command because this action would carry with it the self-incriminating act of ritual impurity. It would not be the only time that Jesus violates a social and health boundary for the sake of restoration. We have no way of knowing if the man eventually went to the priests, because he turns quickly to evangelization, "publiciz[ing] the whole matter." Jesus was unable to appear openly and his fame spread "and people kept coming to him from everywhere." The Word will go forth and will be unleashed no matter what.

Despite disobeying both the Law and Jesus, it is hard to find fault with the newly cured leper, since he seems to be following a higher law, one modeled by Christ himself when he transgresses the Law of Moses in regard to skin diseases. Paul adverts to such actions when he says in the **Second Reading** that the Corinthians ought to "do everything for the glory of God." Paul's argument to the community at Corinth is especially applicable in the context of the Law and its transgressions because he tells them that it is the unity of the Body and the rejection of idols and thanksgiving to God that is at the heart of worship. Like the leper himself, Paul indeed is an imitator (*mimetes*) of Christ, precisely as one who has returned to the foundational relationship with God. That is the example of Christ, who has healed the broken leper not just as a proximate remedy of suffering but as a sign of reconciliation that returns the children of God back to the Father. In a sense, Jesus usurps the role of the priest, who declared a person clean and able to return to the community. Jesus' reconstitution of the human subject restores the wounded into the kingdom of God.

Connecting the Bible and the Liturgy

In the days that followed the promulgation of *Sacrosanctum Concilium*, Vatican II's Constitution on the Sacred Liturgy, Catholic churches all over the world were reorienting themselves (literally) to an inculturated liturgy defined by local language, symbol, and space. The shift in this axis from five centuries of uniformity of the Latin Rite was an invitation to corporate conversion in which the private selves assembling for worship might witness one another in praise of God and exchange greetings of "Peace be with you!" In a sense, the changes initiated in the mid-1960s was a call for everyone living at either the center or at the margins of the church to return to the Body for worship. Not unlike Jesus' laying on of hands and healing throughout the Gospel, the broken and those cut off from community are not only healed but also returned to a Mystical Body.

That return to the heart of community—to Christ's own Body, of which we are *mimetes*, imitators, by virtue of our reconciliation and restoration to the Father through Christ—is at the spine in the **Collect** for today. The Collect, of course, as its name implies, gathers us together at the beginning of the Eucharist, having just confessed our faults to one another and to God. "O God, who teach us that you abide in hearts that are just and true, grant that we may be so fashioned by your grace as to become a dwelling pleasing to you." The force of the word "fashioned" is difficult to grasp, but the meaning of *"da nobis tua gratia tales exsistere"* implies a gift from God that brings us into being. In other words, we ask that we wounded lepers may become not only cleansed but also enter into a new state, a new community in Christ. In so doing, we are following Christ's example and leave all that is not holy behind, for he has returned all things once disfigured by sin to the Father. Now we have been restored not only by ritual but also by Christ's own saving Blood. If the Levitical Code guaranteed the preservation of God's chosen people, then Christ's incarnation, passion, death, and resurrection make possible the transformation through the law of grace, with Christ as the new priest of a New Covenant.

The **Prayer over the Offerings** suggests that we were all once lepers, but we await the Sacrament, the living Christ, to make us whole and ready to return to the Body. "May this oblation, O Lord, we pray, / cleanse and renew us / and may it become for those who do your will / the source of eternal reward." Uniting our wills with the Father is an act of worship that joins us in the reconciliation that makes us One Body; this is the realignment of the sinful and wounded self now plunged into the mercy of God. Like the leper, then, we cannot but announce the Good News as we "Go and announce the Gospel of the Lord."

Strategy for Preaching

It would not be unusual for a fair number of congregants (as well as some preachers) to interpret Jesus' healing ministry, and particularly Mark 1:40-45 as exclusively a private act of healing; but it is clearly more than that. We know that Jesus radically violates purity laws by laying hands on the man who, after being healed, does not go off to some private little island but gathers the community around the word he himself announces. The task for the preacher will be to expand the horizons of the assembly and allow the actions of the Lord to speak of corporate healing, conversion, and evangelization: the dynamics of our restoration in Christ, the Body. Indeed, one way to think about the homiletic core for today is precisely as an invitation to return to the Body, using the leper in the Gospel as a testimony to the act of conversion. So the core homiletic idea might look like this: when Jesus heals he also helps to reconcile and return.

There are three distinct (though connected) active movements to this homily that act as tactics to carry out the homiletic core.

I. Jesus transgresses common sense and the social norms of Jewish laws.

    A. Self-preservation says don't touch dangerously contaminated people; they are contagious.

    B. First Reading (Mosaic Law).

    C. A visual image: perhaps a brief sketch of someone like Rosa Parks who violated a social taboo by not surrendering her seat on a bus.

II. In the process of crossing a boundary, Jesus also heals.

    A. What did this look like in the Gospel for today? This is a restoration of the self as God made the leper, once disfigured.

    B. Collect: the invitation to the whole community to restoration to be "fashioned" by grace.

    C. Prayer over the Offerings.

III. So the wounded are restored to community and spread the Good News.

    A. The leper, now cured, goes out to proclaim.

    B. The Good News cannot be harnessed.

    C. Jesus himself cannot control the healing power of the Word that runs wild with gratitude and joy.

    D. That is the Spirit at work when, by God's grace, we are "formed and reformed," in the words of St. Anselm.

    E. We go too and proclaim (Dismissal).

Seventh Sunday in Ordinary Time

Readings from the Ambo

Isa 43:18-19, 21-22, 24b-25; Ps 41:2-3, 4-5, 13-14;
2 Cor 1:18-22; Mark 2:1-12

We know that the **First Reading** is nested in the larger textual world of Isaiah 40:1–55:13, well known as a series of anonymous oracles or prophecies directed to exiles of Israel living in Babylon (around 540 BC) known as Second Isaiah. The opening of chapter 40 famously begins with "Comfort," a mandate to the prophet to proclaim salvation to the scattered and the lost. The present selection from Isaiah serves as a companion piece, as it were, to God's word of healing: "Remember not the events of the past, / the things of long ago consider not; / see, I am doing something new!" This oracle, then, wants us to understand salvation or comfort in connection with God doing something new, a renovation of the old. Immediately preceding this promise of erasing the pain of the past, God has foretold of a return from Babylon, because he is their Lord, their Holy One, the "creator of Israel." This is a word from the Creator, re-creating his people.

In the context of the First Reading, Second Isaiah sings of God's reformation of Israel, a new exodus out of bondage not from Egypt but the Chaldeans. Not the specific parallels, though, to the events of the Egyptian Exodus: "In the desert I make a way, / in the wasteland, rivers. / The people I formed for myself, / that they might announce my praise." But God recalls these actions not only to illuminate his wonders but to inform Israel that the plan for reconstruction will go on despite Israel's ingratitude. Newness happens because of God's largess and not due to the homage paid to him. God's mercy does not depend on our ability to do good things or even to ask for clemency.

If the exodus from Egypt resulted in a forty-year trek of a defiant and faithless generation who rebelled against God and Moses, this new release from the shackles of the oppressor is a free gift from the God who names himself as nothing less than their redeemer (42:14).

One could name Jesus many things in the course of his ministry in Mark's Gospel, but re-creation could certainly be one of the most important in my estimation. In the complex passage illustrating the healing of the paralytic for today, the immobilized man is re-created by Jesus' power to begin anew, to "[r]emember not the events of the past." That trope encompasses both physical and spiritual healing, something that the moribund scribes were impossibly slow to understand (who is really in paralysis here?). "Child, your sins are forgiven" is a phrase that literally evokes a return to youthful suppleness of limbs and spirit, a return to innocence. In a sense, the man allegorically represents Israel being called into refashioning by the Creator. Moreover, it is fascinating that the scribes are at the root of the cultural paralysis Jesus faces in Mark's Gospel, rejecting re-creation by the Word. In a way, the problem from a Christian perspective that this pericope addresses is that the Living Word is rewriting our lives by forgiveness and redemption, while those bound to their own "texts" cannot imagine the future or forget the past; their own language impresses them too much altogether. All they know is resistance.

That resistance is the profound difference between yes and no, according to Paul. Jesus is rewriting history and our lives because "many are the promises of God, their Yes is in him; / therefore, the Amen from us also goes through him to God for glory." In a way, perhaps the simplest way to name Jesus' ministry in the course of his re-creation of God's people is just "yes." In him there was no resistance, but always the word of salvation.

Connecting the Bible and the Liturgy

We can take our cue from Paul rather substantially in our approximation of Word and sacrament this day. If Jesus is all yes, "the Amen from us also goes through him to God for glory," the chorus of the people of God affirming the saving work of comfort, liberation, and salvation from the Lord in the church's liturgy. Insofar as we speak that word through the liturgy or, indeed, in the course of our daily prayer, we might forget that "amen" is a powerful assent to Christ's "yes." Our "amen" at the Eucharist assents to God's gift of reconciliation in Christ in which our past is remembered no more, and we begin, re-created, anew.

From my perspective, there are at least three conspicuous "yes" or "amen" moments during the Eucharist, beginning with the **Introduction** and the **Penitential Rites**. Having completed the sign of the cross as the visible symbol of the indwelling of the Trinity as the community gathers for worship, the congregation assents to God's unfolding mercy in leading them out of the exile of sin and into the land of redemption: "May almighty God have mercy on us, / forgive us our sins, / and bring us to everlasting life. / Amen." Here, the assembly partakes of God's re-creation and restoration, as they overcome the paralysis of unfreedom and, together with the rest of the church, come into God's house to find forgiveness and healing. Yes, we are brought there by our fellow Christians who, by their witness, have led us to the Lord, opening up the roof so that we might stand in the presence of the saving Christ.

Second, eucharistic doxology also awaits the assent of the assembly of the baptized, after it is sung by the celebrant: "*Per ipsum, et cum ipso, et in ipso, est tibi Deo Patri omnipotenti in unitate Spiritus Sancti, omnis honor et gloria per omnia saecula saeculorum.* Amen." This acclamation of the great "amen" affirmed by the assembly concludes the central action of the Liturgy of the Eucharist, with the elevation of the newly consecrated sacramental elements of bread and wine; it is a moment of communal assent to the work of the Holy Spirit in transforming our oblation into Christ's own offering, "for our good / and the good of all his holy Church."

Lastly, the "amen" after the individual communion with the Body and Blood of the Lord acknowledges consent, a "yes" on the part of all those who have assembled for Eucharist. Having heard the word that affirms God's re-creative power in the world and Christ's own "yes" to engage such a movement of grace from the immobility of sin to the freedom of redemption, each believer assents to his or her own "amen" to God's action in Christ. As a parenthetical aside, a rather confrontational priest who, when an individual presented himself for communion and replied "Thank you" to the priest's "The Body of Christ," said: "The church's response is 'Amen.'" So be it. We might not all take such a tactic, but it should be clear that the communicant's response is a public expression of the gift of God accepted in faith. We take on the characteristic yes, yes, and again, yes. It is the voice of Jesus doing the work of the Father.

Strategy for Preaching

Generally speaking, we might say that human existence lives between the contours of assent and resistance. Read one way, life in the modern age is blessed with a powerful momentum toward the future, re-creative in its own way. Arguably the most important linguistic innovation in English fiction that was written in the last century, James Joyce's *Ulysses* (1922), ends with the word "yes." Indeed, the novel that ends with Molly Bloom's soliloquy casts its afterglow on an age of progress in health advances, technology, air and space engineering, and countless other secular miracles. At the same time, however, original sin threatens to come out of the past and mire the human subject in violence and war, the likes of which are unknown. The people of God casts its "no" to sin and violence and its "yes" to God's power to renovate the world. In a way, the church's action at the liturgy, with its Mystical Body affirming a "yes" to Christ's redemption, is a counterpoint to the corrupt "yes" of hatred and violence. The church, like Jesus, is a "yes" to God's will, but a "no" to all that is not of God. To this we can say with Pope Paul VI in his famous speech at the United Nations: "No more war! Never again war!"

Where does the Christian community's "Amen" stand in relation to the ebb and flow of God's re-creation and humanity's sinful regression into destruction? We face a paralysis of violence, but the Eucharist and the sacramental life of the church, together with the Word of God, reconstitute us, or as St. Anselm of Canterbury said in the eleventh century, *Ecclesia semper reformanda*—the church is always reforming itself. We move from age to age on our respective mats, carried to the feet of the Lord, and beg to be set free. The courageous St. Pope John XXIII called the Second Vatican council to the *aggiornamento*, or updating, of the church. This is a reminder of the continual "yes" in our midst.

The core homiletic idea for today might be: If we acknowledge that Jesus was all "yes," then we are always reaffirming his re-creation in us as we celebrate the liturgy and the coming of the Spirit among us. A convincing homily would note the ways in which our paralysis becomes unbound, and we are set free to take up our mats when we live in God's re-creative light. I suggested some "Amen" moments in the previous section, but there might be others to consider as well. God's love (and our charity that says "amen" to its activity in the world) is endlessly creative. Hate, war, and sin go nowhere; they are dead ends. Was there ever a war that re-created? When we sin, we face paralysis because we are caved in on ourselves. Our "amen" at the liturgy and in our daily lives cooperates with God's love and grace and moves us to say, "We have never seen anything like this!"

Eighth Sunday in Ordinary Time

Readings from the Ambo

Hos 2:16b, 17b, 21-22; Ps 103:1-2, 3-4, 8, 10, 12-13;
2 Cor 3:1b-6; Mark 2:18-22

The initial section of our **Second Reading** from 2 Corinthians hints at Paul's problem of credibility with the Corinthian church. Although reconstructing the Pauline correspondence with the church at Corinth is among the most complex and difficult in New Testament criticism, the very issue of the authenticity of Pauline Epistles themselves serves a modern reader well: Paul makes the most of establishing his own "letters of recommendation" as he uses the idea of writing as a controlling metaphor for solidifying his relationship with his people. With the coming of his opponents to the city, his confrontation with those who live unlawfully and in sin make fertile territory for Paul to develop his theological claims.

Masterfully, Paul turns his disadvantage to an advantage: his real intention is not to rearticulate a new law, but "[y]ou are our letter, written on our hearts . . . written not in ink but by the Spirit of the living God, / not on tablets of stone but on tablets that are hearts of flesh." In one breath, Paul establishes his credibility not through the letter (literally), but in the Spirit is the law of love that allows him justification because his "qualification comes from God, / who has indeed qualified us as ministers of a new covenant, / not of letter but of spirit; / for the letter brings death, but the Spirit gives life." Evidently, Paul could not resist this last play on words, more obvious in Greek than in English. The Corinthians are his "letter," *epistole* (letter of correspondence), written in their hearts and known by all, but the "letter," *gramma* (letter of the alphabet), brings death. In addition to the profound theology that evolves throughout 2 Corinthians, we can see that closely entwined with this marvelous

185

speculative discourse is a brilliant rhetorician who knows how to assail his opponents in Corinth.

Paul never seems to mind pushing the envelope, or the old wineskins, for that matter. Jesus himself makes a good case in the **Gospel**, establishing that the new wine of the kingdom requires the fresh wineskin of a new faith. The letter of the law simply cannot hold the new wine. If the old law of fasting were to be applied to the disciples, Jesus' teaching would burst those old wineskins. The law of love trumps the old way of doing things because the Bridegroom's message will radicalize all we thought we knew and all our former ways of doing things, even how we think. The Spirit of the Lord will not be contained. We see here the Bridegroom's passionate embrace for the people of God, revealing a God who relentlessly searches for his people. "I will lead her into the desert / and speak to her heart," says the Lord through the prophet Hosea. We know that this particular invitation from God alludes to the chosen people's intimate encounter with the Lord in the desert wanderings after the liberation from Egypt. Those were the days of corporate defiance, disobedience, and resistance, despite God's efforts to seduce his people by the good. So too, it is the Bridegroom who also says as he pursues his ministry in Galilee to a people wounded and resistive. But nevertheless, the song of the Bridegroom still reaches out to the ears of his beloved spouse, even as it does today to the church: "I will espouse you to me forever: / I will espouse you in right and in justice, / in love and in mercy. . . ."

Connecting the Bible and the Liturgy

The readings for today strike me as a fabulous example of divine excess: the God who runs breathless with an expanding heart toward his bride in the desert, the Spirit that manifests himself beyond the written word; the new wine of the kingdom served up by the Bridegroom and bursting open the narrow confines of earlier conventions. **Eucharistic Prayer IV** recalls God's pursuit of his people as well: "For you came in mercy to the aid of all, / so that those who seek might find you." That the Bridegroom came to save all is incomprehensible to the Pharisees, whose premium is a measured and calculated fasting rather than limitless love. Not surprising, then, that this same Bridegroom comes to those who are marginalized, who await the new wine of God's mercy: "To the poor he proclaimed the good news of salvation, / to prisoners, freedom, / and to the sorrowful of heart, joy." Jesus fulfills God's promise as it is articulated in the First Reading because he is the Bridegroom who espouses "in right and in justice, / in love and in mercy." These are the excesses of divine love that eclipse our narrow and caved-in sinful outlook.

The **Prayer after Communion** also serves as a gloss to the wine bursting forth in the newness, not yesterday or tomorrow, but now. Jesus implies that his disciples will feast while the Bridegroom is present; so too the church on earth radiates with the sacramental presence of the Lord: "Nourished by your saving gifts, / we beseech your mercy, Lord, / that by this same Sacrament, / with which you feed us in the present age, / you may make us partakers of life eternal." In other words, the Bridegroom is present in this Eucharist who feeds his church now, having lured her into the sanctuary of his divine love. But we also await the age to come, when the church will cross the threshold of the kingdom. So we live now in anticipation, "that the course of our world / may be directed by your peaceful rule / and that your Church may rejoice, / untroubled in her devotion" (**Collect**).

That devotion includes, of course, "the Chalice of everlasting salvation" (*Calicem salutis perpetuae*), which is the new wineskin holding the bountiful and limitless new wine of the age to come. That is the wine of the precious Blood of eternal salvation that is the new wine of the covenant shed "for many for the forgiveness of sins." The Spirit has come to transform the letter into life everlasting, even as our words—weak as they are—are only agents that beg the Lord to come and accept our oblation. Faith alone can grasp such a mystery when it acknowledges that the Bridegroom is here and we run out to meet him now in the present, since he is living and active with his people, seeking out his espoused, the church. When that encounter is reached at the eucharistic banquet, the Lord will speak to us in love and "[s]he shall respond there as in the days of her youth" (**First Reading**).

Strategy for Preaching

Very few people probably realize that God is actively pursuing us. Even for those who are daily involved in religious discernment, we tend to think that we are alone discovering God, or placing ourselves in God's presence, rather than that the Lord is inviting us into the desert of daily life in order to speak to our hearts in love. Yet God does run to meet us—every last one of us. "[Y]ou came in mercy to the aid of all," **Eucharistic Prayer IV** reminds the church. And so we, the espoused, are inextricably joined with the Bridegroom, always holding before us the new wine of salvation that he offers to the church, his Bride.

To understand God's love is impossible; we can only celebrate that it is among us in Word and Sacrament, together with the Bridegroom at the wedding feast. So, being able to be present to the Bridegroom in the Liturgy of the Eucharist as a congregation in faith that rejoices at the presence of God among us is crucial. For the preacher, allowing the congregation to understand the Eucharist as the site of holy encounter with the living God—of communion—may guide the preaching today that focuses on God's excessive love for his people. A core homiletic idea, then, might be a simple but challenging question: can we hold the new wine of the kingdom that has been poured into our hearts?

Notice the imagery in the Scriptures (as always) in a special way this Sunday, together with the liturgical language that supports these associations; the poetics unwrapped here will help to crystalize the direction of the homily. The following is a brief outline supported by particular images that should be expanded, depending on the interest and the prayerful encounter the preacher discovers with God's word. It is good for us who proclaim that God is searching us out; the text is, in a sense, "reading us," even as we meet the Lord in *lectio divina*.

I. God seeks us out in Christ the Bridegroom.

   A. Hosea: God is a *lover* who wants to *espouse* Israel, leading her to the *desert*, speaking to her *heart* (cf. Eucharistic Prayer IV).

   B. Mark: *wedding guests* do not fast when the *Bridegroom* is with them. No one pours *new wine* into old *wineskins* or they *burst* (cf. Eucharistic Prayer I—"Chalice of everlasting salvation").

II. It is an unearned love, *written in our hearts* by the Spirit.

   A. Paul: no *letters of recommendation* needed. The *Spirit* gives *life*; it is God who qualifies us (cf. Collect).

III. That writing establishes the *new covenant,* the *new wine of Christ's blood.*

    A. Paul: written in hearts by the Spirit trumps the old.

    B. Mark: old wineskins burst with new wine.

Ninth Sunday in Ordinary Time

Readings from the Ambo

Deut 5:12-15; Ps 81:3-4, 5-6, 6-8, 10-11;
2 Cor 4:6-11; Mark 2:23–3:6

The Ten Commandments inscribed in the narrative given in the book of Deuteronomy 5:6-21 are, of course, repeated in the book of Exodus 20:2-17 in an almost identical way, albeit with some exceptions. One of those variations occurs in the Third Commandment, the excerpt taken for the **First Reading** for today. At the heart of both versions of the Third Commandment of the Decalogue is the duty to rest, because after six days of work the Lord also rested, and, therefore on the seventh, Israel is to keep *shabbat*. At the same time, though, Deuteronomy appears to add a descant to the core precept found in Exodus: "For remember that you too were once a slave in Egypt, / and the LORD, your God, brought you from there / with his strong hand and outstretched arm. / That is why the LORD, your God, has commanded you / to observe the sabbath day."

This verse introduces another aspect of keeping *shabbat*: gratitude. The keeping of a day of rest not only imitates the pattern of God's creative act but also, according to the Deuteronomic historian, functions as a memorial for liberation. We might say that in some sense at least, this passage in the First Reading adds a theological reflection on the Third Commandment. God not only creates; he also liberates. The implication is that if we are all made in the image and likeness of God, we dwell in that presence in the freedom the Lord has given. Creation, fallen as it is, will succumb to slavery unless the goodness of God intervenes and frees us from the slavery of our modern-day Egypt. Paul will echo such theological sentiments in Romans 8:21 when he hopes that "creation itself would be set free from slavery to corruption and share in the glorious freedom of the children of God." God made the Sabbath holy because he set all creation free from bondage.

That particular issue of the holiness of *shabbat* seems very much at issue with Jesus' confrontation with the Pharisees in today's **Gospel**. As in the previous episode witnessed in last week's Lectionary selection (Mark 2:18-22), the disciples are the proximate cause for the dispute but then disappear from the drama as Jesus takes ownership of the teaching. In a way, the Pharisees' understanding of the Sabbath is quite correct because the disciples are violating the Law. But these legalistic folks seem to have neglected that crucial phrase in Deuteronomy, owing God a Sabbath rest because of a freedom from slavery. Ironically, the Pharisees would enslave Jesus and the disciples in a strict observance of the Law. On the other hand, Jesus appears to be introducing a law of freedom by observing a new way of keeping the Sabbath holy—by a liberation of creation from its bondage to decay and destruction. The man with the withered hand represents all of us shriveling under the devastation of sin and corruption whom Jesus has come to set free. Hence, "the sabbath was made for man, not man for the sabbath" precisely because that day is a marker for human freedom. At issue here is an anthropology of the *imago Dei*, which Jesus himself embodies in its fullness—the image of the invisible God. Paradoxically, the Pharisees attempt to replicate God's act of rest on the Sabbath but only wind up enslaving those who piously try to follow the Law.

Paul is also at pains to enshrine the dignity of the human subject through freedom by insisting on the dignity of the human subject in his reflection to the Corinthians in the **Second Reading**. Paul's anthropology concerns itself with the way "we hold this treasure in earthen vessels, / that the surpassing power may be of God and not from us." Christ will be made manifest—make us holy—as we carry in our bodies the death of Jesus. We might say that it is not sufficient simply to remember the works of Jesus, but the presence must be made manifest in us, his dying and rising, so that "we who live are constantly being given up to death." That is to say, we are made holy, sanctified not by what we do, but through the freedom given to us by the one who makes us holy.

Connecting the Bible and the Liturgy

Paul's remarkable insight that we are always carrying about in the body the dying of Jesus is especially and literally true in a sacramental way, especially in the celebration of the Eucharist. The Body of the Christian faithful gathers precisely so that "the life of Jesus may also be manifested in our body." Indeed, after the celebrant says, "The Mystery of Faith" the congregation echoes Paul in 2 Corinthians with one of the options for the **Memorial Acclamation**: "When we eat this Bread and drink this Cup, / we proclaim your Death, O Lord, / until you come again."

Perhaps this is needless to mention, but we should take the first-person plural very seriously in our response to *Mysterium Fidei*: *Mortem tuam annunciamus*. We are the Body of Christ who now proclaims the death of the Lord because Christ lives in us. In this new identity we who have been withered by sin now have been set free. Our life is now the life of Jesus "manifested in our mortal flesh." The congregation is reminded of this new life that makes us holy—like the new Sabbath celebration that cures us from our shriveling allegiance to the old ways of living for ourselves, echoed in the **Prayer over the Offerings** in today's **Presidential Prayers**: "Trusting in your compassion, O Lord, / we come eagerly with our offerings to your sacred altar, / that, through the purifying action of your grace, / we may be cleansed by the very mysteries we serve." This oration recalls the saving action of the liturgy celebrated for our sanctification in order that the assembly of the baptized might be formed anew into the Body and Blood of the Lord this New Sabbath. Therefore, we profess God's mighty works, not as some remote action seen from afar, not even in a simple compliance with resting on Sunday; no, but we rejoice this day of our liberation because we are made holy and new like the day itself. As we rejoice in our freedom, we rest as the Creator did, who continually renews his work. It is a grateful people who hear the words of the **Prayer after Communion**, recognizing all is made new in Christ, "not just in word or in speech, / but also in works and in truth, / [so that] we may merit to enter the Kingdom of Heaven."

Strategy for Preaching

If we are to think, as *Sacrosanctum Concilium* of the Second Vatican Council does, that the homily is constitutive of the liturgy itself, then we might concede that the very language of preaching—infused as it is by the Holy Spirit—becomes an act of grace and sanctification for the preacher and the hearer. Preaching, then, articulates a saving word to the captive and the prisoner, spoken as Jesus did in the synagogue in Capernaum, to set them free. In a sense, what the individual brings to the altar by way of disposition holds true for those in the listening assembly as well: the Body acclaims the Memorial Action, testifying to the death and resurrection of Christ now living within them. Preaching becomes the occasion for re-creation and freedom, moving the assembly to this very proclamation of the death and resurrection of Christ living within us.

The Third Commandment deals with an observance of God's rest, to be sure, but the Deuteronomic text reflects a theological witness to the Lord's liberation on the day of *shabbat*. What the Pharisees fail to recognize in the **Gospel** today is that it is not so much what we keep, but what keeps us and frees us. God makes us hold, even as he has made and remade this Sabbath the Lord's Day of Resurrection, a day beyond an observance of rest, a new day sanctified by the passion, death, and resurrection of Christ. The New Shabbat is a day of liberation.

Do we allow the Lord of all creation to re-create and free us at the ambo and the altar? How is the Word working within us as Christ's dying and rising to sanctify us so that we profess "not just in word or in speech but also in works and in truth"? (**Prayer after Communion**). Happily, the **Gospel**'s visual description and dramatic action work very much in the preacher's favor to begin to answer these questions. To this end, the homily should be unusually attentive to the cultural details of the Jewish laws of the Sabbath today. These historical observations could form a very useful introduction that might lead directly into the body of the homily and the core homiletic idea: Jesus cured a man with a withered hand; but that was not the only transformation that occurred: he transformed the way we think of the Sabbath as a liberation from our bondage to sin.

Some details to include in the homily are:

I. Deuteronomy 5 as keeping holy Shabbat but also the memory of liberation.

II. Jesus freeing the man and household on Sabbath.

    A. Prayer over the Offerings

III. Image of purification of old into the new taken from an example of the sacraments.

   A. Prayer after Communion

   B. Paul: "we who live are . . . given up to death . . . so that the life of Jesus may be manifested in our mortal flesh."

   C. Mystery of Faith and its corporate response.

IV. Call to mission in freedom: "Go and announce the Gospel of the Lord."

Tenth Sunday in Ordinary Time

Readings from the Ambo

Gen 3:9-15; Ps 130:1-2, 3-4, 5-6, 7-8;
2 Cor 4:13–5:1; Mark 3:20-35

The Yahwistic narrative of creation has become so familiar to us that it seems all the more jarring when part of the account of the Fall becomes cut loose from its usual mooring to the complete creation story, as it is in the **First Reading**. Genesis 3:9-15 relates the immediate consequences of Adam and Eve's disobedience, which are disharmony, shame, and blame. There is a tragic contrast in the relationships among all the principles—God, Adam, and Eve—from before and then after the event we call "original sin." We are signaled to the problem from the start: "Where are you?" aptly describes God's search for the alienated man, now shamed and in hiding among the foliage that was designed for him to enjoy and cultivate. He can only answer, not in righteousness, by blaming his partner for his own act of disobedience. And the woman has no one left to scapegoat but the serpent.

The result of disobeying God can only be described as alienation, which certainly fits our thumbnail definition of sin. Later God foretells that man and woman will both suffer the hardships of toiling in a thorny land and bearing children in pain; these are the residue or the artifacts of a sinful condition, a separation from God and one another played out in the circumstances of everyday life.

In Mark 3:20-35, Jesus does not reference the Fall in Genesis directly but does suggest an image for combating and resisting evil, or Satan. Ironically, this story starts out as an account of Jesus' relatives coming to restrain him, but the Lord then tells a parable about binding a strong man in order to lay hold of his property. It seems that this allegorical parable is specifically addressed to the scribes who have come from Jerusalem claiming " '[h]e is possessed by Beelzebul,' / and 'By the prince of demons he drives out demons.'" So saying, Jesus intends to point out the contradiction of Beelzebul casting himself out, while also referencing himself as the one who is binding the strong man (Satan) and looting that demon's house of its sin and wickedness. This is the act of redemption that reverses the consequences of the Fall, in which Satan came and robbed Adam and Eve of their innocence by breaking through the walls of Eden.

In a sense, then, Jesus becomes our stronger man, more powerful than Adam, who can tie up Satan and plunder his house of death. Christ has left us "a building from God, / a dwelling not made with hands, eternal in heaven," as Paul writes to the Corinthians in the **Second Reading**. With Jesus' act of keeping Satan hostage, we have been given the riches of the kingdom. "Everything indeed is for you, / so that the grace bestowed in abundance on more and more people / may cause the thanksgiving to overflow for the glory of God." This abundance is seen as a gift, of course, the community of faith, "For whoever does the will of God / is my brother and sister and mother."

These three readings form a very interesting connection. The story of the Fall in Genesis maps out the reason and the result of our sin. But Jesus obliquely hints at an autobiographical soteriology in the binding of the strong man and plundering his house. It remains for Paul to tell the Corinthians, and us, what to do with the riches Christ has given us.

Connecting the Bible and the Liturgy

Although we need a continual reminder, the Christian people are well aware of the effects of sin as well as the remedy for this fallen condition. The editors of the book of Genesis set in motion the consequences of the Fall, expressed in a gifted narrative, the results of turning away from love; the Scriptures will detail over and over again the rippling motion created by our First Disobedience and humanity's alienation spinning out from that singular, tragic moment. At the same time, we also witness love's pursuit. Christ has taken on the shame, disharmony, and blame as the supreme act of divine abandonment for the rescue outside the boundaries of Eden.

Baptism grants us a share in this divine life, of course, this divinized indwelling of the Spirit as the neophyte is clothed with Christ as with a garment. The **Communion Antiphon** for today poignantly recalls 1 John 4:16 and the admonition to remain in the love of God as it has been revealed in Christ: *"Deus caritas est, et qui manet in caritate in Deo manet et Deus in eo."* By plundering Satan's gaudy house, Christ has furnished for us a dwelling place—a holy temple that he inhabits, *manet in caritate*—abides in love. This is no divided house, mind you, but one that remains steadfast in love.

The zeal of Christ points us in the direction of our human will, which because of the Fall remains a fateful tree casting the dark shadows of sin and death. So there may be a temptation to falter—as Dante did with his companion Virgil, going up the mountain of Purgatory— and just become distracted, even by good things. What is worse, such delay on the road to love may also lead to despair or hopelessness—to "blaspheme against the Holy Spirit" that divides our house. Therefore, renewing our own zeal by begging God's mercy keeps us abiding in love. The **Collect** witnesses to the healing power of the Eucharist to strengthen the will of the baptized assembly, "we, who call on you in our need, / may at your prompting discern what is right, / and by your guidance do it." Yes, just do it. That is the act of holy zeal when the mind is in the trim. Likewise, the **Prayer after Communion** implores God to continue to abide in his people: "May your healing work, O Lord, / free us, we pray, from doing evil / and lead us to what is right."

So it is all about freedom that, in the end, the will is released from its dark shadows. It should be clear that the Genesis narrative in the **First Reading** discloses the descent into "unfreedom." But as Paul famously tells the Galatians, "For freedom Christ set us free; / so stand firm and do not submit again to the yoke of slavery" (5:1). The liturgy allows us to inhabit God's house, asking for strength of will "so that the grace bestowed in abundance on more and more people / may cause the thanksgiving to overflow for the glory of God." That is freedom in the context of praise and thanksgiving; that is eucharistic worship. Abiding in Christ sacramentally allows us the perfect freedom to move away from our fundamental tendency toward sin and alienation "and lead us to grow in charity" (**Prayer over the Offerings**). The liberation from sin begins and ends with Christ. We are able to say with the psalmist, then, and all the people God has made his own: "For with the LORD is kindness / and with him is plenteous redemption; / and he will redeem Israel / from all their iniquities."

Strategy for Preaching

The genius of the Yahwist creation narrative's depiction of the Fall and its consequences could well form an Elizabethan tragedy: the gift of freedom was so great, the blindness so obvious, the aftermath so immeasurable. Just after the time of Elizabeth I, however, emerged the greatest epic in English, *Paradise Lost* (1667), which managed to capture the intricate contours of the drama of the Fall as a lesson for the ages.

From a preaching perspective, the **First Reading** speaks loudly and clearly about our capacity for denial and blame, and that kind of passage might have elicited a "fire and brimstone" rant. Surely there are other ways of drawing the baptized into a recognition of human sin and our redemption in Christ. Happily, we are long past those days of the, well, "preachy homily"; but breaking open the Word for the people of God today may still capture paradise lost as well as paradise regained. It might be necessary—depending on how one exegetes the assembly—to help the congregation to grasp our capacity for sin and self-inflicted alienation so as to reveal the gift of redemption all the more fully; this recognition of sin on the one hand, and God's goodness and mercy on the other, is a central dynamic in the spiritual life of the Christian soul that will come as no small surprise to the seasoned preacher. But since all of us are so good at lying to ourselves (at least occasionally) about the truth, Word and sacrament can shed the clear light of dawn on the night of our own fateful rejection of God's grace. So the core homiletic idea for today might be: we have a great capacity for filling our house with sin, but Christ has come to rob our homes and set us free.

One way into this focus sentence is to engage the congregation in an introduction that remembers the horrific litany of structural sin perpetrated in the last century, from the Holocaust to the exploitation of farm workers. Sadly, the list is long and seemingly endless because such structural sin continues in a variety of forms today. The point of the Fall story is not to look back at Adam and Eve and blame someone else but to examine our hearts: we need to admit that we'd all find ourselves tempted toward reaching for that fruit of power, pride, and irresponsibility.

The **Prayer after Communion** begs God to "free us, we pray, from doing evil." It is in all of us from the beginning: the bad seed.

The sanctifying power of baptism and the Eucharist set us free from the savage slavery to sin. As an accompanying image, the example of the binding of the strong man that Jesus tells in the **Gospel** can be interpreted as his victory over Satan. What does this look like? Are there contemporary parallels of Christ binding and setting free?

We are liberated by our own gift from God, bestowed on us in Word and in sacrament. Hearing God's Word invites us to ask Jesus to come into our house where the binding of the strong demon will take place. Celebrating the Eucharist takes him to our table. There is no room for the strong man because he has been vanquished by Christ. This is grace bestowed, replacing Satan's presence. And it is grace that has come "more and more," as St. Paul says, and allows us to beckon others to the table of the Lord, the altar of reconciliation to join us in the hospitality we owe to grace.

Eleventh Sunday in Ordinary Time

Readings from the Ambo

Ezek 17:22-24; Ps 92:2-3, 13-14, 15-16;
2 Cor 5:6-10; Mark 4:26-34

As they are presented in the Lectionary this week, the **First Reading** from the prophet Ezekiel and Mark's Gospel form fascinating collaborative partners. Chapter 17 in Ezekiel, from which our selection occurs, begins with the Lord asking the prophet to speak to the people in a parable or proverb—a *mashal* in Hebrew. The imagery of the two eagles and the vine invite a political interpretation concerning the power struggles during the Babylonian exile. The great eagle surely represents Nebuchadnezzar, who is understood by Ezekiel as the Lord's medium of punishment for Israel and transplants a branch of cedar—signifying the destiny of Israel. This metaphor of the cedar is then picked up in verse 22, which may specifically be identified with Jehoiachin, King of Judah, in a favorable way.

The point of this allegorical parable seems to suggest the God who will take over the growth of the original cedar or leadership in Israel and transform it, quite literally, from the ground up. "It shall put forth branches and bear fruit, / and become a majestic cedar. / Birds of every kind shall dwell beneath it, / every winged thing in the shade of its boughs." Clearly, God is active even in exile, lifting "high the lowly tree, / wither up the green tree, / and make the withered tree bloom." In response to this good news, the psalm for today (92) exults, envisioning the cedar to be like the righteous who blossom under God's care. "The just one shall flourish like the palm tree, / like a cedar of Lebanon shall he grow." It is interesting to see the process of movement from Ezekiel to the psalmist. With the use of the metaphor of cedar, Ezekiel allegorizes a king as the one who becomes the new hope for Israel, while the psalmist makes this same cedar as a symbol of anyone who is righteous. In a certain sense, the psalm democratizes a once privileged allegory owned by Jehoiachin; what was once specific has now become possible to all because they have been "planted in the house of the LORD." Paul also wants this holiness to be open to all through the gift of faith. Even though he is at time autobiographical in the **Second Reading**, when he says, "we walk by faith, not by sight," Paul means this to be applicable for every follower of Christ. Paul himself was once restored to sight after his conversion, so he knows personally what true insight is all about.

Jesus deploys a parabolic tradition as we know, but his tactic seems deliberately focused on re-creating Ezekiel's allegory for the purpose of illustrating the kingdom of God. Chapter 4 in Mark introduces the Parable of the Sower that should be read as the background of our present text. Jesus' emphasis on the mustard seed (in contrast with a towering cedar) catches us in the midst of wonder at the coming of the kingdom, even as Ezekiel represents God's power as alive and active in the midst of exile. By using the "smallest of all the seeds on the earth," Jesus illustrates not only the tiny status of the plant (soon to become a shelter) but also the necessity of the earth as an instrument of transformation. It is because of the good soil, then, that the mustard seed becomes something akin to a cedar, for it "becomes the largest of plants / and puts forth large branches, / so that the birds of the sky can dwell in its shade." God's remaking and reconception of even the smallest elements of life allows the Lord to create a space of awe and wonder in the hearts of believers. The kingdom cannot be built by us because it is like nothing we can imagine or invent for ourselves. What we have will be taken up by God's Angel, the true eagle, Christ Jesus, and be made into a vessel of love. That vessel is the church, the people of God, which leaves room always to shelter the poor and those who are oppressed and seek justice.

Connecting the Bible and the Liturgy

If Jesus' parables help us to reconceive the unimaginable presence of the kingdom of God, the liturgy brings our deepest hopes into fruition by recognizing that God hears our cries; this awareness of the nearness of the Lord intuits the *now* of God's kingdom in our midst. Indeed, the **Entrance Antiphon** for today begs for God's mercy: *Ex audi Domine*—"O Lord, hear my voice, for I have called to you; be my help" (cf. Ps 27:7). In some sense, the eucharistic liturgy is the earth that brings forth the Word in the life of faith for the baptized, making a tiny seed grow we "know not how." That is because "we walk by faith, not by sight." We ask the Lord, then, to take the small branch or shoot from the cedar tree and plant it on a high and lofty mountain so that our life of faith might grow ever-deeper in the assembly.

But the real point, it seems to me, is that, like Israel, the community of faith grows *together* as the majestic cedar—or, more to the present circumstances of our lives, like a large shrub from the mustard seed of our baptism. "O God, strength of those who hope in you, / graciously hear our pleas, / and, since without you mortal frailty can do nothing, / grant us always the help of your grace, / that in following your commands / we may please you by our resolve and our deeds." These thoughtful words from the **Collect** increase the awareness of the baptized assembly as a collective witness to the kingdom on the edge of growth, the gathered hope of those who have come to worship in spirit and in truth. It is not just "I" but "we" who walk in the light of faith.

When *Sacrosanctum Concilium* underlined the presence of Christ in the assembly, it imagined moments such as these when the people of God, brought to a deeper awareness of their baptismal life in Christ, would acknowledge their place as creatures ready to be brought forth into full stature in Christ. The Eucharist, then, becomes the fertile soil *par excellence* for a need of the people to ask the Lord to "provide for the twofold needs of human nature, / nourishing us with food / and renewing us with your Sacrament." We face the increase of our faith at the centerpiece of the church's worship because we have asked the Holy Spirit in the *epiclesis* of **Eucharistic Prayer III** to "graciously make holy / these gifts we have brought to you for consecration." Together we implore the Father of all blessings that "thy kingdom come" in our midst as the Word comes to feed us.

And come he will not only for the purpose of strengthening the seed of the baptized but also by attending to the work of the church, so that the gathering of all God's children might find refuge in its branches, sheltering and caring so that "this reception of your Holy Communion, O Lord, / foreshadows the union of the faithful in you, /

so may it bring about unity in your Church." The church itself, then, becomes the largest of plants for the sake of the diversity of humanity. Surely this blossoming of the baptized in Christ is a sign of the kingdom in a world of violence where the unwanted, the condemned, and the unborn are cast aside and left adrift. The living organism of the church, the people of God, becomes a parable for all, a sign of the times in the modern world.

Strategy for Preaching

The readings and the liturgy for today are as much about the charism of preaching as they are windows into the coming kingdom. The liturgical homily enables the baptized assembly to deepen their experience of faith—that is its primary function—the result of which is an astonishing, mysterious, and blithe encounter with God's grace. Preaching allows the flourishing of the kingdom, allowing the people of God to sense that in the midst of the church's sheltering protection "we walk by faith, not by sight."

As suggested, the congregation's awareness of itself as a body of faithful witnesses giving light to its transformation in Christ is key not only to breaking open Word and sacrament this Sunday but to bringing an apprehension that the kingdom is among us in the *now* of God's grace in Christ; that presence is disclosed each day when we ask for our daily bread, together with the coming of that reign of God. So the core homiletic idea for this Sunday might be this: we are assembled as the people of God awaiting the kingdom, but that moment is here among us for the sake of the church and the whole world. The implication here is, of course, that the Eucharist is a visible sign of the now-and-the-not-yet of God's kingdom, which missions us into Gospel proclamation for the sake of that very kingdom. As Jesus makes clear, the reality of God's reign is born of mystery. That mystery comes about by acknowledging the presence of Christ not only in the sacramental elements, the Word, the church's minister but also in the gathered hearers. The **Collect** intends to deepen the awareness of the latter, but the homily can also do so as another conversation partner in the midst of the liturgy by simply making the congregation aware of itself as baptized witnesses. The preacher might call attention to the various ministers serving at the table of the Word or the sacrament, together with the importance of "dialogue" in word, song, and unified gesture during the liturgy. A brief catechetical explanation on the role of the people of God from *Lumen Gentium* or *Sacrosanctum Concilium* could be used then followed by a challenge:

But God intends to make us a sign of the kingdom at this very moment as well. The Collect could be used here in various ways, supported by Jesus' imagery about the kingdom as well as Ezekiel's allegory on Israel. It is Christ who will unlock the doors of the kingdom, which contrasts with our worldly interests to predict, to know, and to figure out. Can we find the humility to receive the kingdom and rest in its branches? That begins now.

So we mission as fellow creatures in the same forest of God's mercy for the sake of the church and the world. What is that mustard tree going to look like?

Twelfth Sunday in Ordinary Time

Readings from the Ambo

Job 38:1, 8-11; Ps 107:23-24, 25-26, 28-29, 30-31;
2 Cor 5:14-17; Mark 4:35-41

With modern conveniences and technology at our fingertips, we forget how vulnerable ancient people were to the elements. At the same time, a hurricane like Katrina that ravaged the Gulf Coast or Super Storm Sandy that brought the East Coast to a standstill can quickly remind us that nature is a force that still defies our comprehension, to say nothing of our control.

Jesus spent a great deal of time in the Galilee region with men who earned their living from the capricious sea. Would the lake yield enough to live on today and the rest of the week? Would their very lives be in jeopardy? In today's **Gospel** we see the fate of the fishermen-disciples go terribly wrong. Suddenly, a violent squall appears from out of nowhere and they, like Job, are caught unaware and in the midst of a potential tragedy. It would certainly not be unusual for such storms to arise from even the calmest of seas, as if to remind those who sail to the sea in ships, "trading on the deep waters" (Ps 107), of their own fragility and that they are staring at the depths of potential oblivion. And so we find the disciples in one of the few moments of collective utter panic in the Gospel narrative.

The plot thickens because they are not alone on the boat but with Jesus, who, curiously enough, is fast asleep. We should not pass lightly over Mark's attention to the contrast between the disciple's trepidation and the Lord's rest. A few things come to mind here. The first is the implication that Jesus is someone of great trust who has taken Psalm 107 (**Responsorial**) to heart. He has seen "the works of the LORD / and his wonders in the abyss." Then again, such trust

205

lends itself to a reading that Jesus remains unsympathetic to the disciples' fear, perhaps a more central (and disturbing) question made quite explicit: "Teacher, do you not care that we are perishing?" This is really *our* question amid the shipwreck of our lives and those we love. Is God asleep when we need that divine presence most?

It is also Job's question. In the final analysis, Job remains faithful but that does not mean he has explained the mystery of God's absence (or silence) amid his suffering. Job had to face the accusations of his friends and wife to give up the ship on the stormy waters. From Job's neighbors' perspective, God seems to have reserved the answer to the question to words that can only emerge out of a storm of mystery. And Jesus does the same by addressing the disciples "out of the storm." In fact, the Hebrew word *se'arah*—often translated "whirlwind"—can also mean divine anger or displeasure (cf. Isa 29:6). The issue, then, is not simply that the Lord stills the sea, but that the disciples come to an understanding of the power of faith and trust in God, even in the midst of turmoil and distress.

The Christian community, for whom, as Paul says, "The love of Christ impels us," faces a challenge of faith and trust as well. The ideal is to "regard no one according to the flesh." Or we might put an action of nature above God's ability to control it, for he "set limits for it /and fastened the bar of its door," as the Almighty tells Job. Rather, the new creation in Christ Jesus sees all things with the mind of Christ, who speaks out of the whirlwind of trust and faith, because "the old things have passed away; / behold, new things have come." The timidity that grips humanity by the neck and keeps us gasping for breath—from before Job up until our present time—need not lay claim on us. It is our sins that have been drowned, not God's beloved humanity.

Connecting the Bible and the Liturgy

The biblical readings touch on the foundational issues present in all humanity—fear, loss of control, and death—and also provide elemental symbols to accompany these emotions: storms, wind, and God's anger. Like the disciples who made their living by the sea, Christians also live by the sanctified waters of baptism. Both the sea and baptism hold the keys to life and death. This liturgy might be a time to take special note of the cleansing power of water, which recalls our baptism.

The *Roman Missal* advises that the blessing and sprinkling of water may occasionally be used on Sundays in order to remind the congregation of their baptism. We recall that, as Paul says in the **Second Reading** (and echoed in **Eucharistic Prayer IV**), "those who live might no longer live for themselves / but for him who for their sake died and was raised." The community of faith no longer fears the violent sea of sin and death because these waters have been made holy: they have been sanctified by Christ's very presence. The assembly will sense the immediacy of God's protecting hand over these waters (as at the dawn of creation) when they hear the **Rite of the Blessing and Sprinkling of Water** at the beginning of the Eucharist, "by which we seek protection on this your day, O Lord . . . that by this water we may be defended / from all ills of spirit and body. . . ." This is the voice of trust emerging out of the human heart amid the stormy sea of life, a refuge for the Christian community, like the Lord's Day itself.

A further resource for the homily in this regard is the under-quoted (in my opinion) **Blessing of Baptismal Water** that takes place during the Baptismal Liturgy of the Great Vigil of Easter. Indeed, the overall "plot" of this magnificent prayer used during the third part of the Easter Vigil explores the dimensions of God's care and love for his people and "whose Spirit / in the first moments of the world's creation / hovered over the waters, / so that the very substance of water / would even then take to itself the power to sanctify." God not only calms those rough waters but also speaks in the midst of the storm to us all, even as Job and the disciples face the darkness of fear. That consummate storm center is the cross itself where the Innocent Victim was given over to the unjust for the sake of all humanity and speaks to us in the language of sacrament as Christ "gave forth water from his side along with blood. . . ." Therefore, far from being a danger, water is the font of life in which human nature "washed clean through the Sacrament of Baptism / from all the squalor of the life of old, / may be found worthy to rise to the life of newborn children / through water and the Holy Spirit." These waters that have destroyed our life of sin, then, purify and sanctify us as we die to the things of the flesh. Along with Paul in 2 Corinthians, then, we say, "Consequently, from now on we regard no one according to the flesh; / even if we once knew Christ according to the flesh, / yet now we know him so no longer. / So whoever is in Christ is a new creation: / the old things have passed away; / behold, new things have come."

Strategy for Preaching

From their particular horizons each of the readings today encourages an interpretation that leans into the unfathomable mystery of God's power. The book of Job and the Gospel articulate a God who speaks in the midst of turmoil, which Paul reminds the church at Corinth that "the love of Christ impels us." Weak preaching will simply posit a rather knee-jerk and naïve response to the Scriptures and the liturgy along the lines of the tiresome cliché such as "all we have to do is trust in God and we will be okay." That kind of sloppy "homiletic" is a sad excuse for entering into the depths of God's Word. The people of God deserve better, and if they are involved in the process of deep listening to a well-crafted homily and come to a realization of the awe-inspiring love of God, then the congregation of hearers will know that "new things have come."

The liturgy makes preaching come alive, certainly the unspoken dialogue for all liturgical preaching. Therefore, accessing the Water Rite as part of the **Penitential Act** clearly sets the stage (and the table) for what *Fulfilled in Your Hearing* calls the preacher's need to name both "demons" as well as "grace" present in the lives of the baptized assembly. The demons are named at the **Penitential Act**, but also the grace of baptism recalled God's saving gift in Christ that will not be defeated by sin. This is the grace-filled moment that calms our rough waters in which God speaks to us out of the whirlwind of our busy and often much-too-selfish lives. So we might consider the following as a core homiletic idea: our darkest moment was when our vessels were still prey to the turmoil of original sin, but Christ has brought our ship safely to port.

There is a lot one could do with an introduction, but if we intend to involve the congregation in an inductive and experiential way, then the homily could deploy the very visual and acoustical elements found in the readings, such as something like this:

"Were you there when the lights went out?" Almost everyone has had the experience of being in the dark without power, and this is an avenue to explore the potential loss of human control and power—a major theme in the readings for today. The theological underpinnings for this loss are hard to avoid in the readings and are brought to mind in the Water Rite at the beginning of Mass. As fallen humanity, we live in a continual state of fear and dread, until God named the grace present in our lives in Christ Jesus, who is living and active among us.

God's work began even before the incarnation. (Quotations from the Blessing of the Font at the Easter Vigil are appropriate enough here.) So Christ has taken us up into his own calming of the waters in the tranquil sea of life: baptism. We are a new creation, no longer fearful but headed toward a promised shore. Consider perhaps an image of a ship entering into port with the Lord bringing us to shore. Gospel quotations and references to the Water Rite find themselves neatly situated at this conclusion.

Thirteenth Sunday in Ordinary Time

Readings from the Ambo

Wis 1:13-15, 2:23-24; Ps 30:2, 4, 5-6, 11, 12, 13;
2 Cor 8:7, 9, 13-15; Mark 5:21-43

Chapter 5 in Mark's Gospel takes us down a fascinating, complicated, and unusual road. This section of the narrative is sandwiched between Jesus' stilling of the sea (last week's sequence) and the return to his hometown. Read the whole chapter to get a sense of what is involved in the excerpt today (5:21-43).

One of the distinctive features we might observe in chapter 5 is the amount of detail Mark lavishes on the chain of stories dealing with exorcism and healing: the shackles of the man possessed that break into pieces; Jairus, a named synagogue official, falling at Jesus' feet; the woman with a hemorrhage and her poignant interior monologue. Taken together, these moments—all of them very human—form a novella of sorts in which we hang suspended, wondering what will happen on the level of plot: what did the exorcized demoniac proclaim to the Decapolis or what will happen to Jairus's daughter or to the woman who becomes Jesus' symbolic "daughter" (he addresses her as *thugater*, not commonly used by Jesus, but here representative of the family into which the Lord seeks to incorporate her by faith: she is a *thugater*, that is, a daughter of God) through an act of tender healing.

These important and colorful details about characters in Mark allow us to put flesh and blood on the God-Man. Like the woman suffering from hemorrhages, we are eventually cured of thinking that Jesus is some magic totem to be touched and that touching him will solve all our problems. Rather, he is intimately involved in the faith lives of those he serves, pushing us beyond the boundaries of idolatry and into a relationship that is familial. A rereading of chapter 5 over and over again yields the meditation on the Incarnate Word restoring God's original grace to humankind, making us all sons and daughters. That is true healing.

Not surprisingly, then, the book of Wisdom contemplates the God who involves himself intimately with creation. "God did not make death, / nor does he rejoice in the destruction of the living." This excerpt comes from the first half of the Wisdom of Solomon and continually exhorts the "ungodly" or the foolish to seek the path of wisdom. (The ungodly and the foolish tend to be one and the same in Israel's wisdom literature, as in Psalm 14: "Fools say in their hearts, / 'There is no God'" (v. 1). Ultimately, the book of Wisdom—a very late composition, probably written in Greek in Alexandria around 75 BC—concerns itself with hope in the God of righteousness and justice. God, who has loved creation from the beginning, will never fail to remember his people: "For he fashioned all things that they might have being." The wisdom here recalls a tradition and a divine Author who remains part of a living memory close to people, despite living under difficult circumstances, such as oppression by foreign rule.

Jesus' restoration of humanity from death reflects the wisdom of God of which he is the supreme personification. As Paul tells the Corinthians, "you know the gracious act of our Lord Jesus Christ, / that though he was rich, for your sake he became poor." Indeed, the incarnation of God in history transforms death to life, restoring not only life but the integrity of the human community. And so those who are completely alienated from the human family (demoniac) become its evangelizers; a lonely woman (that society has rendered unclean) is restored as a daughter; a dead child, returned to life, enjoys a meal with her family. The **Responsorial Psalm** is fitting for those who have been healed and for us: "I will praise you, Lord, for you have rescued me."

Connecting the Bible and the Liturgy

If we are to take the author of the book of Wisdom and Paul and Mark at their word—that is, after all, what the faith community gathers to proclaim in the graced assembly—then God never fails to remember his creation and even now brings them into healing and new life. The gracious act of Christ has given us a new relationship with God, "[f]or God formed man to be imperishable; / the image of his own nature he made him."

The *imago Dei* is underlined in the **Collect** when it prays: "O God, who through the grace of adoption / chose us to be children of light." The immediacy of God's mercy wells up in the church's sacramental life, beginning with baptism and the Eucharist. Clearly, the life of the baptized comes about precisely because the womb of the church has been granted the regenerative power from God through adoption, for we are "God's children now." Indeed, the recollection of God as the sustaining Father of all living things occurs at the beginning of **Eucharistic Prayer III** in a powerful address to the Father: *vivificas et sanctificas universa*—"you give life to all things and make them holy." The Spanish translation of the Latin is even more direct: *das vida y santificas todo*—"you give life and sanctify everything." We ought, then, to pause at the wonder of this address to God. The book of Wisdom and Jesus' own action has witnessed to God's wonders in the world, but the **Eucharistic Prayer** allows creation to speak back a word to the Father, having seen yet again those wonders proclaimed in the Scriptures. Indeed, in Christ, God has drawn all people into the new life of grace, purchased by his own passion, death, and resurrection. In Mark's Gospel, the Lord's healing power encircles all he meets, and very powerfully emerges in the midst of the broken and the troubled—even the dead. The presider, then, says on behalf of the assembly: *"populum tibi congregare non desinis"* ("you never cease to gather a people to yourself") (**Eucharistic Prayer III**). Christ's movement in Mark's Gospel is an increasing swell that brings the lost back to life and into the radiant fire of divine mercy. And we stand now in their company at the Eucharist, well aware that we are ourselves broken and in need of being restored to the human family through reconciliation and healing.

Finally, the congregation of the baptized asks the Father of life to "fill us with life, O Lord, we pray, / so that, bound to you in lasting charity, / we may bear fruit that lasts for ever" (**Prayer after Communion**). We ask that the Eucharist continues to bring us life so that we may bring newness to others—that is, God's life of divine charity. Such is the testimony of the adopted children of God.

Strategy for Preaching

Mary Shelley's well-known novel, *Frankenstein* (1818), makes an utter and complete contrast to God's work of creation and restoration. Unlike God, who made humanity out of nothing, Victor Frankenstein pieces his creature together from dead bodies; the monster becomes an image of the man, and not, obviously, *imago Dei*. More to the point, though, when Dr. Frankenstein sees his creation, he is completely repelled and disowns him. The creature is driven to kill and revenge because he dwells in a world utterly alienated from other human beings.

Happily, life with Christ is altogether something different from an over-reacher narrative. We were all loved into being and will be remembered eternally by the God who made us. In the sparkling words of Gerard Manley Hopkins's "That Nature Is a Heraclitean Fire," we are "immortal diamond." The sacrament of baptism brings this reality home very poignantly. There are some parishes that routinely celebrate the sacrament of baptism throughout the year on Sundays. From the perspective of today's readings, such a baptismal witness makes a fine descant to the already harmonious voice of the church resounding from a response to God. Obviously, preaching liturgically benefits enormously from accessing the natural symbols present in the midst of the assembly, a point clear enough with those about to be baptized, since "God formed man to be imperishable; / the image of his own nature he made him." Whether or not baptism is celebrated, the core homiletic idea for today might be this: we are made in God's own image and through the gracious act of our Lord Jesus Christ, the baptized become God's children forever, healed and restored to the human family.

A very useful and appropriate introduction might involve the hearer in the teaching of the church on social issues upholding life—the rights of the unborn, the stance against capital punishment, the preferential option for the poor. The preacher might approach these in any number of ways so that this introduction leads into a basic two-part structure:

   I. God gives "life to all things and makes them holy" (Eucharistic Prayer III).

     A. The books of Wisdom and Genesis and numerous biblical references.

     B. Creation is also made holy by Christ's healing and restoration (Mark 5).

     C. Baptism makes us temples of God's glory through the grace of the Holy Spirit (image of a building that is restored and becomes a habitation of welcome).

  II. So we are all adopted children of God called to give life to others. (Choose one of the episodes in today's **Gospel** as an icon of the call to restoration to the human family.)

     A. The liturgy draws us into this same gathering of grace; "O God, who through the grace of adoption / chose us to be children of light" (Collect).

     B. And "bear fruit that lasts for ever" (Prayer after Communion).

     C. As a conclusion, consider making a connection between the Eucharist and pro-life justice issues—new life supported by Christ's gracious gift begotten to others.

Fourteenth Sunday in Ordinary Time

Readings from the Ambo

Ezek 2:2-5; Ps 123:1-2, 2, 3-4; 2 Cor 12:7-10; Mark 6:1-6

Scholars date the beginning of Ezekiel's ministry at about 593 BC, placing him as a prophet commissioned by God early in Israel's exile into Babylon. Like most of the prophets of Israel, the vocational call tells us something about them and their ministry. In Ezekiel's case, that Spirit's stirring was dramatic and visionary and follows a kind of ecstatic pattern in which the prophet responds to the urgency of God's *ruah*—the divine Spirit. The opening line of the **First Reading** today says, "As the LORD spoke to me, the spirit entered into me, / and set me on my feet . . . I am sending you to the Israelites, / rebels who have rebelled against me." There is a clear contrast between the docile prophet who becomes an instrument of God's Word and the Israelites to whom God addresses his power; the latter are "[h]ard of face and obstinate of heart."

This description of Ezekiel's encounter with God's spirit and his mission to preach directly precedes the prophet's vision of the scroll of lamentation and woe at the end of chapter 2. At the beginning of chapter 3, then, Ezekiel will be asked to devour the scroll and finds it as "sweet as honey" (v. 3). This is yet one more divine command for the prophet to consume. The summons to eat will be one of two in the book of Ezekiel and underlines the immediate connection of the prophet between doing God's will and consuming the Word: the Word has life-sustaining sweetness, even though the mission is a difficult one. Again, the supportive power of the Word contrasts mightily to the content of lamentations that Ezekiel must deliver to the "rebels" in the house of Israel.

The prophets like Ezekiel were often faced with a striking contrast among three orbits for the Word: the messenger, the message they brought, and those to whom these divine oracles are intended. The tension with these three encounters with the Word becomes readily apparent in Mark's account of Jesus returning to his native place, or *patrida*. Jesus' return home must have been highly significant, since all the synoptic writers have a take on how Jesus was treated in his native place (cf. Luke 4:16-30 and Matt 13:53-58). We sense the resistance of those for whom the message is intended to be hostile and angry, not unlike Israel's tangle with the prophets. Paradoxically, while they acknowledge Jesus' powerful teaching, wisdom in the synagogue, including his mighty deeds, and "were astonished," they took offense at him. The Greek word used here is significant; it is *eskandalizonto*, the root of which means to stumble or trip and, in its most pejorative sense in the New Testament, to sin. Evidently, the people of Jesus' native place could not get past the ethos of Jesus himself, despite the content of his message and the wonders he brings to the community. In this regard, they are linked to the rebellious house of Israel because of "their lack of faith." In a real way, they become trapped in a dragnet of their own making, a diaspora from which they cannot be disengaged. Interestingly, Mark tells us that their discrediting of Jesus (again, very much in the prophetic tradition) provides the reason for the Lord's inability to do much in that place, "apart from curing a few sick people by laying his hands on them." The **Gospel** for today leaves us with a devastating picture of God's silence because of a lack of faith, a powerlessness to disclose divinity.

Yet Paul finds the weakness of his own prophetic call to be a source of strength "for when I am weak, then I am strong." For Paul, it is God's grace in which "power is made perfect in weakness." Whatever Paul's "thorn" in the flesh was, it taught him about reliance on God, which is something that Israel at the time of the exile and Jesus' fellow countrymen and women have yet to believe. It is probably not coincidental that Jesus' ministry in his native place is in curing a few sick people: that is the power disclosed in weakness even amid the faithless.

Connecting the Bible and the Liturgy

The cast of characters in today's readings remind us that human nature is sinfully stubborn and desperately in need of God's grace in order to reform and find true healing. This turn to the Lord means a daily effort at conversion of heart. So the corporate voice of the church begging God's mercy at the beginning of the Eucharist during the **Penitential Act** is the prayer of the faithful to acknowledge God's power and our weakness in the face of sin.

Consider, then, the following option in which the celebrant invites the congregation to engage in the Penitential Act: "You were sent to heal the contrite of heart." And then: "Lord, have mercy." Now there are at least three aspects of this invocation that are important to keep in mind, especially when it comes to preaching. The first is that we are calling on Christ throughout this triple invocation. In a word, we are assenting to the Son and have not become rebels in God's house or strangers to the Lord in his *patrida*. Second, we also note that Jesus was *sent*, implying that he has come forth from the Father as Incarnate Word. In the tradition of the prophets before him, Jesus is the definitive utterance of divine reconciliation. By acknowledging Christ's mission, we are also consenting to the work God is about to accomplish in him for sinful humanity. Third, we might ask: to whom was Christ sent and for what purpose? *Sanare contritos corde*—to heal the contrite of heart. We could easily find ourselves allied with the rebels during the Babylonian exile or those who took offense at Jesus in the synagogue if we lacked one necessary element vital to devouring the scroll of God's Word, the consuming of the Word in its fullness and truth: contrition. Those who are open to the reception of God's power will be contrite of heart and cry, "*Kyrie, eleison*."

In a poetic sort of way, our threefold cry for mercy at the Penitential Act is somewhat analogous to Paul's own struggle, as he suggests in the **Second Reading**, when concerning his thorn, he begged the Lord "three times" that it might leave him. What is our own thorn as we ask God for mercy? Are we able to name the demons in our lives that continually snap at our heels and get us into trouble? Where is the acknowledgment of our own sinful weakness so that we can rely on the strength of God's grace? If we can turn our hearts around, then we embrace the righteous homeland, the *patrida* of Christ, who has come to set us free from all that binds us.

Strategy for Preaching

In a sense, the readings all concern themselves with the difficulty of those charged with preaching God's Word. Ezekiel faces a rebellious people in exile; Jesus confronts a lackluster group of folks from his own hometown, who believe in his works, but not in him; Paul struggles with his own weakness while experiencing the power of grace. Taken together, the Scriptures today deal with the potential loss of heart, lack of faith, and general obstinacy of the people of God. Human nature would suggest that there is a continuity in what we see from the time of the exile until the present day: we are all weighed down by sin and denial. What can the preacher do in order to facilitate the listening congregation to move from hardness of heart and toward conversion?

As suggested in previous weeks throughout the liturgical year, it is important for preachers to regularly take an account of themselves, a kind of spiritual inventory of their vocation as missionaries of the Word made visible; this day is one of those invitations. Am I open to the spirit of the Lord, devouring his Word in immediacy, urgency, and obedience, or am I avoiding this encounter with the Word with a less-than-zealous faith in the one who has called me into that mission of evangelization? A deeper question to explore might be this one: am I allowing myself the vulnerability to be weak in the presence of the Word, so that this divine presence might unfold in the midst of the assembly?

With a little self-examination in mind preceding the preaching event, the core homiletic idea for today may evoke something reminiscent of an old-fashioned altar call, still quite prominent in evangelical churches: are we ready to admit our weakness so the power of God may come through our lives? The strength and import of this question emerges from the **Penitential Act** of the eucharistic liturgy itself. Therefore, one way of structuring the homily might be to use the Penitential Act, the threefold invocation begging for God's mercy through Christ as an organizing principle. Along these lines, a visual introduction leading up to the body of the homily might picture a defoliated landscape, a forest without trees, or a dried-up garden. There are plenty of descriptions to be had in recent dystopian fiction and film, such as Cormac McCarthy's *The Road* (2006) or Suzanne Collins's *The Hunger Games* trilogy (2008–2010).

The body of the homily would then begin to be shaped like this:

I. That is what desolation looks like; no wonder we need contrition and mercy. We say it at the Penitential Act: "You were sent to heal the contrite of heart." "Lord, have mercy." All we need to do is to dispose ourselves to that love.

   A. Ezekiel as an example of one consuming the Word.

   B. Paul as obedient to his mission despite weakness.

   C. Jesus' healing in the midst of lack of faith.

II. But we have to admit our role in personal and structural sin in order for us to be fully alive in God's mercy. So we say that "You came to call sinners." "Christ, have mercy."

   A. It is often difficult to see ourselves as a mixed bag—graced sinners. That God would act in the life of one who has done wrong seems impossible.

   B. The people in Jesus' hometown could not admit that God could dwell in their midst, yet he was that close.

   C. Imaginative illustration, such as a story in which goodness comes to town and everyone misses the miracle.

III. So we continually ask Christ for his intercession, recognizing that he has transcended sin and death. "You are seated at the right hand of the Father to intercede for us." "Lord, have mercy."

   A. Despite our dreary landscape, Christ, the Son of Justice breaks through to reinvigorate us, not just now but forever.

   B. We can learn from the experience of our wounds, even as Paul did. It is in weakness that we are made perfect because of Christ's continual intercession. Our prayers, like our wounds, are joined to him.

   C. The cross of Christ is God's strength acting through weakness.

Fifteenth Sunday in Ordinary Time

Readings from the Ambo

Amos 7:12-15; Ps 85:9-10, 11-12, 13-14; Eph 1:3-14; Mark 6:7-13

This will not be either the first or the last suggestion about the importance of story in the Gospel narratives. As is well known, if we were to read Mark's Gospel straight through from beginning to end in one sitting (a very fruitful undertaking, by the way) then we would make some important and interesting connections. One of these associations establishes a link between the beginning of chapter 6 (cf., last week's Gospel) and today's passage. Jesus left his native place because he found no faith there and experienced an overall hostility to his presence; despite this corporate blindness, the Lord was still able to accomplish healing the sick and the weak, albeit in a limited way. Jesus' response to this seeming setback in his ministry is not dejection but an even further engagement into the work he has come to accomplish by commissioning the disciples: he missions these follows to perform even more mighty deeds by giving them "authority over unclean spirits." This little scenario in today's **Gospel** is a marvelous example of the Lord's ability to delegate power and shows the generative activity of Christ early on in Mark's Gospel. In some sense this passing on of his own charism remains something of a prelude to the post-resurrection community of faith: "The Twelve drove out many demons, / and they anointed with oil many who were sick and cured them."

If Jesus has demonstrated an emptying of his own power for the sake of healing and the promise of the kingdom—an obvious echo of the mystery of the incarnation itself—then he expects no less from his disciples. Curiously, the basic qualifications for performing exorcisms on unclean spirits and preaching repentance to sinners is trust: the disciples are to depend on hospitality and exist in that freedom. The implication here is, Christ is working through his disciples, and the faith of the mission does not depend on the spiritual disposition or condition of the individual disciple but the embodied grace of the Master who has commissioned them into service. Here again, we find that human weakness, far from defeating the mission, becomes its powerful engine. We might say that the personality of the disciple and his or her spiritual condition seem to hold very little sway in the fact of God's intention to bring the Good News of his love to his people. The Baptist reaffirms this in the well-known phrase, "He must increase; I must decrease" (John 3:30). And we see such a transformation again and again in the prophetic tradition, witnessed in the **First Reading** today by Amos. A southerner from Tekoa, Amos's ministry took place in the northern kingdom during the reign of Uzziah of Judah and Jeroboam II of Israel. Much of Amos's prophetic oracles concerned itself with a preaching to the powers about justice for the poor, pitting him against the established status quo and its leadership. Yet he sets the template for self-emptying in his autobiographical account of his call to preach to Amaziah the king of Judah, who tried to prevent Amos from carrying out his mission from God, who said to him simply, "Go, prophesy to my people Israel."

The First Reading and the Gospel carry very particular references to the humility involved with a response to vocation and mission, but the Letter to the Ephesians sets an exuberant tone in the **Second Reading** for a more universal vocational oracle. In his exhortation, Paul (the authorship of Ephesians is controverted) reminds the church at Ephesus that God has "blessed us in Christ." And "he chose us in him, before the foundation of the world, / to be holy and without blemish before him." This exclamation ratifies the universal call to holiness that would be echoed throughout the church over the centuries in various ways, but nowhere more celebrated than in the Dogmatic Constitution on the Church, *Lumen Gentium*. Jesus has already set the priority of delegation in his missioning of the disciples. To this mission all of us have been called, depending on our individual vocational calling and gift. Like the fate of Amos, our life will one way or another be wrapped up with the response to the universal call to holiness as well as our own particular vocational mission: "In him we were also chosen, / destined in accord with the purpose of the One / who accomplishes all things according to the intention of his will, / so that we might exist for the praise of his glory, / we who first hoped in Christ."

Connecting the Bible and the Liturgy

The **Presidential Prayers** for today call the church to acknowledge the universal call to holiness. These petitions are not unusual, of course, but underline Paul's point in the Letter to the Ephesians that we are "destined in accord with the purpose of the One / who accomplishes all things according to the intention of his will. . . ." Indeed, this Eucharist situates us in the midst of "the praise of his glory, / we who first hoped in Christ." The **Collect** begs God to "give all who for the faith they profess / are accounted Christians / the grace to reject whatever is contrary to the name of Christ / and to strive after all that does it honor." Similarly, in the **Prayer over the Offerings** the consecrated gifts brought up to the Lord anticipate their destiny when it says that "when consumed by those who believe, / they may bring ever greater holiness." And finally, the **Prayer after Communion** again begs that what we have consumed "by our participation in this mystery, / its saving effects upon us may grow." All are made holy by the sanctifying power of Christ's action in the liturgy, which empowers the baptized assembly to go forth in mission.

The reliance on the power of grace is certainly clear not only in the liturgy but the **Gospel** for today as well: "The Twelve drove out many demons, / and they anointed with oil many who were sick and cured them." This closing line becomes a biblical mandate (together with its companion, Jas 5:14) for the sacrament of the anointing of the sick, the character of which relies on grace and the power of the Holy Spirit. The anointing signifies the presence of Christ in his Holy Spirit who bestows on those who receive the sacrament healing from affliction. The Blessing of the Oil in the liturgy of anointing accentuates the power of grace to help us grow and to heal our brothers and sisters: "God of all consolation, you chose and sent your Son to heal the world. Graciously listen to the prayer of faith: send the power of your Holy Spirit, the Consoler, into this precious oil, this soothing ointment, this rich gift, this fruit of the earth. Bless this oil and sanctify it for our use." That the call to holiness remains intimately and inextricably bound to our sanctification becomes a lasting sign and a significant reminder to the baptized assembly about our true vocation, which is expressed in the **Responsorial Psalm**: "Lord, let us see your kindness, and grant us your salvation." That sanctification is linked to healing becomes expressed in the mission of the Twelve as they cast out demons and anointed the sick. We find our own sanctification in the work of Christ at the eucharistic liturgy and are reminded of its matchless healing power to draw us all together in peace.

Strategy for Preaching

The prophet Amos certainly had a particular historical mission to accomplish, but his call away from temporal concerns to preach justice as God's mouthpiece remains the archetype for Christian preaching. Clearly, the preacher's call to holiness is allied with the docility before the Word of God: it is only grace that requires our assent. In a sense, the preacher becomes the voice of the church in action, anointing the people of God with the Lord's kindness, so that they might see divine salvation unfold. Sometimes that tender compassion will recognize grace; at other moments it calls to point out demons in the community. This is the mercy that always speaks justice and truth.

The core homiletic idea for today is quite basic and may be something quite blunt and to the point: our vocation as baptized Christians is simply to cooperate with God's grace. Simple enough, yes? Not really. So this call needs to be fleshed out. As we noted in the **Gospel** for today, the sending out of the disciples to cure and anoint could be brought further into focus with reference to the *Rite of Anointing of the Sick*. Moreover, it would be appropriate to invite the elderly or the infirm members of the parish to be anointed at one or all of the Masses for today for obvious reasons. These folks are the natural symbols in the assembly that can only reinforce the Gospel message of the Lord's healing presence through ritual action.

An introduction for the homily might focus on our real (versus imagined) vocation; it takes the congregation through a brief look at the sometimes difficult encounter between grace and vocational discovery. Amos serves as a biblical witness to this reality. Then the beginning of the body of the homily might introduce a short catechesis on the doctrine of grace, supported by sacramental theology and the **Presidential Prayers** for today. Clearly, the text for the Rite of the Anointing of the Sick figures prominently here and, with those to be anointed present, will keep the homily from becoming too abstract.

But grace needs our cooperation. The earlier portion of Mark, chapter 6 (last week's Gospel passage), found Jesus amid a very uncooperative group of people. He was unable to do much because of a lack of faith, of a diaspora of bad will and resistance. Discipleship may struggle with faith issues, but it always strives to be docile before the Lord. That is how God's will is actualized in our presence and how we can recognize grace in our lives and in the lives of others. (A concrete illustration should follow, showing contemporary empowerment for ministry. Optimally, such a situation would be taken from a parish situation, such as recalling the commissioning of catechists.)

There may be times when we are asked to cooperate with God's healing touch, by speaking against the powers, in the style of Amos and Jesus. During this vocational call, we have only to remember that we have been chosen as baptized witnesses (Ephesians). We are fortified by the Eucharist (**Prayer after Communion**) so that we will have the courage to go forth into the world and heal.

Sixteenth Sunday in Ordinary Time

Readings from the Ambo

Jer 23:1-6; Ps 23:1-3, 3-4, 5-6; Eph 2:13-18; Mark 6:30-34

Preaching at the time of the Babylonian exile, Jeremiah indicts Judah's leadership for failing its people miserably. Indeed, the **First Reading** wants to hold accountable those who should have pastored God's sheep but instead brought those chosen people to the edge of destruction. The accusation concerns not only the physical alienation of the people but the marginalization caused by sin and hardness of heart. "You have scattered my sheep and driven them away. / You have not cared for them, / but I will take care to punish your evil deeds." This metaphor of the shepherd losing the flock will be taken up by Ezekiel and, much later, St. Augustine.

At the same time, as searing as God's justice burns against the shepherd leadership of Judah, Jeremiah emphasizes not so much the collapse of these men as he does God's compassion for those who have been neglected. These are those whom Christ would name the lost sheep of the house of Israel or the one lost sheep in Luke's parable and, in today's **Gospel**, the crowds "like sheep without a shepherd" longing to be taught by the Lord. Amazingly enough, in Jeremiah's reckoning, God himself will intervene and become the faithful shepherd and "gather the remnant of my flock / from all the lands to which I have driven them / and bring them back to their meadow."

Perhaps it is just in such a grassy field that Jesus finds the vast crowd, having disembarked and come from a deserted place with his disciples. There is an obvious connection between the First Reading, the Gospel, and the **Responsorial Psalm** in the way that divine compassion has reached out for the lost and helped them to find rest on green pastures. In an interesting sort of way, though, the retreat

225

Jesus makes with the disciples to the deserted place helps them to prepare to feed others who are faced with heartache and abandonment. Having been to the desert of the plain, the ministers of the Lord are prepared to encounter those inflicted with emptiness of the soul. What did these disciples encounter in that deserted place? God's compassion invites both the disciples and the crowds to rest awhile. In a christological sense, this tenderness articulates the "I myself will gather the remnant of my flock." The Son brings God's presence in the midst of chaos and confusion. As the psalm (23) says most appropriately, "The LORD is my shepherd; I shall not want. / In verdant pastures he gives me repose; / beside restful waters he leads me; / he refreshes my soul."

How are the sheep gathered? By teaching. Surely, there were a number of options open for Jesus in terms of his role as Shepherd rescuing the lost sheep, but it is the language of instruction that becomes a unifying element. As the Wisdom of God, Christ helps to affirm the humanity of those who are lost and dispersed. The Letter to the Ephesians is quite poignant in this regard, since that Epistle also imagines the Shepherd gathering in the sheep by his Word: "He came and preached peace to you who were far off / and peace to those who were near, / for through him we both have access in one Spirit to the Father." Jesus brings peace through reconciliation with the Father and so we have "access in one Spirit." The gift of unity ought not go unnoticed here, since fragmentation and meaninglessness are those things facing the wanderer; unity remains the supreme gift of Christ, "in one body, through the cross." In the end, the Shepherd will lay down his life for his sheep so that all may gather into the shadow of the cross.

Connecting the Bible and the Liturgy

There are a number of places in which the liturgical prayers for today interface with the biblical readings in the Lectionary. Indeed, the very paschal mystery itself comes into sublime focus in the opening line of Ephesians: "In Christ Jesus you who once were far off / have become near by the blood of Christ." Perhaps the most obvious theological observation to make here points to the very theological nature of Christ's intercession at the Eucharist and reflects the need to gather in the wanderers and those looking for refreshment around

Word and sacrament. In **Eucharistic Prayer III**, the presider says, "Listen graciously to the prayers of this family, / whom you have summoned before you: / in your compassion, O merciful Father, / gather to yourself all your children / scattered throughout the world." These are the children of the diaspora, the *dispersos* in exile, who remind us of the unity in the church and that the Eucharist is the site in which the Chief Shepherd gathers his flock. Although next week's Gospel passage (from John) will unfold the feeding of the five thousand, the present pericope, with its emphasis on the Shepherd collecting the lost by divine teaching, underlines the emphatic role sacred language plays in drawing those who are scattered together into One Body.

Preface II of the Sundays in Ordinary Time raises our attention to the power of liturgical language to shape the congregation: "For out of compassion for the waywardness that is ours, / he humbled himself and was born of the Virgin. . . ." And again, in **Preface III**: "For we know it belongs to your boundless glory, / that you came to the aid of mortal beings with your divinity. . . ." And in **Preface VIII:** "For, when your children were scattered afar by sin, / through the Blood of your Son and the power of the Spirit, / you gathered them again to yourself." These few instances disclose for whom the church's liturgy holds the power to recollect the sacred story of the incarnation itself, and its very utterance is an invitation to unity in the midst of our diversity and difference. We stand before the Lord God of Hosts utterly unique and gifted, yet drawn together by the saving mystery of Christ Jesus, the Good Shepherd.

All of these selections from the **Prefaces** for Ordinary Time are theological and liturgical descant on the **Responsorial Psalm** deployed for today, as well as the Letter to the Ephesians and Mark's Gospel. Read one way, today's **Gospel** more than hints at the Word emerging from "the deserted place" of solitude, as if he were coming from the womb of the Father; and there, he encountered all humanity in infinite compassion. Indeed, the mystery of the incarnation is God's expression of love when the Son is "moved with pity for them," having himself emerged from perfect union with the Father and the Spirit. These are high christological musings, perhaps strange for a reading of Mark's Gospel. Nevertheless, it is hard to resist the invitation to the mystical that Mark has invited us to share in the dialectic between solitude and compassion that Our Lord exemplifies in his own unique ministry activity.

Strategy for Preaching

The Word is born in solitude and so is preaching; that is, our encounter with God's presence in a lonely place refreshes our soul through the grace of the Holy Spirit. Jesus' healing ministry and his preaching—as well as his disciples' own work—is renewed by going to a deserted place and abiding in God. So, the **Gospel** convicts the preacher in an encounter with interior loneliness in order to be joined with the Lord in faithful service for the sheep. To do otherwise is to succumb to the delinquent shepherd who ceases to gather the children of the Lord around the cross, but promotes superficial agenda. At stake here is the very heart of Christian preaching that must emerge as prayerful sharing of the biblical and liturgical texts in a gifted sharing for those longing to hear the Word. That said, there is a vital homiletic core present in these texts that might be disclosed in any number of ways. Preachers will emerge from their contemplation with their own focus in mind; but here is a homiletic sentence that might gather the congregation, as always, with an eye toward the biblical readings and the liturgical texts. Jesus receives us, reconciles us, and reveals himself to us.

An introduction might briefly hint at the way in which we come to Mass to receive the Body and Blood of the Lord, but it is really Christ who receives us as members of his Body. We become what we consume.

I. Jesus receives us as he encounters the crowds—with compassion God meets us wherever we are.

   A. We are children of God, scattered like the diaspora of Israel, from sin and rejection of the Lord's goodness.

   B. But God wants us back (**Preface VIII**).

   C. Story of a teacher would be helpful here, one who struggles with students (like a shepherd might his wayward sheep) to help them move beyond where they are.

II. Jesus also reconciles us.

   A. The Letter to Ephesians presents several christological examples of this crucial theological reality.

   B. **Preface II of the Sundays for Ordinary Time** as well as selections from the **Eucharistic Prayer for Reconciliation** (**I and II**).

    C. *Catechism of the Catholic Church* (cf. art. 599-618).

    D. Christ senses our need when we are scattered (Gospel).

III. So Jesus reveals God's compassion for us as the Great Shepherd.

    A. (This may be a time for self-examination for the preacher, based on the encounter made in solitude as suggested above.)

    B. An opportunity to share very briefly the preacher's own witness to God's action.

    C. Illustration of a congregation gathering at prayer or a collective ecclesial function. Perhaps an allusion to those keeping vigil in St. Peter's Square when Saint John Paul II died. Or again, those gathered for the newly elected Pope Francis when he invited them to pray for him on a chilly March evening in Rome.

Seventeenth Sunday in Ordinary Time

Readings from the Ambo

2 Kgs 4:42-44; Ps 145:10-11, 15-16, 17-18; Eph 4:1-6; John 6:1-15

The **First Reading** from 2 Kings is Elisha's last miracle story in chapter 4, something that really began after his mentor, Elijah, ascended on a whirlwind into heaven (cf. 2 Kgs 2:11). We ought to see the relationship between the two prophets as exemplary of the way in which the new "hero" comes into his own: it is only after the passing of the mentor when the student becomes empowered to become like him and to disclose wonders. So saying, as Elisha succeeds Elijah, literally inheriting his mantle, he parts the water of the Jordan and crosses that river. Those standing in Jericho were convinced that "[t]he spirit of Elijah rests on Elisha" (2:15). Chapter 4 then invests the text with a succession of miracle stories in order to further validate Elisha's true prophetic lineage: the multiplication of oil (4:1-7), the raising of the son of the Shunammite woman (4:8-37), the sanctification of the pot of poison stew (4:38-41), and finally, the multiplication of loaves (4:42-44).

In the short text for today in the First Reading, scholars tell us that there appears to be some kind of cultic connection with the offering from the man from Baal-shalishah who brought "twenty barley loaves made from the firstfruits, / and fresh grain in the ear." This oblation appears to be a suitable first fruit offering for a priest as prescribed in both the book of Numbers (18:13) and the book of Deuteronomy (18:4). The miracle is without drama, except for the obvious dynamic of the wonder itself, in which we see that a hundred people were fed. And additionally, "when they had eaten, there was some left over." Not coincidentally does the **Responsorial** refrain sing that "[t]he hand of the Lord feeds us; he answers all our needs."

The **Gospel** contains some obvious connections with the First Reading and the **Responsorial Psalm**, with some crucial and notable exceptions. While the Johannine account of Jesus feeding a multitude does establish him as a wonderworker, in the prophetic tradition of Elijah, Elisha, and the prophets of Israel, the Lord has no mentor figure from which he inherits a mantle, but is *sui generis*. Furthermore, Jesus is not linked to a cultic world the way Elisha is associated with the man from Baal-shalishah. On the contrary, Jesus' response in John 6:1-15 is a pastoral reaction to those who were sick and hungry. The cultic aspect of this new feeding of the multitude in John is tied to the Passover meal and emerges not from the mandatory "firstfruits" of priestly offering, but from a boy with five barley loaves and two fish. Like the feeding story in 2 Kings, though, there is food left over. Yet the five thousand who are fed and the twelve wicker baskets left over are a sign that discloses a new order: God's gracious hospitality has been revealed as manna, a transformation of the nation of Israel (symbolically represented by the twelve wicker baskets). A meal of poverty has made not a tribe but a people united by Jesus himself. This unification becomes politically clear to the crowd, but they miss its substantial signification, since they want to make Jesus their king.

Paul expects the same transformation day by day in the lives of the church at Ephesus. He says that they ought to be "striving to preserve the unity of the spirit through the bond of peace." In a sense, what begins as hunger ends in Christ who leads us as "one Lord, one faith, one baptism; / one God and Father of all, / who is over all and through all and in all." The implication we can draw from seeing this text in the context of the first two readings is that while we come to feed at the hand of the Lord who "answers all our needs," we have our part to play as members of this table of plenty. That accountability comes from Paul as an obligation to uphold the spirit of unity, a point he will make elsewhere in his corpus of epistles (see, for example, 1 Cor 12:27ff. and Rom 12:5ff.) as we partake of the one cup and the one loaf.

Connecting the Bible and the Liturgy

The word "abundance" appears twice in the **Presidential Prayers** this Sunday, first in the long **Collect** asking God for mercy (*multiplica* *super nos misericordiam tuam*) and then in the **Prayer over the Offerings** in connection with the gifts (*quae tibi de tua largitate deferimus*). This attention to God's generosity surely highlights a theological aspect of the readings that emphasizes not only multiplication from very little but an excess of food from practically nothing. Indeed, the **Collect** emphasizes God as "protector of those who hope in you, / without whom nothing has firm foundation, nothing is holy, / bestow in abundance your mercy upon us . . ." and again in the **Prayer over the Offerings**, "Accept, O Lord, we pray, the offerings / which we bring from the abundance of your gifts, / that through the powerful working of your grace / these most sacred mysteries may sanctify our present way of life / and lead us to eternal gladness."

It is clear enough that the very celebration of the Eucharist is itself the most powerful connection to the biblical readings we have just heard in their most basic meaning. But the Prayer over the Offerings reminds the congregation that we are returning to God what has been so graciously bestowed on us so that we may be sanctified by the mysteries we celebrate. What is at stake is our personal sanctification, but also our profession to one God and father of us all, to be one in unity. As we consume the Body and Blood of the Lord, we are consumed as well and taken up into the Christ who leads us to the Father. In a certain poetic sense, in John the young man with the five loaves and the two fish remains emblematic of the congregation, since like us the boy returns to God in Christ the gifts that we have already been given. It is Christ who will make these gifts holy—and bringing them, as he did with the six water jars at the wedding at Cana, into the providence of a new order of being, the order of grace, taken from nature itself.

The **Presentation and Preparation of the Gifts** establishes a further connection between the altar and the ambo when it blesses the Lord of all creation "*quia da tu largitate accepimus panem quem tibi offerimus.*" The useful and understandable translation of *largitate* in the *Roman Missal* is the English word "goodness," but that is a weak word (although a very good liturgical word) that unfortunately does not quite grasp what is at stake here: it is through God's excessive abundance, the divine *largess* that we offer this bread and wine. In fact, as noted above, the word *largitate* is used in the **Prayer over the Offerings** precisely to express abundance and is translated accordingly. Semantics aside, God has not only given to his people, he has given his gifts in excess. Ultimately, the theological import of divine gift and graciousness to the point of excess cannot be over emphasized: it spills over not only in the biblical readings emphasizing Jesus' compassion for the crowd but becomes the iconic moment of the cross of Christ itself. Indeed, that God has fed us with his own Body and Blood is not only goodness, it is beyond all telling; it is divine excess. The Eucharist, then, becomes the table not only of plenty (it surely is that) but also of divine *kenosis*, the utterly self-emptying of God for the sake of humanity. In the end, the Lord has not only fed us but has answered the needs of which we do not know, hungers that only God can quench through his Body and Blood.

Strategy for Preaching

The goal for preaching this weekend is not only to make the obvious ties between the feeding stories in the Hebrew Scriptures and the New Testament but also to explore the agency of divine excess into which these stories gesture. As we focus on the supreme offering of Christ's paschal mystery ("we preach Christ crucified"), the homily may be shaped in a number of ways. The preacher might keep in mind that the Lectionary cycle is unfolding the Bread of Life Discourse in John over the next several Sundays (the last of which is the Twentieth Sunday). It would be useful to ask where the preacher wants the congregation to be in regard to the feeding stories, fortified by a faith-filled understanding of the Eucharist. In a sense, of course, this homiletic investigation that deepens the faith of the baptized is central to all good preaching. But this Sunday invites the homilist to unpack how and with whom and where divine largesse unfolds in our lives. The preacher's homiletic core idea, then, could be to help the assembly to answer the following question: how are we surprised by grace?

Such an inquiry cannot even be posed explicitly to the baptized assembly, since to raise it already robs or at least undermines the dynamic of divine excess. We should be overtaken in astonishment that we are not only fed but that there are twelve baskets full, establishing a new order of grace. No, the homily here becomes demonstrative of grace itself, naming God's largesse by its very food preached through the Scriptures. The language of the homily should spill over into abundant insight for the congregation, providing food for the journey and an arena to be ambushed by the holiness of God.

234   *Ordinary Time*

We might consider an introduction that takes a very sober look at contemporary cultural entitlement—not the well-worn Washington cliché "entitlement programs" but an attitude that steals a sense of wonder from the creature for his or her Creator. If we have any rights, they are endowed to us by God. We could allude to a litany of human gifts, reflecting a theological anthropology grounded in the *imago Dei*. It is a gift to be alive. One way in which artistic discourse understood divine excess was through an expression of the baroque (that runs more or less parallel to the seventeenth century in the West): it was a lavish, over-the-top use of colors, emotion, human flesh, nature, and large canvas, all demonstrating that the human subject was in possession of a graced world that could not be measured.

What is our response to just being alive? To take a breath like the first man or woman? We could ask for more and more, but that would put us in the diaspora of fragmented people, scattered everywhere like the crowds Jesus meets in the **Gospel**. Rather, our turning point comes when we can offer back to God something of ourselves, our five loaves and two fish, and place them in Christ's hands. In the tradition of the prophets, the liturgy allows us to return thanksgiving to God for the abundance we have been given (cf. the **Collect** and the **Prayer over the Offerings**). The presence of the eucharistic Lord is the sure sign of God's everlasting abundance in Christ Jesus. There are signs among us that speak this same language after we leave the assembly. (A story focusing on generosity would be useful in this context.) That care for us occurs in the here and now of a grace unexpected, a union of mind and heart with people seen and unseen. There is no end to the Eucharist because it is the unfathomable sign of God's love, reminding us of the kingdom that is even now coming in our midst—immeasurable and beyond understanding.

Eighteenth Sunday in Ordinary Time

Readings from the Ambo

Exod 16:2-4, 12-15; Ps 78:3-4, 23-24, 25, 54;
Eph 4:17, 20-24; John 6:24-35

The **First Reading** from the book of Exodus recounts the Israelites grumbling in the desert and their receiving manna from God in response to their hunger pains. The complaints against God and Moses will be ubiquitous as Israel marches through the desert, murmuring, murmuring, murmuring. They not only register a grievance about bad food and inadequate water but probably a few other things as well. In chapter 14:11ff., for instance, the chosen people prophesy that they will die at the hands of Pharaoh and the Egyptian soldiers.

God's response to these petulant outbursts is sure and certain. The Red Sea opens up and swallows Pharaoh (14:26-31), and manna is served up by divine initiative. God's response to their hunger is read by Israel as wonder, to which they sing, "The Son of Moses," after crossing the Sea. The Hebrew word *manna* is probably related to the expression *mannu*, that is to say, "what is it?" This was the food with which the people would be fed on their journey—simple, sustaining, and providential.

From a symbolic and, indeed, allegorical Christian perspective, there is a lot going on here. The classic patristic interpretation of the crossing of the Red Sea and the subsequent feeding in the wilderness is that these two seminal moments in the history of Israel are typologically associated with baptism and Eucharist. Interestingly enough, the biblical texts suggest that the parting of the sea and the provision for food emerge out of Israel's desperation. The same could be said for the sacramental links as well. Satan, allegorized as Pharaoh, was drowned in the waters of baptism together with our sins, and the Christian community is remembered and fed on our journey through the desert. Freed from the enslavement of sin, that fatal wound has been drowned, together with the Evil One. So the neophyte crosses onto the other side; that is, life in the church when Christ is put on. Needless to say, the result of the crossing becomes wearisome without divine food from heaven to sustain those who have been baptized into Christ. We say, together with Moses, that "This is the bread that the LORD has given you to eat." As the Letter to the Ephesians makes clear, we must put away the old self (read: the self that wants to go back to Egypt) of our former way of life and "be renewed in the spirit." This happens because God continues to sustain us when we "put on the new self, / created in God's way in righteousness and holiness of truth."

Is it any marvel, then, why Jesus tells his disciples, "Do not work for food that perishes / but for the food that endures for eternal life, / which the Son of Man will give you"? The people of Israel believed because they were temporarily satisfied. But Jesus is after something greater than bread in the wilderness: himself. That bread will alone sustain the baptized Christian on his or her journey. "I am the bread of life; / whoever comes to me will never hunger, / and whoever believes in me will never thirst." Jesus makes a crucial connection between the life of faith and consuming the Bread of Life. We must conclude, then, that this Bread is not only sustaining but also *formative*. As the **Gospel Acclamation** makes clear, "One does not live on bread alone, but by every / word that comes forth from the mouth of God" (Matt 4:4b). To participate in the Bread that Jesus has given us is to dwell in his very self, which necessarily means that we leave our own selves behind in the Egypt of our egotistic preoccupations. It is the self that always hungers, but when we encounter the fullness of Christ in the Bread of Life, that appetite becomes satisfied.

Connecting the Bible and the Liturgy

The presider's invitation to the Lord's Prayer that begins the **Communion Rite** suggests our longing for the kingdom; it names that which we desire in our heart of hearts: Jesus, the Bread that has come down from heaven, the Bread of Life. So it is that the great prayer of the Christian people, the Our Father, is introduced as "At the Savior's command," *et divina institutione formati*. In contrast to the people of Israel, who did not know what to ask for or to whom to address their troubles, Jesus has *formed* us as a community of pray-ers by his very teaching, empowering, and daring us to ask the bold demand, "Give us this day our daily bread." This relational formation with the Triune God recognizes our need for the indwelling of the Trinity: our hunger for God as Father, the Ground of all Being and Creator, to live in the poverty of the Spirit, which asks for bread as true disciples: "Sir, give us this bread always." And so we await the Son to feed us at his table, nourishing those who will never go hungry again.

The last line of the Our Father taps another kind of need—"deliver us from evil." Acknowledging that God can bring us out of the grip of original sin (as well as deliver us from its consequences by grace) and answer our profound hungers allows the worshiping community of faith to stand before the Lord, grateful for the bread into which we have been formed—Christ himself. It is Christ who sanctifies us with the celebration of the eucharistic liturgy. The (optional) **Prayers over the People** that may be used by the celebrant at the end of Mass makes it plain that we are always in need of God's protection: "Be propitious to your people, O God, / that, freed from every evil, / they may serve you with all their heart / and ever stand firm under your protection." In some sense, then, this prayer is not only speaking about being freed from evil but also being delivered from the Egypt of the former self and our former way of life.

The true renewal of the mind occurs in the conversion made possible in the celebration of the Eucharist because we come to the Lord who satisfies the deepest hunger of the human heart. At the same time, though, God continues to work on our journey, protecting and encouraging us with consolations. Indeed, the **Prayer after Communion** wisely comingles the plea for God's protection with a simultaneous petition for renewal: "Accompany with constant protection, O Lord, / those you renew with these heavenly gifts / and, in your never-failing care for them, / make them worthy of eternal redemption." The Bread of Life, then, becomes just that: the very life of God reanimating a people lost in the desert wilderness of unbelief and meaninglessness. Those who are discouraged desire the food that will forever banish the hunger from the human heart. Therefore, Jesus advises his disciples, "Do not work for food that perishes / but for the food that endures for eternal life, / which the Son of Man will give you." Manna appeared overnight and was soon turned into vapor with the morning dew. But the Bread that Jesus offers forms us into relationship with him so that we might cry out in the Spirit, "Our Father . . . give us this day our daily bread!"

Strategy for Preaching

When a personal or communal tragedy strikes a community, even those with the hardest of hearts cry out in need. These are desert experiences. When we feel the crushing weight of loss and the accompanying, often indescribable, pain that seizes us, there is nothing much to do except cry out to anyone who will listen. We are apt to recognize our need the most when we are trapped in this dry and arid time of deep emptiness and longing, like our ancestors, the chosen people.

But Ordinary Time is often just that—not a crisis to be dealt with or solved. So, the preacher faces a challenge on this Sunday: how to unfold a homily that challenges a fairly comfortable congregation to recognize their need and dependency on God, their hungry hearts, in the midst of America the Plenty. No easy task, to be sure. A former generation of preachers might have held the threat of hell or divine displeasure over the heads of the assembly, but this instills and generates fear, not a recognition of dependence, still less of hunger. What is going to help the congregation stand before the altar of God and say with one voice: "Give us this bread always!" That is the deep prayer of desire at the heart of the eucharistic celebration. So, the homiletic core idea could be to allow the congregation to explore the question of divine dependency from the point of view of eucharistic desire: all of us have received the Bread of Life throughout our lives, and what would it be like not to encounter Christ in the Eucharist in this assembly? This is a fairly open-ended question, and it may not have been pondered widely. Yet I think it bears some reflection not only from the perspective of today's readings but also from time to time as a eucharistic assembly.

    I. Most of us will not go hungry tonight, although there have been times when all of us feel a longing to be filled.

        A. Human reactions: we could steal, we could complain, we could curl up and die.

B. Israel in the desert represents the paradigm of spiritual and physical hunger, waiting to be fed.

II. What is our real hunger? Food? Lack of peace? Longing for what we left behind, or the "old self" as Paul tells the Ephesians?

A. Image of what it means to be truly hungry: people in a fancy restaurant talking about nothing, calling on their cell phones, drifting off to sleep before the meal is even completed.

III. We don't seem to be able to satisfy our hunger, so Jesus proposes himself as the Bread that will feed us.

A. He does not call himself the Bread of Life for nothing. We come alive when we eat—no longer spiritually hungry.

B. **Prayer over the People** (optional and cited above) and **Prayer after Communion** express God's protection and our constant renewal.

C. We are formed as a community of faith, crying "Our Father, . . . give us this day our daily bread."

D. We become bread for each other and for the world; that is, life in Christ.

Nineteenth Sunday in Ordinary Time

Readings from the Ambo

1 Kgs 19:4-8; Ps 34:2-3, 4-5, 6-7, 8-9; Eph 4:30–5:2; John 6:41-51

This Sunday's **Gospel**, like last week's text, is part of the Bread of Life Discourse in John, in some ways an extension and interpretation of the feeding narrative that occurred in John 6:1-15. The Johaninne text, like the Synoptics, accounts in the narratives for a feeding story (cf. Matt 14:13-21; Mark 6:30-44; Luke 9:10-17), but only the Fourth Gospel labors to provide Jesus considerable contemplative and personal reflection on the meaning of the miracle of the loaves (6:26-71), which is an extended dialogue between the Teacher and his disciples.

Since we are dealing with a kind of evolving text throughout these weeks in the Lectionary cycle, dispersed like sacred bread on the hills, it is helpful to consider this "discourse" more like a drama than a theological interpretation in an abstract sense, especially when it comes to preaching. In this particular section, we note the resistance Jesus faces concerning his proclamation that his own self-giving as Bread is present among them as real food. From the looks of things, it appears that some Jews complained (an echo of last week's Exodus reading where the people of Israel were also grumbling against God and Moses), ironically protesting that the one who says he is already present among them as everlasting life is altogether too familiar: " 'Is this not Jesus, the son of Joseph? / Do we not know his father and mother?' " The drama that emerges here is precisely the murmuring that resists faith, or receiving the Bread of Life versus disbelief. " 'Everyone who listens to my Father and learns from him comes to me.' "

Elijah faces his own series of difficulties regarding faith on his flight through the desert from Jezebel. The prophet is on a journey of forty days and nights, a parallel with the journey Israel and Moses experienced; both encounter a theophany at Mount Horeb. Elijah's feeding is followed by the divine presence in unexpected stillness and silence. The presence of God hidden away in nature's shadows discloses the subtle way the Lord has made himself known in the familiar circumstances of daily life, a reality that seems to have escaped some of Jesus' hearers. "I am the bread that came down from heaven."

The **Responsorial Psalm** presents us with the challenge of God in our very midst, not unlike the offering Jesus himself makes to the people of his time: *Gustate et videte quoniam suavis est Dominus* ("Taste and see the goodness of the Lord"). We indeed "bless the LORD at all times" because God is present in the still, silent wind and in a tiny morsel of bread, present among us even in the desert of our unbelief. We may turn to grumbling or complaining, but we do well to remember the constancy of the Lord and that our faith is being tested. Paul's admonition comes to mind as a sober antidote to these moments of disbelief: "Do not grieve the Holy Spirit of God, / with which you were sealed for the day of redemption." Can we reconcile the Christ who is present among us in our brother and sister with the bread that came down from heaven? This bread comes to us in the Christ who dwells very near, maybe too near for some—in every person we meet. It is the everyday familiarity of those living among us that causes our most profound resistance but, undoubtedly, may also be the wellspring of our conversion. Can we recognize God in the still, small voice as well as at Mount Horeb? To do so we will need to follow a simple exercise: "All bitterness, fury, anger, shouting, and reviling / must be removed from you, along with all malice."

Connecting the Bible and the Liturgy

Although John's Gospel has come to us as a high christological text, the Jesus who presents himself in those pages remains intimate and close at hand—perhaps a little too close for comfort for some of Jesus' historical listeners. But the Lord is at pains in chapter 6 in the most intimate *ego emei* language (the "I am" trope is well known to be a specialty in the Fourth Gospel) to tell us that he is present to his disciples as the real bread come down from heaven, the Bread of Life. But this is only one of the many times when Jesus has been pointed out to us so uniquely. "Behold, the Lamb of God," says John the Baptist, which is, of course, echoed in the liturgy itself: *"Ecce Agnus Dei, qui tollit peccata mundi."* And even, *"Ecce homo,"* says Pilate. Here, we have the Bread of Life in our midst being pointed out by Jesus himself. If last week's biblical texts and liturgy challenged us to recognize our need for God's bread, this Sunday holds before us a mirror to our response to that offer of life-giving food come down from heaven. The key is recognition, which the *Agnus Dei* begs to hold up (literally) as waiting for our response. The liturgy here exercises the utmost freedom for the assembly, allowing for our response in faith to affirm our belief that this is Jesus the Bread come down from heaven.

At the same time, though, the bread that we all acknowledge as Christ must be recognized in one another as well. For the assembly of the baptized present and gathered for bread broken and wine poured out in his memory remains one of the constitutive signs of Christ's presence in the sacrament of the Eucharist. The **Collect** implicates all of us together as one in the same family, fed by the same God, the Father of us all. "Almighty ever-living God, / whom, taught by the Holy Spirit, / we dare to call our Father, / bring, we pray, to perfection in our hearts / the spirit of adoption as your sons and daughters. . . ." The prayer here expresses an intention that is both vertical and horizontal: it is vertical in daring to call God Our Father, but it is horizontal with its desire to see all of us as adopted sons and daughters brought to perfection in charity for one another. As Ephesians tells us, we do not want to grumble or reject the God in our midst by grieving the Holy Spirit. The liturgy binds us together as "one body, one spirit in Christ" (**Eucharistic Prayer III**). Paul urges forgiveness as the way to be like Christ: "be kind to one another, compassionate, / forgiving one another as God has forgiven you in Christ. / So be imitators of God, as beloved children, and live in love." Indeed, when the celebrant prays the **Prayer over the Offerings**, it is not only the gifts of bread and wine but our very lives, as children of adoption, which are also to become a new reality, part of this Bread of Life come down from heaven. "Be pleased, O Lord, to accept the offerings of your Church, / for in your mercy you have given them to be offered / and by your power you transform them / into the mystery of our salvation." So, these gifts become for us the Bread of Life because our very salvation hinges on it, as well as the day-to-day life in the Christian community. The words of the angel of the Lord to Elijah might figure prominently to anyone in the Christian assembly gathered to celebrate the Eucharist: "'Get up and eat, else the journey will be too long for you!'"

Strategy for Preaching

If the overall strategy for last Sunday focused on our need for God—and allowing the faith community to lean into the experience of desire for the Bread that gives eternal life—then this Sunday calls our attention to the potential resistance of the Christian community to that invitation. How do we resist God's life? Why would we not wish to engage in the fullness of Christ?

The Scriptures bear witness that those who have come before us have also been hesitant in accepting God's invitation to the Bread that brings new life. Fear and desolation plagued Elijah (and for good reason); the folks listening to Jesus were clearly puzzled at his offer to feed them with himself, together with a self-reference as the bread "came down from heaven"; Paul had to address the church at Ephesus concerning bitterness and hardness of heart, which was certainly a legacy stretching back to the Israelites wandering in the desert. Although we are still unfolding chapter 6 in John's Gospel (and will again next week), the homily has a different core idea for each of these weeks. Based on the Scriptures and the liturgy for today, the core homiletic idea today might be this: Jesus is the Bread of Life, but we have to want to engage that divine life as it is being offered to us here and now—at the Eucharist and beyond.

I. Some have given up on living, perhaps not totally but half way. Or maybe they "half-believe."

    A. Paul cautions the Ephesians that if they give up on the Holy Spirit they will become bitter.

    B. In the **Gospel**, Jesus is offering the crowds a chance in a lifetime—actually a shot at eternity—but their doubts and fears get the better of them. Jesus is too close for comfort.

    C. Illustration: a story that recounts someone who was once hopeful but now lacks trust. Perhaps someone who was rejected by love and is now bitter. They are weary from the journey.

II. Elijah seems to be at this point of exhaustion—weary and downtrodden—until God sends an angel to sustain him and invitation to break bread.

    A. That is grace in action: God interrupting our fall in the darkness to pick us up again.

    B. Somewhere there is an angel waiting to feed us the Bread of Life. Paul tells the Ephesians that they should be compassionate and kind to one another.

    C. We are feeding each other as brothers and sisters with one Father (Collect).

III. That feeding comes first from Christ himself at this Eucharist.

    A. In "Behold, the Lamb of God" we have a chance to recognize Christ in the breaking of the bread and to be broken and consumed by him. How deeply do we believe that? Or are we resisting?

    B. We might not have completely rejected Jesus, but are we allowing ourselves to be fully known?

    C. The call to recognize the Lamb in the Eucharist is the invitation to know Christ more deeply by faith and to be more fully known by him. He is very near.

    D. We approach the table of the Lord knowing that what we will eat—the Bread of Life—will confirm us in the light of God's truth (cf. Prayer after Communion).

Twentieth Sunday in Ordinary Time

Readings from the Ambo

Prov 9:1-6; Ps 34:2-3, 10-11, 12-13, 14-15;
Eph 5:15-20; John 6:51-58

For three successive Sundays we have had the same **Responsorial Psalm**: "Taste and see the goodness of the Lord." There are other ways of saying this or translating the Hebrew text, but Psalm 34 vividly echoes the overall dynamic of the Scriptures and the liturgy during these weeks, which has emphasized the Lord as a providential caregiver, the only one who bestows holy bread on his people in his Son. The close reading and parsing of chapter 6 of John's Gospel that has interrupted the Markan Cycle until the Twenty-Second Sunday in Year B (when we return to Mark), allows for the Christian community assembled for Eucharist to pause, take a collective breath in the Spirit, and *gustare et videre* the Eucharistic Lord. The very repetition of the psalm these weeks and the recurrent admonition coming from the Lord that he is "the living bread that came down from heaven" invites us to feast on the Word as well as sacrament. In a sense, these weeks permit the baptized assembly to dwell deeply in the eucharistic Lord's presence.

In this regard, the church is like the wisdom figure in the book of Proverbs, a selection of which is used for the **First Reading** for today. In its liturgy of Word and sacrament, the church has sent out its maidens all over the city to come and taste of God's goodness of the One Bread and One Cup. " 'Let whoever is simple turn in here'; / To the one who lacks understanding, she says, / Come, eat of my food, / and drink of the wine I have mixed!' " The Letter to the Ephesians admonishes the community as well to be "filled with the Spirit, / addressing one another in psalms and hymns and spiritual songs, /

singing and playing to the Lord in your hearts, / giving thanks always and for everything / in the name of our Lord Jesus Christ to God the Father." In other words, the invitation is the same: come and partake of the table that Wisdom has set, Christ himself is the host at the table set by the church. We taste and see the goodness of God as the community of the baptized, sustained in our journey in the wilderness.

The catch is that we have to chew on the Word. To really embrace Wisdom's invitation, we must encounter divine self-giving at its most basic level. Not surprisingly, we find resistance to embrace God's self-gift, much like last week. And, yet again, it is difficult to find fault with our brothers and sisters in the crowd who bristle about eating the flesh of the one standing before them. The account in John is actually quite graphic. In speaking about consuming the flesh of Christ, John deliberately uses the Greek verb *trogon*. This funny little word really means "to chew" or, more colloquially, "to munch." So, put most obviously, Jesus is asking the crowds to munch on him. Surely, this is a way of pushing the limit, asking how far we would go to partake of Wisdom's banquet. Would we seek Wisdom out in the streets and turn in because we lack understanding and chew on the Word for understanding and salvation? In a sense, the church has allowed us to chew on chapter 6 of John's Gospel during these weeks, as we delve ever deeper into a particular aspect of the Gospel in the Bread of Life Discourse. Do we dare to match our encounter with the Word with a consummation of the flesh of the Son of Man and drinking the cup of his blood? To commit to this sacramental reality of ambo and altar joins us to the Body of Christ in Word and sacrament, quite literally. The hope in the resurrection becomes more than a dream but a faith-filled reality because Christ himself has been raised, and we, his Mystical Body, along with him: "Whoever eats my flesh and drinks my blood / has eternal life, / and I will raise him on the last day."

Connecting the Bible and the Liturgy

As suggested several times in the last few weeks, chapter 6 of John's Gospel faces us with the complexity of encountering him as the Bread of Life, sometimes faithless, sometimes resistant, and sometimes just plain skeptical. In today's passage, Jesus proclaims the Trinitarian relationship we have in receiving him as the Bread of Life: "Just as the living Father sent me / and I have life because of the Father, / so also the one who feeds on me / will have life because of me."

The biblical reflection on the Trinitarian indwelling in the Eucharist can be brought into sacred relief through an encounter with the **Eucharistic Doxology**, which the celebrant sings at the conclusion of the eucharistic prayer; it discloses in a powerful way just how we remain in him and he in us through the Trinity. *Per impsum, et cum ipso, et in ipso, est tibi Deo Patri omnipotenti, in unitate Spiritus Sancti, omnis honor et Gloria, per omni saecula saeculorum.* In the eucharistic liturgy, we have already been brought near to the Lord in the Word proclaimed, and now, with the gifts of bread and wine that Wisdom has prepared for us at the table, the reality of the Trinity among us is acknowledged with the great "Amen." Moreover, the **Eucharistic Doxology** testifies to the degree into which we abide in the Lord, or "munch" on this flesh. We are through him; we are with him; and we are in him. It does not get more thoroughly relational than that, does it? In a certain sense, the assent the assembly makes with the Great Amen already testifies to that which they will become when the Body and Blood of the Lord is distributed in their midst and consumed. This **Eucharistic Doxology** is Wisdom calling out to us, saying, "Come, eat of my food, / and drink of the wine I have mixed!"

The assembly, then, is asked to lean into the experience of consuming the word in faith, to affirm its taking possession of us as a baptized assembly. The Living Bread is made welcome for the congregation of believers; will we come to the table? This very corporate action encourages the faith community to come in from the highways and byways of the lonely road and affirm "Amen" to the living God. As the Letter to the Ephesians tells that community, they ought to live out of a spirit of praise and thanksgiving for God and one another, "in psalms and hymns and spiritual songs, / singing and playing to the Lord in your hearts, / giving thanks always and for everything / in the name of our Lord Jesus Christ to God the Father." Our assent to Christ's life in us to the glory of the Father—*per ipsum*—is our identity as a eucharistic people, dwelling in Christ the Word made flesh not only in history but also in and through his people today.

The **Prayer over the Offerings** for this Sunday strengthens our awareness of the indwelling of Christ's presence when it says, "Receive our oblation, O Lord, / by which is brought about a glorious exchange, / that, by offering what you have given, / we may merit to receive your very self." With this gift in mind, surely there is a cause "to give thanks always" for this glorious exchange where we receive Christ's very self. The baptized assembly, of course, already moves *per ipsum* and *cum ipso* by virtue of that sacrament; we have put on Christ as a garment. But the eucharistic meal sustains the community of love with the indwelling of Love, of the Beloved, so that those who receive him anew will have life eternal. That we have been baptized is a fact. But how far we will allow the grace of the Eucharist to deepen our faith commitment is a question for a lifetime as we remember the promise: "Whoever eats my flesh and drinks my blood / remains in me and I in him."

Strategy for Preaching

Chewing on the word: it is not a particularly pious phrase, yet the desert fathers and patristic authors spoke about eating the Word of God much like cows consume their food, endlessly recycling this nourishment as it moves toward digestion. Earthy, isn't it? The prophet Ezekiel and John the Evangelist were both commanded by God to eat a scroll. So it is Jesus' invitation to the community of believers to feed on him; the command is baffling and scandalous to some of his hearers, yet this is the invitation to the Christian congregation that preaching enlivens and in-fleshes. For what is Christian preaching if it is not a scattering of the word to be chewed by the hearer in order to deepen the person's understanding in wisdom and knowledge and, most of all, faith? The growth in faith to live as a eucharistic people in Christ—and through Christ—becomes an essential goal for liturgical preaching. The core homiletic idea for today could be something like this: we come together as a eucharistic assembly, and leave this church consumed by life with Christ.

The theology here is rich, integral and paramount. The question is: what does this homiletic core look like? A homily might be structured around the first part of the **Eucharistic Doxology**—"Through him, and with him, and in him"—with very specific (often visual) attachments to these organizing principles. This language looks at our relationship with Christ—not from the outside but from the center of our being.

An introduction might simply ask the congregation to consider the various ways Christ has manifested himself during the past week, including some brief examples of Christ's work in the parish or the local community. All of these activities have flowed from the eucharistic table, from which we take the Living God dwelling within us. How?

I. Through Him. We pray that we act through Christ routinely at the liturgy, but also consider its implications when we leave this worship space.

   A. Trust that Christ will be the one to bring our prayer to the Father.

   B. We are filled with the Spirit as we praise him in "hymns and spiritual songs" (Ephesians).

   C. The abiding presence of Christ in all those we encounter throughout our day.

II. With Him. We are Christ's instruments as we carry on his work through mission.

   A. We pray that we may be conformed to his image on earth (Prayer after Communion).

   B. Brief story perhaps about someone who grew in the apostolic life of the church, such as Dorothy Day.

   C. Conforming to Christ as we hear the Word and devour it together.

III. In Him. There is permanence about our consuming the Bread of Life that is like nothing else. Jesus has taken us to himself.

   A. Gospel: "Whoever eats my flesh and drinks my blood / remains in me and I in him."

   B. This is the way for the wise because it is the avenue to rid ourselves of foolishness by living in him in a deeper relationship of trust and love.

   C. As we consume him in Word and sacrament, we become indwellers in the Trinity—intimate in our relationship with Christ Jesus—closer to him than we are to our very selves because we are the Body of Christ.

   D. Christ is so close we can taste and see his goodness (Responsorial Psalm).

Twenty-First Sunday in Ordinary Time

Readings from the Ambo

Josh 24:1-2a, 15-17, 18a; Ps 34:2-3, 16-17, 18-19, 20-21, 22-23;
Eph 5:21-32; John 6:60-69

The **Gospel** today includes the last portion of John 6 (vv. 60-69) that focuses our attention on the evolving revelation of the Bread of Life to those closest to Christ. Indeed, the chapter began as an encounter with the feeding of the five thousand, then Jesus explicated the meaning of true bread to believers and unbelieves alike. The last portion of chapter 6 invites a kind of theological reflection for the sake of the disciples as to how they will respond to Jesus' challenge that unless they eat his flesh and drink his blood they will not have eternal life. They struggle with this, even in their belief. "This saying is hard; who can accept it?"

So, we are brought back to the reality of discipleship, faith, and rejection. The overall trajectory of chapter 6 is shaped along the following lines: it begins with a challenge to the Twelve to distribute bread for the many and ends with Jesus' haunting question to Simon Peter that could be posed to any Christian during troubled times: "Do you also want to leave?" Having faced the reality of faith, including the darkness of its eclipse and absorbing the weight of consuming (read: chewing on) the flesh of the Son of Man in all its stark reality, we are all left in freedom with a choice to come to the banquet or not. It is sobering to remember that "As a result of this, / many of his disciples returned to their former way of life / and no longer accompanied him." The question has brought Simon Peter to a kind of existential awareness, a crisis of meaning, when he answers, "'Master, to whom shall we go? / You have the words of eternal life.'" Jesus has pushed and deepened the question of absolute meaning

250

and relationship with him all the way through the Bread of Life Discourse, and we have wound up with a crucial moment: together with the disciples we must answer with an assent toward faith or reject Jesus and depart.

Paul has a hard saying all his own (and I am not speaking of the controverted phrase "Wives should be subordinate to their husbands as to the Lord"), involving mutual dependence, love, and responsibility. In a sense, Paul brings the monumental decision at Shechem, recorded in the Hebrew Scriptures, and the ratification to serve the Lord from Joshua's household into a new context—the everyday, the practical, and, in a modern theological sense, the sacramental. Indeed, Israel was on its way to becoming a nation under the leadership of Joshua, peeking out of the loose gaggle of tribes and associations. But the unification of the people of Israel occurs as a renewal of a covenantal relationship with God by acclamation: "But the people answered, / 'Far be it from us to forsake the LORD / for the service of other gods. / For it was the LORD, our God, / who brought us and our fathers up out of the land of Egypt, / out of a state of slavery.'" But Paul's version of a covenantal response consists of the small moral choices that govern everyday lives. The analogy of husbands and wives as subordinate is like the church's submission to Christ. The life of marriage, then, becomes a covenant of (mutual) obedience in love and nothing less, and this sacrament embodies and incarnates the life of faith. To assent in faith and receive the Body of Christ as eternal life means loving the spouse, "even as Christ does the church, / because we are members of his body." That day-to-day covenant that consumes the Body of Christ in an act of love also renews our covenant with the Lord. It comes not in the voice of many tribes by acclamation, as it did at Shechem under Joshua, but our participation in the life of the Body of Christ.

Connecting the Bible and the Liturgy

In the Sundays leading up to the conclusion of chapter 6 in John's Gospel—that is, our present passage—there are seemingly endless connections to be established in the liturgical texts for the Mass of the Roman Rite with the Bread of Life Discourse. The dialectic between John 6 and the liturgy seamlessly reminds us that biblical texts continually circle back to our liturgical practices in various and diverse ways. Both the Lectionary and the liturgy for the past several weeks have raised issues of faith and resistance appropriate for the community of the Beloved Disciple, which is to say the baptized assembly; Jesus and the church challenge us to grow ever deeper in our love for the Body of Christ, the Bread of Life.

Yet there remains another opportunity to proclaim a strong tie between ambo and altar today, this time through the words of Joshua's house at Shechem and a response of the faithful at the heart of the eucharistic celebration. The congregation is asked to affirm the eucharistic mystery by responding to the presider's proclamation of the *mysterium fidei*: "We proclaim your Death, O Lord, / and profess your Resurrection / until you come again." Like the people encamped at Shechem at the edge of renewing their covenant with the most High God, this proclamation takes us to the world of remembering the deeds and wonders of the Lord, "those great miracles before our very eyes." We recall that God has "protected us along our entire journey / and among the peoples through whom we passed." Appropriate enough, we are responding to the great paschal mystery itself, the dying and rising of Christ. Therefore we face a kind of ultimate question not unlike the disciples and Simon Peter. Having seen the Lord revealed in the Eucharist before our very eyes, we are free to accept or reject this divine presence, this mystery of faith. Moreover, we might also observe that, since we are at the end of the Bread of Life Discourse and have traveled through the desert with the chosen people (and grumbled with them, perhaps), the previous Sundays' episodes, beginning with Elijah's flight in the desert read at the Seventeenth Sunday until the renewal of the covenant at Shechem, linger with us as a chance for an acclamation of the mystery of faith. It is as if we have come to ground zero and now Jesus asks us to cut to the chase, as he does with Simon Peter: "Do you also want to leave?" If we would stay with Jesus, then let us proclaim the mystery of faith. All of us will take a lifetime to grow into the reality that Jesus has "the words of eternal life." Yet it is our very relationship with the Lord that grows into full bloom when we realize that there is no one else to whom we can go because the Bread of Life has the words of eternal life.

A liturgical connection outside the eucharistic liturgy may prove fruitful for homiletic development. In the *Order for the Solemn Exposition of the Holy Eucharist*, the church offers the following oration (used during Morning Prayer), just before the presider blesses the people with the monstrance: "Lord Jesus Christ, we worship you living among us in the sacrament of your Body and Blood. May we offer to our Father in Heaven a solemn pledge of undivided love. May we offer to our brothers and sisters a life poured out in loving service of the Kingdom where you live with the Father and the Holy Spirit, one God, for ever and ever." What comes immediately to mind here is the new covenant at Shechem: "As for me and my household, we will serve the LORD." The contour of the prayer said at Solemn Exposition takes us through the oath of Shechem and the promise to live with "undivided love" to the one God, Christ who has the source of eternal life. But even further, the offer to bring ourselves into "loving service" for our brothers and sisters presupposes what Ephesians says is the normative behavior for the truly Christian community: submission to the Lord in love to the other—my spouse. It is an act of Christian service and responsibility of love to dwell in a relationship that nourishes the partner as one's own flesh. In our everyday acts of love, we offer ourselves to be consumed by Christ who has loved us and given his own body for the redemption of the world.

Strategy for Preaching

The preacher who exegetes the congregation will recognize that the longer version of the **Second Reading** is a contemporary land mine that needs to be confronted in a pastoral way through the appropriate scriptural study and modern cultural analysis. Some will only hear that "wives should be subordinate to their husbands" and miss an opportunity to see that this contemporary observation in patriarchal first-century Palestine cannot be the single horizon from which we see this text. Paul's metaphor stretches all of us to mutual self-giving to the Body of Christ in love, which is a hard saying, especially when lived honestly in a covenantal relationship of mutual respect. Obviously, we can extend this teaching from spouses to single-parent families and relationships between parents and children, friends and relatives, those with whom we work or with whom we travel on the bus or subway. What if mutual self-giving is extended to those driving cars at rush hour?

With all this in mind, the homiletic core idea for today should take into account the way in which the Bread of Life Discourse has been building over the last few weeks and entertain a question that echoes the commitment to discipleship we see today in the book of Joshua and John's Gospel. Are we ready to fully embrace the demands of Christian discipleship, together with the hard sayings that come from dwelling with the Word made flesh?

One way of structuring the homily, based on this focus statement or something resembling it, is to break down the oration alluded to in the previous section (during Solemn Exposition) into three distinct parts, all of which create a fairly organic and unified homiletic narrative.

I. We worship Christ living among us in the sacrament of his Body and Blood.

   A. This is a hard saying, isn't it? (cf. all of chapter 6, especially vv. 16-69).

   B. This commitment to the Incarnate Word implies the difficulty of the Body of Christ living among us, not far away. That means we have to deal with the members of his Body.

   C. The Letter to the Ephesians becomes very quickly applicable as a hard saying to any who are ready to renew their covenant to living sacramentally in Christ: mutual submission and self-giving to the Christian community means being consumed by Christ. Can we grasp that in its fullness?

II. We ask for the grace to offer our solemn pledge of undivided love.

   A. An illustration here might be the best way into this statement, a short narrative of a couple whose struggles with their relationship made them steadfast for fifty years of married life. Depending on the congregation, the subject might be two friends or two coworkers.

   B. Israel in the desert also offered themselves through an oath at Shechem, after a long period of testing.

III. So we offer to our brothers and sisters a life poured out in service.

   A. If we have learned anything in these past several Sundays about Jesus, the Bread of Life, it is that he is offering himself up for the sake of the church (Eph 5:21-32)

B. The call to consume the Eucharist is the vocation to be poured out for one another in mutual service.

C. That giving in love is the only path for meaning; we can go nowhere else (Simon Peter's declaration to Jesus).

Twenty-Second Sunday in Ordinary Time

Readings from the Ambo

Deut 4:1-2, 6-8; Ps 15:2-3, 3-4, 4-5; Jas 1:17-18, 21b-22, 27; Mark 7:1-8, 14-15, 21-23

Overall, it seems clear that the readings for today take us in a very different direction from the last several weeks. The Letter of James begins a series of selections for the Second Reading and will continue to (and include) the Twenty-Sixth Sunday. The Gospel returns to Mark, posing the commandments and righteous behavior, with the book of Deuteronomy as a partner text.

The selection from the book of Deuteronomy in the **First Reading** engages us in a short remembrance of Israel's relationship with the Lord, which functions as an exhortation to the chosen people. Moses is careful to drive home the corporate identity of the Israelites, a reality that was solidified precisely because of the commandments. "[W]hat great nation has statutes and decrees / that are as just as this whole law / which I am setting before you today?" Moses holds the key to the deposit of historical memory, as well as leader, mediator, lawgiver, and, in some places, priest and prophet as well. The text immediately preceding the present selection, however, points to the ambiguous relationship God has with Moses. Time after time we have understood Moses to be God's chosen one not only because of his many roles and service but because he saw God "face to face." Yet at the same time, God deprives Moses of crossing over the Jordan to the Promised Land, telling the leader that he was angry on account of the people and would charge Joshua with the succession of leadership into the Promised Land. Despite his setbacks, however, Moses speaks to Israel the truth: "hear the statutes and decrees / which I am teaching you to observe." Although he has encountered an angry God, Moses nevertheless acts justly and articulates the necessity of obeying the laws and commandments God has given. Moses may have faltered, but he was true to the law that he was passing down to the nation of Israel.

Perhaps Jesus has Moses in mind when he faults the Pharisees for not honoring God with their hearts. Moses clearly offers the Lord an act of worship by recalling God's command to follow divine teaching, despite his own difficulty with God and the people who were the cause of that anger. If Moses slipped and paused at the rock in his trust in God's power to bring forth water in the desert, he shows no such lack of trust now; he is the example of righteous obedience to the law in the midst of the desert of desolation. Indeed, Jesus becomes a kind of new Moses by glossing the reality of the law Moses set forth, the internal motivations of which drive the engine of sin behind the breaking of the commandments: "'From within people, from their hearts, / come evil thoughts, unchastity, theft, murder, / adultery, greed, malice, deceit, / licentiousness, envy, blasphemy, arrogance, folly. / All these evils come from within and they defile.'" This is a fairly comprehensive list of human weaknesses that lie behind breaking the commandments. Moses himself seems to have known that the interior disposition can make one unclean or not. But from Jesus' perspective, most of the Pharisees in his day, as well as the institutional religion that supported them, had yet to learn such wisdom.

The Letter of James ratifies the experience of one who, like Moses, has humbly bid "welcome" to the Word that has been planted in us and is "able to save" our souls. Far from being just a hearer of the Word, Moses and the devout disciple of the law that Jesus has in mind is a righteous doer of the law as well. Paradoxically, the Pharisees and the scribes claim to follow Moses, but do so only with their lips, that which the lawgiver himself, the meekest of men, honored with all his heart.

Connecting the Bible and the Liturgy

The **Collect** for today enunciates an important foundational moral principle: true worship emerges from the heart (not from the lips alone) and finds its origin and its culmination in God, the giver of grace. "God of might, giver of every good gift, / put into our hearts the love of your name, / so that, by deepening our sense of reverence, / you may nurture in us what is good. . . ." The adherence to God's commands is an affair of the heart, something that the Pharisees and scribes fail to see in themselves. As Jesus tells them, "You disregard God's commandment but cling to human tradition."

The church desires to save us from this fate of hypocrisy by locating the source of our deepest motives in our hearts' desire, the white hot furnace that God fuels by his love. As the **Collect** goes on to address God, "by your watchful care, / keep safe what you have nurtured." Why? It is because "[f]rom within people, from their hearts, / come evil thoughts," and so on. It seems that, like some kind of faulty and twisted assembly line, we have an endless capacity for generating sin from the depths of ourselves. But it is only God who can provide for us ways of escape. The commandments are there not to be followed by those who congratulate themselves for keeping them, but for those who need to preserve what is already within them, their interior disposition sacred to the Lord.

Worth attention in a special way along these lines is asking God to be the agent of "deepening our sense of reverence." The implication for this request, of course, is that true reverence comes from deep within the human heart, for which no amount of proliferation of external practices may overcompensate. That is Jesus' point. When it comes to true worship and reverence for the commandments, we are called to embody in our hearts what we profess with our lips.

The Eucharist also becomes the site for the Christian faithful to express their adherence to the love of God from their heart. Like Moses, we might find ourselves experiencing desolation, seemingly cut off from the Promised Land. We discover a dislike for one of our neighbors or anger at a parishioner. But we press on, not with a fake smile (in his Rule, chapter 4:24, St. Benedict advises his monks to never give a "false peace") but with an authentic desire for reconciliation, always interiorizing the commandments in our actions. In the words taken from the Letter of James, we become "doers of the word and not hearers only," deluding ourselves. Indeed, when we receive the Word at the ambo and the table of the Lord, we partake of "[r]eligion that is pure and undefiled before God and the Father." In a sense, the proclamation of the Word and the partaking in the one bread and one cup teaches us how to allow the Word to dwell deeply within our heart. The **Prayer after Communion** urges the congregation that has just received the Body and Blood of the Lord to live that sacrament in love and self-giving: "Renewed by this bread from the heavenly table, / we beseech you, Lord, / that, being the food of charity, / it may confirm our hearts / and stir us to serve you in our neighbor." That is why we "[h]umbly welcome the word that has been planted" in us and that God deepens in our hearts: it is for the sake of the love of God and our neighbor. No external discipline will account for the heart's disposition toward love; it is only God who can invite us into the ever-increasing desire to love more in our heart of hearts. As the **Gospel Acclamation** (from Jas 1:18) reminds us once again, "[The Father] willed to give us birth by the word of truth / that we may be a kind of firstfruits of his creatures." Bearing fruit from the eucharistic Lord, we are destined to love.

Strategy for Preaching

Over the last decade or so, Valentine's Day has become practically a secular solemnity (if that makes sense), with stores and advertisers gearing up for the high holy day of love soon after the celebration of the New Year. We could chalk up such cultural behavior to a commodification of romantic love (so what's new?) or a silly midwinter distraction to brighten up the landscape with hearts and flowers. That said, we might consider these boxes of chocolates and red roses strewn throughout the land, together with the animated email cards to every possible relationship we may have (including our pets), as a deep longing for real love. Jesus confronts his own age with the challenge of loving from their heart and not human tradition. In the American culture, though, we just create more shallow human tradition, disposable and expensive, to answer deep questions. Red balloons, anyone?

By contrast, Christian worship is a response to live at the deepest center of who we are, the creature speaking back a word of love to the Creator for what St. Benedict refers to as an "expanding heart." So the core homiletic idea for today could be this: our challenge from the Lord is to live in authentic relationship with him from our heart and not just our lips. This may sound simple, but the congregation will consist in a variety of dispositions in regard to this provocation to a fuller indwelling with our heart. Some parishioners have become lifelong contemplatives who would shame any monk or nun; others are still progressing as they learn to deepen their faith experience.

An introduction might concentrate on a human longing already present in our lives, which seeks to move beyond mere externals. Cultural observances like Valentine's Day come to mind as a way of contrasting deeply mediated human longing and love. Moses is an example of the "meekest of men" who lived within the space God created in his heart, even with disappointment. The deepening of love does not bracket discouragement or even desolation, and a brief recounting of the life of Moses in the introduction would underscore the importance of holding steadfast to God, despite setbacks.

The body of the homily would then move to suggest that the church today invites us through the readings in Scripture and the liturgy to live from our heart, which is nothing less than an invitation to respond to our baptismal call. The **Collect** is a useful gloss here. Our lifelong response in baptism is a deepening that takes us beyond just shallow observance. Yes, we can come to Mass every Sunday and still not deepen our faith by attendance at worship. It will mean shedding the illusions of ourselves and living honestly before God, something that Jesus shows us in his dealings with the Pharisees. Here, an illustration could be used that would avoid examples so lofty that the congregation could not possibly aspire to such heights or could find them completely inaccessible. If a saint could be pictured as one of us transformed, perhaps someone like Dorothy Day, then this example would work well. Otherwise, there are countless men and women who strive each day to live honestly in their relationships with each other. Another good example could be drawn from human development: maturity comes when we move from shallow relationships as preteenagers to more substantial and rewarding ones as we become young adults. In the end, our goal in our relationship with God and one another is what Blessed John Henry Newman called *cor ad cor loquitur*, "heart speaking to heart."

As always, the Eucharist becomes the occasion and the opportunity to renew our commitment to God and one another. Where does the encounter with the Word at the ambo and the altar take us? We might follow this with a brief example taken from a parish community who were doers of the Word. At an extraordinary parish in the Archdiocese of Los Angeles, every Wednesday after the daily Mass the deacons organized an absolutely huge food drive, stretching from one end of the school cafeteria to the other. People came from miles around with bags and bags of food and grocery items; it went on all day. Righteous action follows closely on the heels of those who abide in the Word.

Twenty-Third Sunday in
Ordinary Time

Readings from the Ambo

Isa 35:4-7a; Ps 146:7, 8-9, 9-10; Jas 2:1-5; Mark 7:31-37

The **First Reading** sounds like it belongs to Advent rather than a
Sunday in Ordinary Time! Listen and see if this does not sound like
the expectant church at the dawn of the new Liturgical Year: it is the
promise that the eyes of the blind be opened and the ears of the deaf
to be cleared, together with the utopian vision that "[s]treams will
burst forth in the desert, / and rivers in the steppe. / The burning
sands will become pools, / and the thirsty ground, springs of water."
All this may strike us as a bit effusive for an ordinary day. And, in
fact, there is reason to believe that this particular portion of Isaiah is
also a bit out of place in the text itself, with some scholars observing
that this particular section of Isaiah's text may have been written
later than the eighth century (when we believe chaps. 1–40 to have
originated), placing it around the time of the Babylonian exile and
Second Isaiah.

But an oracle containing a message of freedom "out of season,"
as it were, reminds us how near God is to us at *every* moment; our
redemption is at hand, a liberation from the captivity of sin and death
is waiting for the Christian community as we enter the waters of
baptism. God's moment of salvation will not be held captive by our
time-bound conventions. Ordinary Time is quite extra-Ordinary.
Indeed, Jesus' encounters with the deaf man with a speech impediment in the district of the Decapolis appears rather ordinary at first
glance, considering the amazing number of those troubled in mind
and body we take to be rather normative anywhere and at any time.
But the exchange between Jesus and the man is far from ordinary;

it is a sign of the divine recompense "which has come to save us." That salvation comes not in a general way but in the very particular person of Christ we know from our faith in the incarnation. Here is the utopian vision of Isaiah rendered absolutely particular by the mouth of one formerly confused but now bursting into speech.

Additionally, the passage in the **Gospel** hints of the importance of Jesus in foreign territory, having just come from the district of Tyre and exorcising a Greek, Syrophoenician woman's daughter. Now in the district of the Decapolis, Jesus is again in Gentile territory. At least one point to be made here is that "divine recompense" has come not only to the house of Israel but to Gentiles as well. The beginning of the **Second Reading** seems most appropriate in this regard, when it advises the Christian community to "show no partiality / as you adhere to the faith in our glorious Lord Jesus Christ." It is surely faith emerging in a Gentile community that Jesus finds in the Syrophoenician woman and then, later, the people who brought him the man with the speech impediment. Faith knows no borders. Neither does the heart of God.

A secondary effect of this healing through faith is proclamation, even when Jesus "ordered them not to tell anyone." The so-called "Markan secret," which attempts to repress the announcement of the Messianic news, seems irrepressible even to the most unlikely of sources and one that cannot escape dramatic irony. Ironically, while Jesus cures speech, he cannot stifle proclamation. Although here and elsewhere in the Gospel of Mark the disciples remain fairly clueless to Jesus' identity as son of God, it is the demons who voice "I know who you are—the Holy One of God!" in chapter 1:24; and in chapter 7 it is the Gentile population of the district of the Decapolis who are spreading the Good News. These are extraordinary events either in or out of season, when "the ears of the deaf be cleared . . . then the tongue of the mute will sing." A river has come forth from the desert.

Connecting the Bible and the Liturgy

The readings for this Sunday disclose a certain power of what was either hard or broken into a new beginning for "those who were bowed down," as the **Responsorial Psalm** (146) has it. Even the very landscape of "burning sands will become pools, / and the thirsty ground, springs of water." The overall sense from these readings is that fractured nature, wounded humanity, scared creation longs for its true vocation: breaking away from the harness of affliction of body—deafness, impediment, even class distinction of rich and poor, Jew or Gentile—and into the freedom of faith, a joy in our Lord Jesus Christ. What is the true destiny of this restored creation? It is not just repair, but praise and proclamation. So this is why the deaf and the mute sing and "the lame leap like a stag . . . the tongue of the mute will sing."

In other words: freedom. That is the word that sings of our salvation gained for us by Christ, who has restored creation to its beginning. The **Collect** for today acknowledges this reality when it prays that our own liberation from sin and our faith in Christ yield a loosening of what binds us: "O God, by whom we are redeemed and receive adoption, / look graciously upon your beloved sons and daughters, / that those who believe in Christ / may receive true freedom / and an everlasting inheritance." In this regard, faith becomes the arena for perfect liberation, the expression of those who have been unbound from what has held them in chains. Clearly, one of the best applications for interfacing with these biblical texts is the *Rite of Baptism* and the *Ephphata* Prayer, performed over the ears and the mouth given to the neophyte after baptism. We recall that the presider says that "the Lord Jesus made the deaf to hear and the dumb to speak. May he soon touch your ears to receive his word, and your mouth to proclaim his faith, to the praise and glory of God the Father."

In a sense, the *Ephphata* prayer makes all the baptized free to proclaim, even as we long for completion in Christ Jesus. A biblical parallel that comes to mind is Paul's majestic reflection in Romans 8:18-25 on the future destiny of the created world that, though mired in corruption, awaits future glory. "For creation awaits with eager expectation the revelation of the children of God . . . in hope that creation itself would be set free from slavery to corruption and share in the glorious freedom of the children of God." The **Communion Antiphon** for today seizes on the opportunity to remind the congregation that every creature awaits perfection in God: "Like the deer that yearns for running streams, / so my soul is yearning for you, my God; / my soul is thirsting for God, the living God" (Ps 42). Jesus' liberation of us all is the reconciliation of us all at the very same moment: to be made whole is to be restored as a child of God. Those who have been far off have now been brought near the running stream of baptism to drink of its life-giving waters. And like Dante at the end of the *Purgatorio* (XXXI), who drinks from the River Lethe, we drink from a stream that restores us to lost innocence. That return to the origins of creation is witnessed today by the man with the impediment, which was both physical and spiritual; once cured, his faith rejoiced in praise. Then again, the cure was a sign of what has come to us in baptism and that which awaits us as children of God in future glory. That future glory is already singing God's praise with a newfound voice.

Strategy for Preaching

The readings for this Sunday are unusually visual: dry landscape bursting into water; a mute and deaf man liberated into speech; the shabby poor placed ahead of one with fine gold rings and fancy clothes as "heirs of the Kingdom." The preaching for today, then, might consider the wealth of visual images that could be deployed for the sake of the listener's visual imagination; these would account for God's liberating presence, even in a world of brokenness. So, the homiletic core idea could be that the Lord is nearer than we imagined, and even in our shattered lives we will find mending and liberation to spread the Good News.

One possible introduction would draw from the most visual season in our grasp and lead the assembly into a consideration of the Isaiah text as God's liberating initiative. Sketch out a winter scene (the Western Hemisphere will be far from this on the Twenty-Third Sunday of Ordinary Time!), perhaps with carolers, Christmas lights, poinsettias, and crib sets. It sounds like Christmas, looks like Christmas, smells like Christmas, but here we are far from Advent. Yet Isaiah announces in the First Reading that the nearness of God is always with us, liberating us in season and out.

In a way, we are always keeping vigil for the Lord's coming, even outside of Advent. We await completion. We are divided by politics, class, religion—the haves and the have-nots—just as they were in the early church (cf. The Letter of James). We are injured and broken, unable to speak the truth in our disabled tongues and live the faith like the speechless. This is a good opportunity to really lean into the experience of the man in the **Gospel** who is unable to speak; perhaps it is a chance also to use some other characters in Mark who also long for healing and completion (Rom 8).

Yet the incarnation tells us that there is nothing God desires more than to make us whole again: Jesus' healing ministry in Mark discloses our reconciliation. Our sacramental life is an ongoing process of restoration, beginning with our baptism. "*Ephphata!*" "Be opened." That is the word that opened the dry landscape of original sin and gave us a river of new life. This is the true freedom purchased for us by Christ, allowing us to live in perfect freedom.

An important related issue here concerns not only individual freedom but corporate liberation as well. One of the greatest hardships occurs for people when they are stifled from proclamation and forced to be mute. Tragically, many in our world face terrible persecutions for expressing the religious language of what is deeply held in their heart, their faith in God. They, more than anyone, await the glorious freedom of the children of God. The liturgy for today is a source of faith-filled expression for all God's people (**Collect**). We the baptized must cry, "Be opened!" for all our brothers and sisters throughout the world who long to be made whole as God's children. (A gloss from the *Declaration on Religious Freedom* of the Second Vatican Council or another citation from Catholic social teaching would be very useful here.) Jesus frees us, so how can we keep our tongues silent?

Twenty-Fourth Sunday in Ordinary Time

Readings from the Ambo

Isa 50:5-9a; Ps 116:1-2, 3-4, 5-6, 8-9; Jas 2:14-18; Mark 8:27-35

If last week's **First Reading** from Isaiah was reminiscent of Advent, this week's text from the same prophet has a Lenten character running through it. Indeed, as the third of the three Servant Songs, Isaiah 50:5-9a articulates the obedient one who has not rebelled even under difficult circumstances. The passage focuses on the servant who has surrendered absolute trust to the divine will. "The Lord GOD is my help, / therefore I am not disgraced; / I have set my face like flint, / knowing that I shall not be put to shame." This is the voice of absolute confidence in God for the sake of mission. It is important to note that the verse immediately preceding this selection is the call to service itself: "The Lord GOD has given me / a well-trained tongue, / That I might know how to speak to the weary / a word that will rouse them" (v. 4). In other words, the Servant is precisely that: a servant for the sake of others sent into mission with the steadfast faith that God will aid him in carrying out that which he was asked to accomplish. Verses 5-6 verify that the Servant has fully embraced his vocation, even in the face of the malignant who seek his destruction: "I have not rebelled, / have not turned back. / I gave my back to those who beat me, / my cheeks to those who plucked my beard; / my face I did not shield / from buffets and spitting."

When this passage is viewed alongside the **Gospel**, there are some interesting christological implications, as we might imagine. We know that the early Christian community appropriated the Suffering Servant songs of Isaiah as constitutive emblems of Jesus' identity. Jesus himself implies that his own personhood remains very much

267

like the Servant we see portrayed in Isaiah 50:4-9. "He began to teach them / that the Son of Man must suffer greatly / and be rejected by the elders, the chief priests, and the scribes / and be killed, and rise after three days." Not everyone's idea of Messianic kingship, to be sure. But from Jesus' perspective, the destiny of the Son of Man is to claim the role of the Suffering Servant and no other, which the Markan Christian community appears to see as absolutely foundational. Indeed, the Gospel begs for a definition of this Jesus. The conversation along the way to the villages of Caesarea Philippi is precisely one of discovery, as the Lord puts the question to them quite bluntly: "Who do people say that I am?" Peter undoubtedly represents those past and present who claim Jesus as the Christ but jettison his role as the Suffering Servant on the cross. According to Jesus, however, the mysterious role of the one who "must suffer greatly / and be rejected" is thinking "as God does." There is a subtext here if we allow ourselves to think about it: the Son of Man's union with God through suffering occurs in the context of an acceptance of the divine will.

The mission of Christ as one who suffers and surrenders—thinking as God does—becomes generalized as a principle for Christian discipleship at the conclusion of this Gospel passage: "For whoever wishes to save his life will lose it, / but whoever loses his life for my sake / and that of the gospel will save it." This submission for the sake of the Christian vocation and the call to service for God and the neighbor demonstrates complete trust and confidence in God; it is a rock-solid faith that endures the trials of faith, hope, and love even in the midst of human rejection. For James, faith is the doorway to tireless performance of good works—that is, service in love. The Christian is able to say that "I will demonstrate my faith to you from my works": because we lose our lives for the sake of Christ and the Gospel.

Connecting the Bible and the Liturgy

Despite the Lenten ambiance with which the readings are cast, the Scriptures and the liturgy orient us toward the everyday life of the Christian community, one dedicated to self-giving and service without cost. Indeed, the Eucharist itself without the Christ who embraced the Suffering Servant becomes empty and void of its christological core, which is the role of a servant who washed the feet of his disciples during the Passover meal, even as he handed himself over to death for the sake of the world. Therefore if we recall that the eucharistic liturgy remains focused on God's consummate love as the Suffering Servant, giving his people his own Body and Blood, then what liturgical texts speak to the center of this soteriology and highlight the biblical language that supports them?

Preface I of the Passion of the Lord fully embraces the reality of the Suffering God when it says, "For through the saving Passion of your Son / the whole world has received a heart / to confess the infinite power of your majesty, / since by the wondrous power of the Cross / your judgment on the world is now revealed / and the authority of Christ crucified." The ability to "confess the infinite power" of God's majesty is exactly what is missing from Peter's confession at Caesarea Philippi—a Christ without a cross. But the **Preface** is at pains to point out that it is precisely in the cross where true power resides—*dum ineffabili cruces potentia*. In the face of the "authority" of Christ crucified, we may still be helpless to think the way God thinks, but we are given a heart to confess the reality of God's love either at Caesarea Philippi or elsewhere. Jesus' vision of discipleship, then, is a heart that confesses the love of God, one that literally takes to heart the Suffering Servant.

With an acknowledgment of the saving work of Christ as the backdrop, we may speculate on the christological implications of the Letter of James, when the author acknowledges that faith without good works "is dead." Christ himself set the blueprint and the gold standard for joining faith and good works because his very faith and trust as the Suffering Servant—his identity as the Son of Man who came to suffer for the sake of humanity—is one with the redemptive work of salvation. From the perspective of his identity as Servant, how is it possible to separate the faith of Christ from his work of redemption? Indeed, the Servant proclaims that he has come to speak a word to rouse the weary, a work made possible by faith and trust in the God who sent him into mission. Similarly, the **Collect** prays that our own faith in God will enkindle in us the work of service: "Look upon us, O God, / Creator and ruler of all things, / and, that we may feel the working of your mercy, / grant that we may serve you with all our heart." It is God's grace that gives us the consolation of faith, which, in turn, helps us to serve "with all our heart."

This is the heart given to us "to confess the infinite power" of God's divine majesty. As we are drawn into Christ's redemptive work by our celebration of the Eucharist, the Father sees and loves in us what he sees and loves in Christ. The corporate Body of Christ surrenders to the Father as the Suffering Servant. In a sense, each time the Christian faithful gather to celebrate the Eucharist we are answering the question, "Who do you say that I am?" We answer as the voice of the church in Christ as we do at the Pauline **Gospel Acclamation**: "May I never boast except in the cross of our Lord / through which the world has been crucified to me and I to the world."

The **Prayer after Communion** suggests that, like the Suffering Servant, we have allowed God to open our ears that we may hear and "have not rebelled," but said, "See, the Lord is my help; who will prove me wrong?" In a very real sense, then, we offer ourselves with Christ as an oblation and allow the communion we celebrate to bring us into that union with the Trinity: "May the working of this heavenly gift, O Lord, we pray, / take possession of our minds and bodies, / so that its effects, and not our own desires, / may always prevail in us." This "working" of our communion is the work of Christ, the true heavenly gift, who leads us by sacramental ways to offer our life in service, losing our life for the sake of the Lord and the Gospel.

Strategy for Preaching

There are obviously a number of theological issues at stake this Sunday that might bear fruit in evangelization. The first of these is the faith of Christ that led him to suffer the agony and humiliation on the cross as a saving work for the people of God. The second of these important theological reflections is the identity of Jesus as "the Christ." As noted, it is possible to affirm Jesus' identity and get it wrong, as Peter does by rebuking Jesus for appropriating the cross as his true mission. An interesting contrast would be to refer to Matthew 16:22-23, in which Peter repeats his denial of Jesus' suffering; but this naysaying occurs, interestingly enough, after Peter's confession and the commissioning as keeper of the keys of the kingdom. Third, if Jesus has laid down the condition of discipleship in saying that "[w]hoever wishes to come after me must deny himself, / take up his cross, and follow me," then, we might ask: what are the implications for contemporary Christian discipleship and our own affirmation of Jesus' identity as Christ the Suffering Servant? So, the core homiletic idea might embrace this threefold challenge and project a structure that would apply each of these statements within a coherent narrative homiletic text. Such a statement might look something like this: we know that Christ suffered and died for us, a reality we might prefer to deny, and yet true discipleship always embraces the Suffering Servant and his cross. It is necessary to join crucial theological/catechetical teaching with a focus that is coherent and easy to understand. The remainder of the homily will unpack this statement and make it real in the hearts of the baptized assembly so that their faith is deepened at the Eucharist.

The biblical and liturgical witnesses we have discussed above help to inform our structure for the homily. The introduction may be something like a description of a painting depicting the crucifixion or agony in the garden, a visual mystery of our Lord's passion that is well known and brought to mind even outside of Lent.

I. Christ's faith and the work he accomplished remains part of the paschal mystery we continue to celebrate.

    A. Historical background of the Suffering Servant.

    B. Preface I of the Passion of the Lord. Illustration of crucifixion in art, perhaps a contrast between the highly graphic versions often seen in Latin America and Spain versus the more tame variety in North America. We often turn our heads at such disfigurement; we like our Jesus sanitized.

II. We are not alone in our denial.

    A. Peter in Mark's Gospel today (contrast with same incident in Matthew) denies the cross.

    B. Contemporary versions of a sanitized Christianity, a refusal to pick up our own cross or walk with another who has to endure such suffering.

III. Our true discipleship means losing our life for the sake of the Gospel.

    A. Think of what this means! Everything we do is usually oriented toward self-preservation and working to get ahead, but faith tells us to let all this go and live for Christ and the cross; it is tough.

B. Collect prays that "we may serve you with all our heart. / Through our Lord Jesus Christ, your Son." Christ redeemed us so we do all things "through" him. That is our work. That is our faith.

C. Prayer after Communion helps us remember that we ask God to "take possession of our minds and bodies."

D. That reality of being caught up in Christ's Body at the Eucharist is what we do here, or rather, has been done for us.

Twenty-Fifth Sunday in Ordinary Time

Readings from the Ambo

Wis 2:12, 17-20; Ps 54:3-4, 5, 6-8; Jas 3:16–4:3; Mark 9:30-37

Context matters. In the passage taken for today's **Gospel** it is especially important to see the text within the framework of the rest of chapter 9. As suggested earlier, when preaching from the Lectionary, the proclamation of the Word often needs to be situated within the textual environment of the *whole narrative* from which it has been selected. Indeed, the transition from the beginning of chapter 9 to our current pericope may be viewed by some as going from the sublime to the ordinary. Jesus had taken Peter, James, and John up on a high mountain and was transfigured before them, while Elijah and Moses appeared and conversed with Jesus. Finally, the theophany concludes with a voice from a cloud, " 'This is my beloved Son. Listen to him' " (9:7).

By contrast, our current passage forms a somewhat tragic-comic commentary on this transcendent event of the transfiguration of Jesus. For the second time, Jesus announces a prediction of his passion (liturgically speaking, the first time was last Sunday in 8:31) but the disciples have done everything but "listen to him," as the Father has commanded. Instead, they appear to be consumed with "discussing among themselves on the way / who was the greatest." Jesus senses that the Twelve were arguing, convicting themselves in a dispute that eventually will be construed by the early church as corrosive to Christian living. The **Second Reading** then is a kind of gloss on this competitive behavior from the disciples. The Letter of James says that it is the undoing of real wisdom to be caught up in power struggles and envy: "Where jealousy and selfish ambition exist, / there is disorder and every foul practice. / But the wisdom from above is first of all pure, / then peaceable, gentle, compliant, / full of mercy and good fruits, / without inconstancy or insincerity."

The **First Reading** shows an even more draconian version of the passion of ambition and jealousy. The selection from the book of Wisdom is part of a larger whole (2:12–5:23) that scholars tell us is drawn form Deutero-Isaiah chapters 52-62. In the mind of the author of the book of Wisdom, the wicked are driven by angry passions against the righteous in order to test him. (This does have the ring of a prophetic oracle, doesn't it?) The passage here seems especially appropriate for the events of Holy Week: "Let us see whether his words be true; / let us find out what will happen to him. / For if the just one be the son of God, God will defend him / and deliver him from the hand of his foes."

While James and the author of the book of Wisdom concentrate their efforts in a plan to guide and teach those who have ears to hear, Jesus demonstrates his point more vividly than a written discourse. By putting a child before the disciples as an example of the way one is to receive him, Jesus forces the Twelve to encounter what they would rather not hear: that the one reckoned least in society (children had no social status at all in this period) becomes a parable illustrative of hospitality and divine mission. "Whoever receives one child such as this in my name, receives me; / and whoever receives me, / receives not me but the One who sent me." It seems to be that Christ chooses a child because this little one has yet to be caught up in the snare of passionate "jealousy and selfish ambition," certainly a telling and stinging example for those arguing on the way about "who was greatest." But even further, it is well to note that the lesson again goes unheeded, at least in the long run. The disciples James and John will repeat this encounter with ambition, in chapter 10:35-45, when they ask to sit at Jesus' side, one at his left and the other at his right.

Connecting the Bible and the Liturgy

In my experience, there is often a misreading that occurs in Mark 9:36 that deserves clarification today. Jesus is not discoursing on the quality of children who are exemplary in their disposition toward the Christ, as in Matthew 19:13-15, and should not be prevented from coming to him. Nor is the Markan passage for today about humbling oneself in order to be the greatest in the kingdom as in

Matthew 18:3-4. Where Mark and Matthew both agree is in the current selection for today and Matthew 18:5. "Whoever receives one child such as this in my name, / receives me." (Matthew omits the Markan rejoinder concerning the Father.) The point here has to do with reception of children, the condition of which mirrors welcoming Jesus and the One who sent him.

Why labor over this distinction? The subtle shift in meaning is significant in a liturgical context, especially as we ask the Lord to receive the gifts we offer at the Eucharist, even as we prepare to receive him in that sacrament. True hospitality is the antithesis of pride and ambition, graphically portrayed in the **First Reading**. Receiving a child in our midst is not, then, unlike receiving the eucharistic Lord. As the priest prepares the bread and wine at the eucharistic table, he makes an offering on behalf of the congregation, not with clerical privilege or status but in service and simplicity. "*In spiritu humilitatis et in animo contrito suscipiamur a te, Domine; et sic fiat sacrificium nostrum in conspectu tuo hodie, ut placeat tibi, Domine Deus.*" The emphasis is clearly on humility and contrition of heart, so that we may "be accepted by you, O Lord," asking that "our sacrifice" may be pleasing to God. The first-person plural announces the intention of the church to bring the whole assembly into this offering, this oblation, in humility and true reverence. The Lavabo follows, not as a sign of ritual purity but as "*a peccato meo munda me,*" a cleansing of my sins—of the very things that the Letter of James says "make war within" our members. The presider at the table of the Lord receives the Lord as a child, while the church's ritual renders him simple and contrite of heart.

And so the **Prayer over the Offerings** implores, "Receive with favor, O Lord, we pray, / the offerings of your people, / that what they profess with devotion and faith / may be theirs through these heavenly mysteries." Baptized in union with Christ, all come to the table of the Living God as little children, waiting to receive and to be received. We do so for the sake of our good and for the whole church, through the one who came as a little child.

Strategy for Preaching

The challenge for the homily this week is considerable: the Scriptures and the liturgy explicitly run counter to our preconceived notions of what our society tells us is important. And it is not only the world that falls into the category of the marketplace: the church at large has had its political struggles, priests compete for larger parishes, parishes vie for more students for their schools. Even if we succeed in yielding a significant core idea for our preaching today, the congregation faces a world of competition in and out of the parish doors. And that way of life persists not because of malice but because we are driven to do so often out of necessity to put bread on the table.

And it is putting bread on the table that might become a significant point of departure and a controlling metaphor this day. We cannot change the often brutal economics of late capitalism, but we can allow the congregation to lean into another, divine economy similar to the way in which Jesus challenged the disciples to understand their own ambitions. So, the core homiletic idea for today might be this: we tend to be guided by the need to succeed, but that is not the only way to put bread on the table. In other words, use the Eucharist as an alternative way of seeing our economy, one that potentially undermines the competitive Darwinian allegiance to success and achievement. So, we receive the Lord with gratitude at the eucharistic celebration, like a child in our midst.

If there are children present in the congregation, they represent the natural symbols worth a thousand words. In our busy world we tend to forget that children are signs of unconditional love: they deserve unreserved respect and love, and return the same. When we receive them in our midst, it is outside the economy of success. We receive these children in a divine economy that mirrors the eucharistic offering of praise and thanksgiving. (Support here comes from the Priest's Silent Prayer while preparing the Offerings, together with the **Prayer over the Offerings** and these could be deployed to show the humility we bring.) The gifts at the altar are not purchased by the rich but brought as "fruit of the earth."

In this celebration we leave behind not the world but ourselves as described in the book of Wisdom, the self that is arrogant and full of pride. An allusion might be made here to the events of Holy Week (yes, even in Ordinary Time) where Jesus' innocence is contrasted with the plot against him by ambitious and sinful men. A contemporary example might follow, perhaps an example from fiction or film. Robert Penn Warren's novel, *All the Kings Men* (1946), comes to mind as well as Alexander Mackendrick's film, *Sweet Smell of*

Success (1957), as examples of politics, greed, and ambition in post-war America in the midst of a booming economy. There are scores of others.

The last section of the homily should emphasize that the Lord has provided the Eucharist for our table without cost (**Responsorial Psalm**). Bread has come to us without need for pride and ambition. We face a world of competition, but it does not have to be that way since the Eucharist provides an alternative perspective to living with one another where everyone has plenty. We can return to our jobs and homes, knowing that being top dog really means very little when it comes to receiving one another and the Lord as a little child.

Twenty-Sixth Sunday in Ordinary Time

Readings from the Ambo

Num 11:25-29; Ps 19:8, 10, 12-13, 14;
Jas 5:1-6; Mark 9:38-43, 45, 47-48

Representations of leadership and authority are complicated in the Hebrew Scriptures, as we might expect. The **First Reading** presents us with a scenario that is deeply seeded in the Scriptures: the sharing of *ruah*, or God's Spirit. Perhaps the most well-known of these prophetic confluences occurs when Elisha asks his mentor, Elijah, for "a double share" of his spirit before the latter is taken up to heaven in a fiery chariot (2 Kgs 2:9, NRSV). We might see this as an instance of the charismatic spirit bestowing itself on the next generation. But there are other instances not necessarily associated with prophetic identity but heroic leadership that occur, for example, in the book of Judges when the Lord raises up Othmel, son of Kenaz, Caleb's younger brother, and again in another Messianic leader, the first of the Servant Songs of Second Isaiah, where the spirit of the Lord rests on this chosen one, who will "bring forth justice to the nations" (Isa 42:1). Finally, Luke depicts Jesus (in chap. 4:16ff.) as precisely the fulfillment of the legacy of prophetic witness, giving sight to the blind and setting the captive free.

At the same time, however, there appears to be another tradition that understands the working of the spirit a bit differently, directed toward the sharing of responsibilities (and even prophecy) rather than resting on a single head. The collegial distribution of God's *ruah*, from this perspective, becomes an important aspect of carrying on the tradition through collaborative efforts. In Exodus 18:13-26, for instance, Jethro, Moses' father-in-law, proposes that seventy men be selected to help Moses carry out responsibilities so that his son-in-law does not wear himself out. A parallel instance occurs in the book of Numbers (in the First Reading): "Taking some of the spirit that was on Moses, / the LORD bestowed it on the seventy elders; / and as the spirit came to rest on them, they prophesied." A similar instance (with an important distinction) occurs in Acts 6:1-7 when the Hellenists complain that "their widows were being neglected in the daily distribution." As is well known, the early church chose *hoi diakonoi*—seven of them—to be of service to the community. These folks who are first named in chapter 6 fulfill an important administrative function but are already "filled with the Spirit and wisdom" (v. 3). We might remember that this is the post-Pentecost church where God's Holy Spirit has already come down and shared itself with the disciples gathered together in one place.

Jesus seems to suggest in the **Gospel** that the disciples are not to interfere with the workings of those who perform a mighty deed (literally: accomplish an act of power) in his name. Here again, we notice a sharing of divine *ruah*. The spirit has been distributed on those who lay claim to service in the name of Christ. Competition, so much an issue in these last few weeks of Mark's Gospel, seems completely ridiculous when it comes to vying for a place in Jesus' inner circle. We follow the will of the Spirit, not a pecking order for power seekers. In fact, Jesus does not really have an inner circle as such; he just has disciples who follow. If there are insiders to the Messianic secret in Mark's Gospel, they exist for ironic purposes, since the ones who are closest to the Lord do not understand him and flee at last. The Lord is well within his own tradition when he tells his disciples that "whoever is not against us is for us." Additionally, the Lord offers a rather sobering social take on the sharing of power when he links the sharing of his divine power to the work of charity. Whoever is with Christ, or belongs to Christ, and "who gives you a cup of water to drink . . . will surely not lose his reward." To be a disciple means carrying on the work of charity, a sharing of Christ's mission on earth.

James is equally clear about the distribution of power and wealth when he accuses the rich of withholding wages from the works of the field. But the Lord of hosts hears their cry. This text will become one of the foundational documents for Catholic social teaching concerning the "just wage," an issue that became particularly important during the economic crisis of the Great Depression. The Letter of James is still a viable lens for contemporary instruction on fairness to immigrants in the United States; it also establishes a paradigm for a just global economy that does not exploit developing nations and indicts those wealthy countries who do so.

Connecting the Bible and the Liturgy

As God's Spirit is poured out upon the baptized assembly gathered to celebrate the eucharistic liturgy in the name of Christ, the readings for today form a natural and strong alliance with the liturgical texts.

The **Collect** acknowledges in the first instance God's freedom to bestow the Spirit wherever he will. In some sense, then, this freedom is what Jesus accuses his disciples from preventing. The issue of distribution of God's spirit is, of course, God's concern and not ours. We domesticate the Creator into our own image if we think or act otherwise. "O God, who manifest your almighty power / above all by pardoning and showing mercy . . ." This Collect is an immediate acknowledgment of the divine freedom to which no one has access except the Son, who himself acts in God's name through the Holy Spirit. When we accomplish mighty sacramental deeds, we always do so in the name of Christ in the unity of the Holy Spirit, and therefore are not against him but (literally) with him.

And so, like the prophets, we ask for a share of God's spirit when we say, "bestow, we pray, your grace abundantly upon us / and make those hastening to attain your promises / heirs to the treasures of heaven." The grace of the Spirit is what the baptized assembly asks not only as individuals but "upon us" the people of God, since we are gathered, "hastening to attain your promises."

It may be too obvious to mention, but we might remember the point of departure for our liturgical celebrations that involves a mutual sharing, so to speak, of God's Spirit: "The Lord be with you." And the response: "And with your spirit." This exchange, a bit controverted at times, desires an outpouring of the Spirit, an opening of heavenly grace. I am also thinking here of that famous moment in the homily by an ancient author in the Liturgy of the Hours of the Roman Office for Holy Saturday (Vol. II, 496–98). After his death on the cross, Christ descends into the netherworld to free Adam and Eve and all the righteous in "hell." "At the sight of him, Adam, the first man he had created, struck his breast in terror and cried out to everyone: 'My Lord be with you all.' Christ answers him: 'And with your spirit.' He took him by the hand and raised him up, saying, 'Awake, O sleeper, and rise from the dead, and Christ will give you light.'"

The Spirit seems destined to be shared, especially at the eucharistic liturgy. Someone once told me that a good translation of "And with your spirit" in Portuguese is "He is present here among us." Accurate or not, this translation and the many other global inflections interpreting the sharing of the Spirit of the Lord is worth pondering; the Spirit will distribute himself where he wills and on whom. We can only ask. In any case the point is that there is a mutual exchange at our liturgical celebrations in which the Spirit is moving, sharing, and sanctifying. All of us awake as the Spirit of God is bestowed on God's people, the ministers, the assembly, the elements, and the Word. These are the visible signs of Christ in whose name these works of power are accomplished. Finally, when the presider implores the Spirit to descend on "these gifts," we ask only to be filled with that same Spirit that comes to us once again, even as it did for Moses, the chosen people, and the early church: in Body and Blood poured out not for a select few but for all the baptized who act in Jesus' name.

Strategy for Preaching

The readings this weekend provide great witnesses for collaborating in Christ's church and demonstrate the legacy of the Spirit, who labors to accomplish God's will in ways outside of our power and control. The Spirit's freedom, which is not ours to manipulate, places all the faithful in a position of challenge and potential resistance. Who knows to whom the Spirit will be granted? Now there is a threatening question for those in power, or the inner circle elite. We know that in the sacramental life of the church, the Spirit has already been given to the baptized, empowering them as instruments of Christ's name to spread the Good News. Recognizing the Spirit's powerful presence in oneself becomes a discernment issue for a lifetime. So, the core homiletic idea for today might be that Christian discernment calls us to acknowledge God's presence in our lives and sometimes that Spirit of the Lord will surprise us—even challenge us.

An excellent introduction or point of departure for the homily in this regard is *Lumen Gentium*, the Constitution on the Church of the Second Vatican Council. Needless to say, the church as the people of God is the founding principle of how the church finds its identity—through dialogue and mutual exchange of gifts, which are empowered by the Spirit of Christ himself. It was as if those at the council emerged from Rome with Moses' words on their lips: "Would that the LORD might bestow his spirit on them all!"

The homily could then go on to speak of the dialogical character of the eucharistic liturgy, beginning with the exchange, "The Lord be with you." The congregation and the celebrant ask for a portion of the Lord's spirit to come upon them, even as the prophets of old shared in the outpouring of God's presence. This exchange admits to a diversity of roles but not honorific status. Preachers who are parish administrators will necessarily be challenged to look deeply into their own practices of collegiality with the laity. And this collegiality is especially true in the homily itself in which the preacher is the first of listeners of God's Word, sharing the faith of witness and becoming a "mediator of meaning" as *Fulfilled in Your Hearing* refers to the preacher. An often overlooked reality is that just as the Spirit empowers the preacher to speak in Christ's name, so also that same Spirit gives strength and inspiration to the hearers. At this point the homily might encourage the listeners in their discernment process, unpacking each day the voice of the Spirit deep within them in discernment. The first of these discernment moments occurs with the greeting, "The Lord be with you," and finds itself coursing throughout the biblical texts as well as the **Collect** for today.

Jesus implies in today's **Gospel** that the disciples need to be on guard from thinking themselves as privileged followers. A good illustration for how we are to see Christian discipleship might be to contrast the ways of Christian living with more secular behavior. (Admit as well that sometimes a good number of Christians act as if they are an elitist group with special access to Jesus.) Our culture strives toward marginalizing the accidentally rich, while placing these favored in enclaves of special safety and treatment. But the more the Christian discerns the working of the Spirit within him or her, the more the name of Jesus becomes identified as a life-giving agent for giving a cup of water to the thirsty and all those in need. And the more the Spirit is recognized in us, the more we can see that same spirit poured out on others, uniting us as brothers and sisters in the same Lord.

Twenty-Seventh Sunday in Ordinary Time

Readings from the Ambo

Gen 2:18-24; Ps 128:1-2, 3, 4-5, 6; Heb 2:9-11; Mark 10:2-16

With all the talk spilled over the years by Fundamentalists about the one week God spent on creation, together with their failure to account for God's active role in science and the details of an evolution the Lord himself designed, the Yahwistic portrait of creation somehow gets lost. But not today. The **First Reading** is an excerpt from the Second Creation Story (Gen 2:4b–3:24), the first line of which immediately shows the Lord God's compassion on his new creation and desire to form a community of love. "It is not good for the man to be alone." It is notable that while the first action in the Yahwistic account is the creation of a human being, this deed is followed closely by a marvelous environment of creatures over which the man will preside, name, and function as their steward.

With the introduction of a "suitable partner" in the creation of a woman, the emphasis seems to be precisely that: partnership. To underline their (semantic) link with each other, the woman is referred to in Hebrew as *'ishshah* and the man as *ish*, clearly a play on words for the sake of the woman who is fashioned from a part of man (usually translated as rib). The awkward realities of a patriarchal society notwithstanding, it is still remarkable that the emphasis in the narrative is on shared bodily, social, and environmental partnership. "That is why a man leaves his father and mother / and clings to his wife, / and the two of them become one flesh." From the point of view of Christian anthropology, equality between husband and wife, man and woman, this text from Genesis is rooted in the sacramental reality that these two are joined in one flesh; one cannot dominate the other. Yet this pre-lapsarian vision makes the Fall Story that is to follow all the more tragic, since with the introduction of original sin the first captive is the partnership of equals.

Jesus himself is clearly rooted in biblical anthropology when he addresses the Pharisees about the question of divorce granted to them by Moses. Jesus reckons this aspect of creation as part of a sinful world introduced by the Fall. This "hardness of heart" to which Jesus refers is the unfortunate result of living in the shadow of a broken and sinful world. Jesus has been restoring creation throughout Mark's Gospel through healing, casting out demons, and now envisioning a world where two are again one flesh. Mark's introduction of children as signs of the kingdom of God becomes another sign of such restoration—a time before humankind lost its innocence. That lost innocence was fully restored by Christ's own suffering on the cross and victory over death. He will bring back all creation to its original state of perfection that was once lost to us. As the Letter to the Hebrews says, "For it was fitting that he, / for whom and through whom all things exist, / in bringing many children to glory, / should make the leader to their salvation perfect through suffering." The text from the Letter to the Hebrews, which will begin to run for several weeks in this Lectionary cycle, forms a useful theological bridge for the First Reading and the Gospel. It is, after all, Jesus the High Priest, who was not ashamed to call us brothers, bringing many children to glory. "He who consecrates and those who are being consecrated / all have one origin." In Christ, man and woman return to the Garden as one flesh.

Connecting the Bible and the Liturgy

Perhaps the most obvious, useful, and important connection available today between the Scriptures and the liturgy is the *Rite of Marriage*. Indeed, the texts for the marriage ritual present a wonderful gold mine of liturgical vocabulary for a homiletic structure on an ordinary Sunday.

The marriage ritual (option A) celebrated during Mass uses a **Collect** that focuses on the goods of marriage, unity, and procreation, when it says, "Be attentive to our prayers, O Lord, / and in your kindness uphold / what you have established for the increase of the human race, / so that the union you have created / may be kept safe by your assistance." Notable here are the key words "kindness," "increase," and "union." These are words spoken back to the loving God, the Creator and Father, which Jesus himself references when he tells the Pharisees that there was a divine plan "from the beginning of creation" that created man and woman, "*and the two shall become one flesh. /* So they are no longer two but one flesh." In other words, God has made holy our nature, allowing the coming together in order to procreate and to love that is sanctified in a covenant.

There are further connections. As the **Preface: the Dignity of the Marriage Covenant** expresses it, "For you have forged the covenant of marriage / as a sweet yoke of harmony / and an unbreakable bond of peace, / so that the chaste and fruitful love of holy Matrimony / may serve to increase the children you adopt as your own." The **Preface** points not only to the sacrament of marriage but also to the common origin of all creation and its renewed sanctification in Christ Jesus. As the Letter to the Hebrews points out in the **Second Reading** for this Sunday, "He who consecrates and those who are being consecrated / all have one origin. / Therefore, he is not ashamed to call them 'brothers.'"

Finally, arguably the most beautiful and substantial connection between the Scriptures and the liturgy this weekend occurs at the pronouncement of the **Nuptial Blessing**, which in one paragraph provides an eloquent summation of Jesus' own teaching on marriage and the origins of our theological understanding of creation through the lens of Christian anthropology: "O God, who by your mighty power / created all things out of nothing, / and, when you had set in place / the beginnings of the universe, / formed man and woman in your own image, / making woman an inseparable helpmate to the man, / that they might no longer be two, but one flesh, / and taught that what you were pleased to make one / must never be divided." Since Jesus is restoring all creation to its lost image, the *imago Dei*, the way God intended creation to flourish from the beginning is the "loving favor . . . to make of one heart in love / those you have already joined in this holy union" (**Prayer after Communion**).

Strategy for Preaching

The **Gospel** for today is one of the more challenging passages to preach because it can be read very naively. Jesus appears to be giving black-and-white instructions to hopeful but uninformed engaged couples. As such, the passage lends itself to knee-jerk hermeneutics for preachers short on time and ideas: "I know what this passage is all about: Marriage is forever. God made marriage. We should be faithful." Now there are few in the faith community who would argue with this teaching, but is it a core homiletic idea for these hearers? When preaching for a diverse congregation (some of whom are divorced, remarried, or separated, and others are gays or lesbians with partners), this pericope represents nothing less than a hornet's nest, waiting to sting just about everyone in sight. Therefore I think that an informed homily that is both faithful to church teaching and an encounter with Christ in the Word would artfully manage a blending of the scriptural and liturgical texts.

In fact, the readings and the liturgy for today suggest our points of origin with God as the source. So, the core homiletic idea for today might be that God created us out of his own goodness, and we continue to mediate that love in our relationship with each other, especially in marriage and friendship. Notice how broad this sentence is, as it attempts to embrace the **First Reading** as a point of departure and then gradually moves into more specific territory. The key word to consider is *mediate*, for relationships of all kinds are instruments of love disclosing God's presence. When God tells the man that the woman is a helper, we might read this as most optimal: an aid in finding true happiness. So, by extension, our closest relationships—especially those under the covenant of marriage—mediate our journey toward the Lord. We are different at the end of our life because of the partner, the friend, God has given us. Here is a potential homiletic structure to consider or something like it.

For the introduction, the preaching for today could emphasize the very broad theological question of love itself, a movement toward the other and out of the narcissistic concerns of the self, an absence of self-interest. In this regard, the *imago Dei* acts for the good of the other, even as God completely, utterly, and always moves toward the good for us.

I. We were made in God's image and so we reach out for completeness in love to another in love.

    A. First Reading and Gospel serve as images to support this initial sentence.

II. Jesus understands a lifelong commitment in love (marriage) as a way to return to God.

    A. Rite of Marriage, especially **Collect**, **Preface**, **Nuptial Blessing**.

III. Our wounded nature prevents us from experiencing this permanent mediated love for a variety of reasons.

    A. Some have been wounded by divorce and separation but still find God in hope and faith.

    B. While Christian marriage is not a possibility, those of differing sexual orientation can find meaning in true friendship that mediates the experience of God.

    C. There are many different avenues to find God, but the key is remembering the covenant with the other in either friendship or marriage.

IV. In the end, Jesus the Bridegroom is mediating for the Bride, the church, so that all our imperfections will amount to very little. The reality is that we are imperfect, so we will mediate imperfectly as well.

    A. Letter to the Hebrews.

    B. Illustration of hope through a story of covenantal relationship either in marriage or friendship.

Twenty-Eighth Sunday in Ordinary Time

Readings from the Ambo

Wis 7:7-11; Ps 90:12-13, 14-15, 16-17;
Heb 4:12-13; Mark 10:17-30

As is well-known, the authorship of the book of Wisdom has been the subject of frequent scholarly inquiry over the last several years. Originally thought to be the work of Solomon because of references in the text itself (such as the assignation in 9:7-8 as the one who was commanded to build the temple), the historical identity of the writer of the book of Wisdom has been in debate for centuries. Complicated questions remain about why monarchy, the temple construction, and the pursuit of wisdom could be consolidated into one person, Solomon or anyone else.

The issue of authorship notwithstanding, the **First Reading** has a great deal to teach us about personal discernment in the Wisdom Community. The First Reading is a rarefied look into the subjective consciousness of a narrator exploring the depths of God. Of particular interest is less a connection with Solomon the Wise than with a persona who embodied the value of wisdom in Israel and was heard by God because of a steadfast focus on righteousness and pursuit of the one thing necessary. "I prayed, and prudence was given me; / I pleaded, and the spirit of wisdom came to me." It is this desire for obtaining wisdom that becomes the real spine of the current selection, a longing for a transcendent value beyond material wealth or power (again, the historical construction of Solomon as monarch was useful to Israel because the king is construed as a leader who preferred wisdom over control and domination). "I preferred her to scepter and throne, / And deemed riches nothing in comparison with her, / nor did I liken any priceless gem to her. . . . "

Jesus engages the man in the **Gospel** in a moral assessment of the one thing necessary when the earnest person runs up to him and says, "Good teacher, what must I do to inherit eternal life?" Indeed, the Lord taps into the very desire of the heart clearly present in the author of the book of Wisdom who says, when contemplating wisdom, that "[b]eyond health and comeliness I loved her." In a sense, wisdom in Israel transforms the commandments from an external observance into a heartfelt desire for eternal life. The young man is almost there, but not quite. According to the Gospel for today, to follow the commandments from youth is paramount, but the invitation to leave everything and follow is the real test of discipleship and the interior disposition to love. The man falters. "At that statement his face fell, / and he went away sad, for he had many possessions."

Jesus promises an abundance of riches "a hundred times more now in this present age" for those who understand true wisdom, or giving up everything and following him. That includes imagining oneself as a pious follower of the Law from youth, which is among the riches of pride. We will nevertheless be subject to persecutions besides, since those who embrace Christ's wisdom also devour the Word of God, which is "living and effective, / sharper than any two-edged sword, / penetrating even between soul and spirit, joints and marrow, / and able to discern reflections and thoughts of the heart." This discernment granted to those who encounter the Word, according to the author of the Letter to the Hebrews in the **Second Reading**, is wisdom itself—and indeed Christ, the personification of wisdom, the following of whom gives eternal life. By this author's reckoning, nothing is hidden from God: "No creature is concealed from him, / but everything is naked and exposed to the eyes of him / to whom we must render an account."

Connecting the Bible and the Liturgy

Like the Word of God itself as envisioned by the Letter to the Hebrews, Jesus cuts like any two-edged sword through our meek observances to pious religious devotions, asking us to go deeper into the caverns of our hearts. The reality check here is that the encounter with Jesus in the **Gospel** with the young man is meant for all of us—every last one of us—since we are always able to go deeper, not by adding a new practice or commandment to our list, but by letting go of those things that possess us and obscure our true desire—the wisdom and knowledge of God.

Seeking God with all our heart as a liturgical assembly brings us face to face with the eucharistic Lord. Facing the congregation with the desires of their heart, the **Collect** for this Sunday becomes the voice of wisdom searching out its proper end. "May your grace, O Lord, we pray, / at all times go before us and follow after / and make us always determined / to carry out good works." To carry out these good actions, we ask God for grace in order to *iugiter praestet esse intentos* ("make us always determinied"). Grace must be *semper et praeveniat et sequatur*, behind and before us, penetrating us like wisdom, just so we are able to set our priorities straight. Like Christ's encounter with the young man, grace stands before us to provoke us and lead us into the good. It is our willingness to set Christ above all that moves us away from pro forma participants in the liturgy to beggars of grace. We are asking here for the Word of God to cut through our hearts as the psalmist implores in the **Responsorial Psalm**, "Fill us at daybreak with your kindness, / that we may shout for joy and gladness all our days."

It is the wisdom of the church's liturgy to act so as to transform God's people into hearers of the Word who long to free themselves from anything that weighs us down from seeking God or the desire to serve him and "to carry out good works." As we are reminded in the **Prayer over the Offerings**, the gifts we bring are our very selves, our most precious possession, now freely given "that, through these acts of devotedness, / we may pass over to the glory of heaven." This heavenly, eternal life is also promised to the disciple who has left all things behind. Surely, the eucharistic liturgy intends the baptized assembly to abandon their possessions—that is to say, the sins we possess and that possess us—when we engage the **Penitential Rite** at the invitation of the presider at the beginning of the liturgy. We acknowledge in our sins "*ut apti simus ad sacra mysteria celebranda.*" Freeing ourselves from sin with the help of grace, which is already given to us before we ask, allows us to participate in the foretaste of eternal life.

It is Christ himself, the Word of God, the Wisdom of God, who cuts through our sins, which liberates us for true worship. "You were sent to heal the contrite of heart." When we are contrite, we surrender all the things we possess and place them before God's merciful care. The promise Jesus gave his disciples that they will in inherit eternal life that, for those present at the Eucharist, "comes from the most holy Body and Blood of your Son, / so you may make us sharers of his divine nature" (**Prayer after Communion**). The Eucharist then becomes both the agent of our conversion and the promise for those who pursue the Word of God, Christ himself, receiving him with true devotion.

Strategy for Preaching

The goal for preaching this Sunday is to imagine with the hearer the extent to which the two-edged sword of the Word of God engages us. The book of Wisdom and Jesus' teaching to the man with many possessions ask for a hearing that is deeper than the surface of intellectual knowledge but enters the realm of moral conversion. As suggested, the author of the book of Wisdom moves us beyond the commandments into the world of desire for God—even at the cost of "health and comeliness." The desert fathers, like Cassian, acknowledged spiritual growth in much the same way when a monk reaches a state of *apatheia*: the monk cares little even for interior possessions (such as opinions and pet peeves) and reaches a state of detachment from everything except the love of God. Writing in the sixteenth century, St. Ignatius of Loyola would later say that Christian discernment should eventually move toward "holy indifference," recognizing the things that are not of God. The classic writers of spirituality remind us that after a period of purgation and illumination, the advanced Christian disciple enters a "unitive way," made possible by abandoning the possessions of the self to divine providence. This abandonment is what Jesus is asking the man in the Gospel to do. So, the core homiletic idea for today might recognize the ways in which the Word of God moves us into freedom and away from the things that bind us.

Consider using the idea of an imaginary journey for this homily, built, as always, around the listening assembly; it would focus on the redemptive Word of God, cutting as a two-edged sword. From a christological perspective, this homily is as much about Jesus as it is the man with many possessions: it is Christ who has abandoned the riches of the Godhead in order to become poor and share in our nature; grace becomes the riches of the kingdom that we all share because of Jesus.

Suppose, as part of this imaginative homiletic narrative, we follow the man with many possessions into a past and future. He observed the commandments from his youth, he tells us. He must have been a worthy character, then, zealous for God and good works. So Mark tells us that "Jesus, looking at him, loved him." The man is where most of us discover ourselves: full of possessions, mostly of the interior variety, which weigh us down; we are at the edge of conversion, moving from good to better. But how to get there?

There is something holding us back or we would be there already! The shorthand language for possessions in this Gospel is "unfreedom." What are these "unfreedoms" if we could name them and put them in a big bag? Jesus encourages the man as he asks us at this liturgy to follow and leave behind what holds us back. There are numerous invitations in the liturgy and the Scripture for today inviting us to live on grace and let go of what we think we need. (See, for instance, the Collect, First Reading, Prayer over the Offerings, and Penitential Rite.) The liturgy places us not as greedy children coming to get our favorite food at grandma's table, but as adult baptized Christians awaiting God's gifts in our poverty of spirit.

That is what it means to enter into eternal life—foretasted at the Eucharist. We can let everything go and approach God with open hands. Speaking of which, what happened to this man in the Gospel? One theory might be that Jesus' words cut into his heart that day like a two-edged sword, even though the poor guy ran off into the midst. It's unimaginable that he ever forgot that encounter with the "Good Teacher." There is, in fact, a man who shows up in Mark's Gospel in the Garden of Gethsemane who loses all his possessions. Remember? He loses his cloak and runs away naked, just as Our Lord is hauled off to his passion and death. Some scholars think the man appears again, clothed in white (emblematic of the baptized) at the empty tomb. Maybe, just maybe, we see him here for the first time. He finally let go of everything and found eternal life for real in the middle of a very unlikely encounter with the Teacher who would help him to understand true wisdom and what it means to empty the self of all possessions. May it be so for us at the Eucharist and what that meal signifies! (See Prayer after Communion.)

Twenty-Ninth Sunday in Ordinary Time

Readings from the Ambo

Isa 53:10-11; Ps 33:4-5, 18-19, 20, 22;
Heb 4:14-16; Mark 10:35-45

Although we know that the four Suffering Servant songs (the last of which figures in today's **First Reading**) were appropriated by the Christian community in order to foretell Jesus' messianic ministry, it is important for the baptized to lean into the historical experiences of God's chosen people from whom these magnificent songs most immediately refer. This historical reality, though far from our sight in the twenty-first century, becomes especially clear in a post-Holocaust world. In a sense, it is only by recalling very deeply the affliction of Israel from Assyrian aggression to Nazi fascism that we are able to grasp the cost of suffering of millions and millions and, in the end, begin to understand the cost and the profound mystery of redemptive suffering.

The price of human death and suffering cannot be glossed over as pious platitudes but must be faced as the silence of God, even as Jesus himself stared at this emptiness squarely on the cross. The cross, then, takes up the very suffering Christ himself represents for all humanity past, present, and future: the Man of Suffering is acquainted with grief so that through his suffering, he "shall justify many, / and their guilt he shall bear."

But at what price is this precious oil, this pearl of great price sold? We know the answer to that question: our redemption. But we also must recognize the role God plays as the one who "was pleased / to crush him in infirmity . . . and the will of the LORD shall be accomplished through him." The righteousness of God can sometimes only

293

be accomplished in the midst of suffering because of the world of sin. And so the innocent suffer. The chosen people. And God in Christ.

Whether we willingly embrace the redemptive cross becomes quite clear in the **Gospel** for today. The disciples James and John may be representative of the Israel that seeks a champion, a messiah of power and not one who is called to servanthood. In this regard, the two sons of Zebedee want to participate in messianic power but understand the leadership of Christ as one who lords this authority over his people like the Gentiles appear to do. Rather, Christ's authority comes from the quality of his suffering for others: "whoever wishes to be great among you will be your servant; / whoever wishes to be first among you will be the slave of all." Slave? Servant? In describing his own call as the servant who suffers, Jesus also introduces a new economy into the human sphere: the first will be last and the last will be first. This is a world turned upside down, "[f]or the Son of Man did not come to be served / but to serve and to give his life as a ransom for many." Is it any wonder why the early Christian community saw the life of Jesus through the lens of the Suffering Servant Song: "If he gives his life as an offering for sin, / he shall see his descendants in a long life, / and the will of the LORD shall be accomplished through him."

In this regard, the **Second Reading**'s selection taken from the Letter to the Hebrews is perfectly positioned to recognize the priestly aspects of Christ as the Suffering Servant as well as the theological aspects of the Servant Lord. But this priesthood is not hierarchical, emerging from a clerical family or privileged status. No, the priesthood of Jesus is distinctly and uniquely an inseparable aspect of the incarnation, which itself draws from the Suffering Servant: "For we do not have a high priest / who is unable to sympathize with our weaknesses, / but one who has similarly been tested in every way, / yet without sin." The Christ's free gift of himself as the one who redeems cannot be erased from the incarnational God who is one of us.

Connecting the Bible and the Liturgy

The baffling and distressing aspect of the **First Reading** that speaks of the Suffering Servant is redeemed by virtue of itself, since the man of sorrows "gives his life as an offering for sin, . . . and the will of the LORD shall be accomplished through him." That the baptized embrace the Servant and his mission remains an incarnational reality (as we see in the Letter to the Hebrews) and formulated in a creedal reality: *"Et incarnatus est de Spiritu Sancto ex Maria Virgine. Et homo factus est. Crucifixus etiam pro nobis sub Pontio Pilato, passus et sepultus est. . . ."* Therefore we understand the biblical text today as forming the architecture for the house of God, inside of which the community of faith makes its profession during the eucharistic liturgy.

At the same time, the Eucharist asks us to participate in the reality of our redemption not only on the level of belief but also through our experience of Christ, the Suffering Servant, who was handed over for our redemption, crucified, and was raised. The invitation, then, is for the congregation to become a community of disciples, hearing the Messiah as a Servant Leader and embracing the same obedient offering to God for the sake of others. The most important level of religious experience becomes, for the Christian soul, the surrender to the will of God, even as the Suffering Servant has done so. The language of the liturgy, as always, embodies our participative experience as we become "one Spirit in Christ." The **Collect** implores God to align our wills to his through obedience when we pray, "Almighty ever-living God, / grant that we may always conform our will to yours / and serve your majesty in sincerity of heart." This is the invitation to become what we will soon consume, the Body of Christ, by offering our very selves as servants to God.

The call to service, then, takes on many shapes, but most basically this mission seems to emerge from the one who has a sincere heart, according to the **Opening Prayer**. How does this conformity to God's will and a sincere heart become more perfect? By celebrating Word and sacrament. In the words of the **Responsorial Psalm**, we ask God to "let your mercy be on us, as we place our trust in you." Moreover, Jesus implicates the power of sanctification (as opposed to its earthly corollary of a will to power) to make us servants when he asks James and John: "Can you drink the cup that I drink / or be baptized with the baptism with which I am baptized?" The Eucharist becomes the cup of the servant, granting a union with the Servant Christ, even as we bring our gifts to the altar. "Grant us, Lord, we pray, / a sincere respect for your gifts, / that, through the purifying action of your grace, / we may be cleansed by the very mysteries we serve." It is *"tua purificante nos gratia"*—the action of grace given from God that sanctifies the faithful through service for service. The cleansing of sanctification comes in the eucharistic celebration even as we serve these mysteries. In a word, there is only service at the core of the eucharistic liturgy—Christ's table service on the night he allowed himself to be handed over for our redemption. And our participation as a Servant church and Servant leaders joins in these sacred mysteries for "our good and the good of all his holy Church."

Strategy for Preaching

Christian preaching is not able to account for human suffering as much as provide a faith-filled context that explores its mysterious nature. We stand convicted of afflicting suffering on the countless innocent by our own sin. We have brought the Suffering Servant to the final hour of his end and, paradoxically, his triumph over that same sin and death. To comprehend such suffering (even in some basic way) is also to grasp our role as those who thirst, not for justice but for a need to triumph and succeed. Needless to say, we can never allow the pride that demands a place at the Messiah's hand to control our understanding of God's unfathomable rule; instead, we are called to the kind of service that gives endlessly, the sacrifice of Christ for all. The homiletic core idea for today might be that we are called to profess our faith in the Suffering Servant as well as to become one with his self-gift for our redemption.

An introduction might begin to parse what we consider to be part of the word service today. The word has become a bit of a mishmash because we are not altogether clear about the sacrificial aspect of service. We think of self-service, checkout service, table service. But what are the services that we connect to self-gift? Perhaps nursing, parenthood, teaching. In the first few weeks of Pope Francis's days after his election, his unassuming manner, the washing of men's and women's feet in a prison for youth in Rome, the associations with everyday folks on the street, all spoke of pastoral outreach and service, and not monarchical privilege.

Christ's gift was completely "for our sake" as it says in the Creed. The Suffering Servant Song of Isaiah could be discussed in this context as part of Israel's identity and history, and then attached with a Christian assignation for understanding Christ as the Redeemer. With the Creed and its incarnational dogmatic formula in mind, we could expand on the dynamics of the **Gospel** and the role of baptism as an invitation to share in the One Bread and One Cup Servant-hood. That meal participates in the cross as we are conformed to God's will (**Collect**).

So, our suffering is transformed from meaninglessness to a salvific act through Christ as we participate in the Eucharist, by asking for God's mercy in the purifying action of his grace at the Liturgy. We are expiated from our sins through Christ's dying and rising. Our weaknesses are accounted for, according to the Letter to the Hebrews, by the priestly role of Christ, by the Suffering Servant, the Son of Man, who "did not come to be served / but to serve and to give his life as a ransom for many."

Thirtieth Sunday in Ordinary Time

Readings from the Ambo

Jer 31:7-9; Ps 126:1-2, 2-3, 4-5, 6; Heb 5:1-6; Mark 10:46-52

When the book of Jeremiah is taken as a whole, chapter 31 represents something of an anomaly in an otherwise difficult and painful text. Most of Jeremiah's emphasis to Israel is about dispersion and fragmentation, but the present selection for today's **First Reading** promises a gathering of the tribes of Israel, not because of anything inherently wonderful about these folks, but because of the unique paternity of God: "I am a father to Israel, / Ephraim is my first-born." One gets the sense that amidst the tribulation of wandering, rebellion, and downright bleakness of exile, God has stretched forth his hands and recovered his beloved child. There is much joy promised by the Lord in this text, much of it the result of God's intention to yoke Israel home from exile, "from the ends of the world."

But there is an added feature to note here. Not only will the Lord deliver the remnant of Israel, but God will bring these chosen people back "with the blind and the lame in their midst, / the mothers and those with child." In other words, those who are the most neglected of society will not be left behind; all will be led "to brooks of water, / on a level road, so that none shall stumble." God's invitation is not for the strong or for those who may have surfaced as elite groups in the community: this invitation is for the outcast, those who have been trampled and forgotten. Later in chapter 31, God will offer a "new covenant" to the remnant of Israel; it is a promise to begin all over again, renewed with another pair of eyes in order to apprehend another reality—the poor, God's *anawim*, are invested with dignity by the Holy One who loves them and will not allow them to be lost.

It would appear that not everyone in the crowd collecting around Jesus and the blind man as the Lord was on the way out of Jericho got the memo Jeremiah wrote centuries earlier. The scene with Bartimaeus, the son of Timaeus (one of the only people named in Mark's gospel whom Jesus healed—all the more unusual because he was a beggar), is a poignant one, with the blind man gradually being coaxed by Jesus to discover the impact of an important question that is put to him: "'What do you want me to do for you?'" Perhaps this forgotten son of Timaeus, now seemingly abandoned and in his own exile from his family, is being asked to form a closer, paternal attachment to the Lord, not unlike those in Israel at the time of Jeremiah. Clearly, Jesus wants to draw this blind man into his care, but he also wants Bartimaeus to discover what he really wants (he answers the question—"'I want to see'") and what holds him back from a relationship with Christ (the cloak is cast off).

Yet that is not the only thing that holds Bartimaeus back. The dark side of this pericope is that Bartimaeus is marginalized intentionally by a crowd who continues to rebuke and humiliate him. That is the ugly little secret in this passage: there are some who do not want everyone—particularly those who are outcast in society—to be healed and be returned to community. There will be those who want to stifle a cry for help and mercy. At the very least, these folks' naysaying the blind man's efforts to seek Christ are ambivalent, even if they encourage Bartimaeus to eventually get up and go to Jesus. Perhaps more to the point: one cannot really rely on the crowd for guidance but must seek the Lord by asking what is most important and necessary. That is the question that saves Bartimaeus in the end: "What do you want me to do for you?" Society fails those in difficulty, despite the promises and the political negotiations. There may be some voices in the crowd who encourage others: these are the faithful helping the homeless and the destitute in a secular society that has cast the poor, the elderly, and the unborn aside like so much trash. This passage is an invitation to throw off the cloak of abuse and humiliation and put on Christ.

The **Second Reading** from Hebrews recognizes that even the most desperate among us have access to God in Christ. "He is able to deal patiently with the ignorant and erring, / for he himself is beset by weakness / and so, for this reason, must make sin offerings for himself / as well as for the people." Making our way through the crowd, which is a mixture of those who have heard God's words on salvation and those who have not, we will find Jesus the High Priest, who offers "gifts and sacrifices for sins." All of us are poor and blind and in need of mercy. In Christ, the whole Christian community can proclaim with Bartimaeus, "Jesus, son of David, have pity on me."

Connecting the Bible and the Liturgy

The **Entrance Antiphon** for today could well be Bartimaeus's refrain after he was cured of his blindness and followed Jesus on the way: "Let the hearts that seek the Lord rejoice; / turn to the Lord and his strength; / constantly seek his face." The liturgy immediately positions the congregation to identify with the principle object of Jesus' healing. Indeed, the **Gospel** focuses our attention on the reality of seeking and, sadly, those who discourage that seeking. The heart that looks for the Lord in mercy and forgiveness is capable of rejoicing and "following him on the way." That exultation and movement toward following the Lord emerges not only from being healed but because we have asked to be healed by God's mercy. We have to know what we really want: God's merciful love. Similarly, the **Penitential Act** asks the religious subject to account for him- or herself in the midst of the baptized assembly, to "acknowledge our sins" in order to "prepare ourselves to celebrate the sacred mysteries." The congregation asks Christ to have pity and to heal our blindness.

It is worth pondering what—or more precisely who—is prompting this Penitential Act. The priest, on behalf of the church, begins this invitation to the Penitential Act at the beginning of the Eucharist. The church is encouraging us to move away from the crowd of naysayers who wish to dissuade us from the mercy of God. "'Take courage; get up, Jesus is calling you.'" This is the voice of the church asking the congregation to cast off our cloak or whatever else weighs us down. What drives this impulse toward repentance for both Bartimaeus and the eucharistic congregation is *penthos*—the tears of sorrow. This movement toward the Lord in order to be healed from the blindness of sin allows our healing to unfold: *"qui peccatores vocare venisti."* Yes, this is the call for all those who name themselves with Bartimaeus as in need of God's embrace. With the children of Israel we can say, "proclaim your praise and say: / The LORD has delivered his people, / the remnant of Israel."

With the Gloria following immediately from the *"Kyrie, eleison,"* there is a sublime transition from the contrite heart to the soulful praise of the Lord. We are on the way. The relationship between sorrow for sin leading to gratitude and praise becomes especially lucid in the triple attributes lifted up to Christ: "You take away the sins of the world, / have mercy on us; / you take away the sins of the world, / receive our prayer; / you are seated at the right hand of the Father, / have mercy on us." These are the collective prayers of the grateful hearts who have recognized their blindness and have been illuminated by the face of Christ and, like Bartimaeus, follow Christ the Lamb where his offering for our sins will be completed at the altar once again.

Strategy for Preaching

A very colloquial way of expressing the motion and energy behind the biblical readings and their associated liturgical texts for today is a version of a movement from "stuck to unstuck." The remnant of Israel is stuck in the diaspora of despair and loss, and so God desires to transport them to a new covenant by gathering them "from the ends of the world, / with the blind and the lame in their midst." Bartimaeus is stuck in the ghetto of blindness and humiliation and kept there, in part, by the social order that tells him to stay put. Jesus' voice strikes a note in the man to free him for enlightenment and discipleship. That call to walk on the way may also be to recognize the sinful structures that have allowed him and others to be marginalized in the first place. The Letter to the Hebrews presents "the ignorant and erring" being ushered in by God's patience and the priesthood of Christ brought by the incarnation and the paschal mystery. So the core homiletic idea for today could be something along the following lines: if we find ourselves trapped in sin or despair, God's liberating voice desires to move us toward him and to discipleship. An interesting way to structure the homily might be to use the threefold attributes of Christ deployed in the Gloria as a way to allow the hearers to come from their own alienation to corporate praise and thanksgiving.

An introduction might take a number of routes but could focus on the general aspect of how we manage to get "stuck" on the side of the road in so many different ways. Details, preachers, details! These are extremely important and evocative elements to remember, as always. There is often a dramatic turning point when we reach rock bottom, or that place where we find Bartimaeus. As suggested, the **Penitential Act** allows us to voice our need for mercy and to ask to be set free from sin, that is, what is keeping us from true freedom.

An outline could be shaped like this:

I. Introduction (as above).

II. We move toward Christ in the church by crying out for healing in the Gloria: "You take away the sins of the world, / have mercy on us."

    A. Letter to the Hebrews: Jesus has had mercy on us because he experiences our weaknesses, except for sin. A brief catechesis here on the incarnation, with an appropriate image to accompany this teaching.

III. We also say with Bartimaeus, "You take away the sins of the world, / receive our prayer."

    A. Bartimaeus cries out and the Lord hears him and cures him. He is held back by his cloak that must be cast off.

    B. We pray in the mist of resistance from others so we must have courage.

    C. We need the church to keep us encouraged and to remind us that "Jesus is calling us."

IV. With the whole church we cry out: "You are seated at the right hand of the Father, / have mercy on us."

    A. Jesus continues to intercede for us.

    B. Jeremiah 31 presents us with a "new covenant" that will gather all people from the ends of the world. Christ forever intercedes in the new covenant of his blood for all people (cf. Letter to the Hebrews).

V. Conclusion: we are drawn to the altar of the Lord where we will be healed from our blindness once again in the presence of Christ made visible. (Image)

Thirty-First Sunday in Ordinary Time

Readings from the Ambo

Deut 6:2-6; Ps 18:2-3, 3-4, 47, 51; Heb 7:23-28; Mark 12:28b-34

The book of Deuteronomy, which is voiced, according to the Deuteronomic historian, by Moses himself, consolidates the identity of the people of Israel as those who follow the Law of the Lord and abide in his divine covenant. Chapter 5 sets the context for the **First Reading** today because it lays out the Ten Commandments. In context, then, chapter 6 functions as a kind of high gloss or commentary on those divine mandates. In a sense, if chapter 5 contains the letter of the Law, the chapter that follows demonstrates how the inherent disposition orients the self in carrying out these precepts and statutes. The First Reading provides us with a window into the heart that has internalized what the Lord God has asked of his people.

That heart begins with "fear of the Lord," an often confusing description of a humble disposition before God. Rather than a false fear of the Lord—linked to feeling unloved or unworthy—a genuine fear of the Lord maintains a realistic self-assessment before God. Here, the virtue of humility becomes indispensable because only when we can honestly look at ourselves as creatures and God as Creator are we able to hear the commandment clearly and loudly without pretense or, in the common parlance, projecting a "false self." God asked Israel to hear intensely and deeply with what St. Benedict would later call "the ear of the heart." Indeed, the Christian community could replace itself with "Israel," for the invitation is the same for us as it was for God's chosen people. The soul or *nephesh* names the entirety of our being—not just our mind or the physical strength of our body. Even our modern religious culture tends to live out of its mind more than the fullness of our heart until we become entirely identified with our mind. We have a lot to learn from Israel. We are only able to love God with all our heart, soul, and strength if we understand that this foundational relationship between the author of life and ourselves involves our entire self.

Clearly, Jesus was to follow these three attributes of love more than any other as he gave himself utterly to the Father's will for the sake of humankind. In the paschal mystery, Christ is not simply repeating the Great Commandments; he is embodying them. For in following God alone with the substance of his being, Jesus also showed perfect love of neighbor by laying his life down for all flesh. As the **Second Reading** from Hebrews says, "He is always able to save those who approach God through him, / since he lives forever to make intercession for them." Christ's submission to the will of the Father was the perfect act of charity, the expression of divine self-gift present in the two Great Commandments. Jesus' offering has taken us up into himself and, therefore, into God: we are freed from the Law to act in accordance with the one who has been united with us through the paschal mystery. In Christ, we say with the **Responsorial Psalm**, "I love you, Lord, my strength." Jesus told the scribe that his answer brought him "not far from the kingdom of God." But Jesus has brought us into the very kingdom of God itself.

Connecting the Bible and the Liturgy

The two Greatest Commandments name the integrated, interior disposition of the friends of God whose whole self follows the Lord without reservation. Christ himself becomes the iconic model of perfection in this regard; he has emptied himself completely: soul, mind, and body at the service of the Father's will and for the service of all humanity.

The new and more literal-minded translation of the Niceno-Constantinopolitan Creed professes an immediate claim on the individual speaker when it says in English, "I believe," or simply *"Credo."* We ought to see this simple statement as a profession involving the entire self—mind, soul, and body. Having heard the readings from the Lectionary this Sunday and the homily that preaches through them, the baptized Christian stands up to be counted in the midst of the assembly with a clear "Credo." In a sense, the creed we profess during the liturgy is a doctrinal expression of the Responsorial Psalm,

"I love you, O LORD, my strength, / O LORD, my rock, my fortress, my deliverer." This is the refrain of the Christian community and the individual baptized subject, willing once again to commit to a belief in God with a full heart, mind, and body.

In a mystical way, the **Creed** itself positions those who profess its precepts to carry out the two greatest commandments; it does so by expressing its belief in the incarnation, which is the divine disclosure of self-giving in human flesh, the engine behind these commandments: "*Qui propter nos homines et propter nostram salutem descendit de caelis.*" This creedal formula majestically captures the way in which Christ the God-Man took up what was not his (our human nature) while remaining fully divine. And so, whole soul, mind, and body were embraced for "our salvation." "*Et incarnatus est de Spriritu Sancto ex Maria Virgine, et homo factus est.*" As we know, the *General Instruction of the Roman Missal* inscribes a bow up to and including "became man." It is easy to see that what began as an individual profession of faith has become, quite graphically, a corporate response through the common gesture of the assembly. "I believe" becomes "we believe." This action, of course, involves the soul, mind, and body—a singular intention—not only of the individual but of the whole church in an assent to Christ's incarnation. Indeed, the church as the mediating presence of Christ on earth bows as a sign of gratitude to show its own profound humility; it is a doctrinal confession of faith, unified through a liturgical gesture. As the Body of Christ, the assembly of the baptized discloses its attributes as the presence of Christ at the Eucharist, thereby bowing in assent to the Father's will and for the sake of divine charity. All become one as we worship with all our hearts and we are joined to one another in a common baptism and common eucharistic table.

Strategy for Preaching

Pastoral preaching desires to move the congregation of hearers from those who simply listen to those who accomplish the will of God through the entirety of their being—soul, mind, and body. Our culture tends to prioritize the mind to such a high degree that it is the region from which we understand everything—including God. "I think, therefore I am" became the watch-phrase of the Enlightenment for a good reason. We do a lot of shallow listening as well. We tend to be out of touch with our bodies when it comes to the way they are temples of the Holy Spirit, to say nothing of our care for the soul. But there is a reason that *nephesh* has played such a crucial role in the Judeo-Christian tradition: "the heart has reasons which reason cannot know," to quote the famous words of Blaise Pascal. Indeed, the noetic experience of faith articulated in the **Creed** at the eucharistic liturgy must be embodied by the Christian who professes these beliefs, even as Christ himself took on flesh. We form a corporate, living Body as we the church say what we believe and consume the one who died for our salvation. We are incarnated by the Christ who *homo factus est.* Therefore the core homiletic idea for this Sunday might be that we are called to love God and our neighbor with all our body, mind, and soul. We might notice a slightly different nuance with this core statement, since it does not include the traditional "love your neighbor as yourself." An option is made here to conflate a focus on both the love of God and the love of neighbor around the single encompassing strategy of the entirety of love that these two ideals require.

As we might expect, these three components of the self (body, mind, and soul) and the call to love form a kind of skeleton for the homiletic text. Further, an introduction might consider which of these aspects of the human person are encouraged in our society and which are not. For example, the ghettoization of the elderly and the poor certainly encourages a youth (body) culture to the exclusion of wisdom (mind). But paradoxically, we are frenetic about losing our memory in old age and divinize the mind. Similarly, we do not seem to have a language for the human soul, even as some attempt to capture rights for the pre-born; these children do not signify potential human souls in the making, but prehuman, nonlegal entities.

I. Loving God and neighbor demands everything we have—body, mind, and soul. The body is the first and most obvious way in which we account for our loving.

   A. Marriage as giving of body to the other.

   B. Creed and the doctrine of the incarnation as sanctifying the body.

   C. Liturgy emphasis on corporate gesture.

II. But also our whole mind.

    A. Church helps us in articulating the self-giving in the Creed when we say, "I believe."

    B. Contrast "freedom of speech" in the First Amendment with the Two Great Commandments, given by Christ.

    C. The act of will is involved by all who love. (Illustration)

III. So the soul becomes the true test of our degree of loving.

    A. It is possible to love halfway, but that is not what was commanded by God through Moses.

    B. Deuteronomy, Gospel references.

    C. Christ's priesthood accomplished by his entire being an offering, even as we offer ourselves together with the bread and the wine as living sacrifices.

    D. A conclusion might pose to the congregation that there is a process to loving into which mature disciples grow. (Image: the assumption of the Virgin Mary, who was taken up to heaven body, mind, and soul; that is, the human subject comes to full stature as she surrenders herself utterly to God's will.)

Thirty-Second Sunday in Ordinary Time

1 Kgs 17:10-16; Ps 146:7, 8-9, 9-10; Heb 9:24-28; Mark 12:38-44

The **First Reading** relates an episode in the life of Elijah the Tishbite, but in order to understand this scene more fully, we will have to go to the beginning of chapter 17 where the present selection finds its plot origins. Elijah announced to Ahab that there will be neither rain nor dew but only a life sustained by God's Word. Elijah himself will be tested along these lines, as he flees amid a drought when he goes into hiding east by the brook of Cherith (that in Hebrew simply means "gorge") before the Jordan. God provides drink and food by means of ravens for Elijah until the river dries up, at which time he must move on to Zarephath, where he will be provided for again, this time by a widow.

Elijah will have a significant relationship with the widow at Zarephath (in Luke 4:24-27 Jesus will reference Elijah in 1 Kgs 17:10-16 as an example of a rejected prophet who is provided nourishment by God and the widow), who will sustain the prophet out of her poverty. Elijah will restore her son to life through the Lord's intercession. This encounter exemplifies the wonders that confirm Elijah as *'ish Elohim*—a man of God. Elijah exists solely on the promise of God, and the widow shows a similar trust when the prophet repeats God's pledge to her, saying, "'The jar of flour shall not go empty, / nor the jug of oil run dry, / until the day when the LORD sends rains upon the earth.'" There seems to be a clear instance here of prophetic faith sharing a charismatic movement of divine trust. The simple *anawim* we encounter with Elijah is meant to contrast the vicious lives of Jezebel and King Ahab, whose will to power and idolatry will eventually cause their downfall. The provision of food for both Elijah, the widow, and her son ultimately extends to a renewal of life for the boy; these wonders are made possible by the good will of those who cooperate with God, even in desperate (i.e., drought, hunger, and starvation) circumstances. The *anawim* of God, like the widow herself, live by trust and divine promise because they have been witnessed to by others, such as the prophet Elijah, who hold fast to the Word of God despite persecution.

There is a parallel we can infer between the First Reading and the **Gospel**, since Mark describes a widow putting two small coins into the treasury. She is not unlike the widow of Zarephath, who takes what she has and prepares a cake for Elijah, herself, and her son. Generosity becomes the unmistakable sign of trust in the providence of God, especially from those who have little.

But there might be something a little less obvious when it comes to associating these texts in today's Lectionary that operates on a symbolic, indeed allegorical, level. I offer this interpretation as a kind of patristic reading in order to understand how Scriptures can invite us ever deeply into its secrets, even beyond a necessary and vital historical-critical understanding. Perhaps others have seen similar connections. Following the Letter to the Hebrews, we might say that Christ himself has given all that he has into the treasury, which is to say the sanctuary, not made by human hands but established as an eternal priesthood, a passageway that has guaranteed our salvation. The two coins he offered were his divinity and humanity, a full deposit of all he had in order "to take away sin by his sacrifice." That is how our redemption was purchased. The scribes in the long robes Jesus describes are the ephemeral offerings of those whose lengthy and ineffectual prayers do not intercede on our behalf. Christ, like Elijah before him, lived on the Word of God, and out of his poverty contributed his very Godhead into the sanctuary for our salvation and justification.

Connecting the Bible and the Liturgy

In the last half of the twentieth century, the church had, for a variety of reasons, become more and more vocal in its social teaching about God's "preferential option for the poor." Much of this teaching is deeply embedded in traditional Catholic thought, but the practical reasons for understanding the role of the poor surfaced in a special way during the leadership of the Latin American Catholic Church in the 1960s and '70s and the USCCB stance on economics and immigration from the early 1980s until the present. From a biblical perspective, the *anawim* of God have been more or less rejected by the powerful and have been lifted up by God, a celebration resonant with the gift of the incarnation itself, as Mary of Nazareth vocalizes in the *Magnificat*. Jesus notices the widow in today's **Gospel** in the tradition grounded in the Hebrew Scriptures and highlights her devotion out of all those who give from their surplus. The return to God in the midst of want echoes one of the stories in the Elijah cycle from the **First Reading** today as well, but we might say that the widow of Zarephath can trace her origin to all the *anawim* of Israel. Trust in God comes to those who have nothing, and so God provides for these poor out of divine mercy.

The eucharistic assembly stands as always poor before the Lord, waiting to be fed in the midst of our hunger, a famine longing for nourishment in the landscape of sin and evil. The **Collect** for today is a reminder of the intensity of our own want and our need for God's help when it says, "Almighty and merciful God, / graciously keep from us all adversity, / so that, unhindered in mind and body alike, / we may pursue in freedom of heart / the things that are yours." This Collect, then, begs God's merciful protection from adversity, but also that we be unhindered "in mind and body alike." So we are praying, in other words, for the ability to accept the Providence of God in "freedom of heart," or to give out of our poverty all that we have, even to the last penny of our service for one another. The freedom of heart requires nothing else except to live on the Word of God. The Collect puts us at the disposal of God's Spirit, even as Elijah was positioned in his flight to Zarephath. That same Spirit will come down at the Eucharist, like a raven from heaven, and feed the faithful with food that will sustain us in our journey.

A further reminder of the need for God's protection in the midst of our poverty occurs in the **Communion Rite**, after the Our Father and the presider says, "*Libera nos, quaesumus, Domine, ab omnibus malis . . . et ab omni perturbatione securi.*" We have asked in our prayer to the Father to "Give us this day our daily bread," and so we await the Providence of God as Elijah did before us to feed us at his table. Christ has become the grace to all those who seek him in their poverty, the divine gift of charity to those on pilgrimage to their heavenly home. "The jar of flour shall not go empty" until that eternal banquet feeds all of God's people and Christ appears "a second time, not to take away sin / but to bring salvation to those who eagerly await him."

Strategy for Preaching

A golden thread of sorts, woven by providential righteousness, glistens throughout these texts for today, giving special attention to trust in God, generous giving, and caring for the poor. Elijah receives God's gifts through nature and humanity, a divine mediation that clearly sustains him and those he encounters. The Word himself speaks up for the widow and so feeds the disciples with justice for God's *anawim*. Christ will become bread for all through his priesthood of divine charity. So, the core homiletic idea today might be to consider the immeasurable generosity of God in Christ unfolding in the Eucharist as a sign for the poor of hope and eternal life.

An introduction might account for the life of Elijah leading up to the present reading in 1 Kings; such a retelling sets the context for Elijah's response to God's Word. As a general principle, the preacher should not presume that the congregation will fill in the blanks in Scripture. Rather, it is up to the preacher to stitch together a fine quilt of the Scripture that will make the Lectionary speak more fully to the hearer. We model ourselves after God's weaving of salvation history.

 I. Elijah lived only on promise and God's Word. A very visual description of what it means to be in a drought and to thirst could companion this story of Elijah.

   A. God's generosity as the giver of all good gifts.

   B. We have a hard time understanding Providential generosity because we can control everything—turn on the air conditioner when it is hot, go to the faucet when we are thirsty.

   C. One of the few things left we cannot control is the weather, more specifically, a natural disaster. That is when we are forced to trust God—and one another.

 II. This kind of situation of dependency on God and the widow he meets in Zarephath. Both are fed by bread, but more than that: they are nourished by God's sustaining promise to the *anawim,* the poor.

   A. Example of how people reach out to each other during natural disaster. That is where God is present to those in need.

III. The Eucharist presents us each Sunday with a way in which we are poor before the Lord and respond to God's generous love to the Bread we receive in Christ—Word and sacrament.

   A. Collect

   B. Communion Rite ("Deliver us, O Lord . . .").

   C. We are all poor as we stand before God waiting to be fed.

   D. Jesus offers himself for our salvation into the divine treasuring (Letter to the Hebrews) to purchase our redemption. Like a poor widow, he gives everything he has for us.

Thirty-Third Sunday in Ordinary Time

Readings from the Ambo

Dan 12:1-3; Ps 16:5, 8, 9-10, 11; Heb 10:11-14, 18; Mark 13:24-32

As we move toward the end of the church year, it is appropriate enough that the **First Reading** for today is taken from the book of the Prophet Daniel, whose name means "God is my judge." During these "final days," so to speak, we are reminded of the last things—that is to say, the important things—a reality that will become clearer in the weeks to come with the celebration of Christ the King and the Advent season.

The author of the book of Daniel was writing during a time of huge tragedy and difficulty for the Jewish people. Antiochus IV Epiphanes, the Greek tyrant who ruled the Seleucid Empire from 175 BC until his death (by assassination) in 163 BC, defiled the temple and killed righteous Jews. The final edited version of the book of Daniel occurred sometime around mid-200 BC. The first six chapters relate the events of Daniel and his companions—all observant followers of the law—and the Gentile rulers during the postexilic period. Chapters 7–12 tell of four apocalyptic visions, detailing God's vindication over unjust rulers.

The apocalyptic visions in the First Reading belong to the way the author of the book of Daniel conceives of God's relationship with his people and the divine ownership of history. Apocalyptic language becomes a window into the present difficulty by projecting the future. God justifies the righteous through Michael "the great prince" and with the inscription of names written in a book: "At that time your people shall escape, / everyone who is found written in the book." The author of this fascinating text affirms the God of history who keeps a record of human life and the transgressions of justice and mercy. An obvious parallel with the book of Daniel, the book of Revelation was written at a time of persecution for Christians, and that similarly accounts for the just and their fate as those who have been inscribed in "the book of life" (20:15). The **Gospel** for today has also absorbed the apocalyptic imagination as well, as Mark relates the immediacy of the return of "'the Son of Man coming in the clouds' / with great power and glory, / and then he will send out the angels / and gather his elect from the four winds, / from the end of the earth to the end of the sky."

With the voice of the apocalyptic dominating the ethos of this Sunday, the continuation from the Letter to the Hebrews seems like an odd choice as a reading companion, even though it is part of the *lectio continua* from the previous weeks in Ordinary Time. On balance, however, we might read the apocalyptic through the lens of the Letter to the Hebrews, meaning through Christ's priesthood, which stands permanently fixed for our intersession: "But this one offered one sacrifice for sins, / and took his seat forever at the right hand of God; / now he waits until his enemies are made his footstool. / For by one offering / he has made perfect forever those who are being consecrated." In other words, Christ's self-gift has already vindicated the just and vanquished the unjust persecutors by taking away sins. In this regard, it is the same victorious Christ who has offered himself up, who will come "with great power and glory." Rather than his name in a book, we will see his signature in the wounds he discloses as a sure sign of victory over the enemy, death itself.

Connecting the Bible and the Liturgy

On some level the **Presidential Prayers** for this Sunday function as stabilizing language for those who wait for the coming of the Lord. Although the Markan community largely believed that the return of the Son of Man was imminent, our contemporary scene (rightly) dismisses the "end of the world" scenario as emerging from fringe groups, often associated with paranoid individuals threatened by society and its norms. To understand the apocalyptic is not to predict the end of the world, but to grasp the triumph and vindication of God's reign over early power, sin, and death. In a very real sense, the Eucharist becomes the eschatological meal precisely because of its disclosure to the baptized of the coming kingdom in our very midst. **Preface VI of the Sundays in Ordinary Time** expresses the "now but not yet" status of the Christian assembly who have died to sin and death and live in Christ, clothed as baptized members with the garment of Christ: "For in you we live and move and have our being, / and while in this body / we not only experience the daily effects of your care, / but even now possess the pledge of life eternal." As Christians, we look to the apocalyptic of the Lord's Supper as an eschatological meal to remind us of the sober lesson of the fig tree: that we may sense the summer of the Son of Man is always before us since "[his] words will not pass away." Such liturgical language will take us into the end of the church year as we welcome soon the Feast of Christ the King and then the First Sunday of Advent.

As we abide in Word and sacrament, the faithful embrace the priesthood of Christ, while living for that which was promised. The **Collect** prays that our eucharistic praise and thanksgiving becomes eternal bliss: "Grant us, we pray, O Lord our God, / the constant gladness of being devoted to you, / for it is full and lasting happiness / to serve with constancy / the author of all that is good." The use of the word "constant" (or a form of that word) twice in a single sentence could strike us as redundant, but we get the point: constant gladness is a gift from God, and serving in that same faithfulness to the Creator makes us happy. This "devotion and gladness" and "full and lasting happiness" is a mirror of those who are singing a new song before the Lord in the book of Revelation: "These . . . are the ones who follow the Lamb wherever he goes" (14:4-5). Like the Letter to the Hebrews, the liturgical prayers provide a gateway into the eternal, while we also experience the coming of the Son of Man. So we pray that the gifts we bring through the eternal priesthood of Christ "obtain for us the grace of being devoted to you / and gain us the prize of everlasting happiness" (**Prayer over the Offerings**).

Strategy for Preaching

When the **Gospel** tells us about Jesus forecasting tribulation and darkening skies, this language is not asking for a response to a spectacle but for hopeful vigilance. Why? "And then they will see 'the Son of Man coming in the clouds' / with great power and glory. . . .'" While apocalyptic language may trigger some edgy individuals and groups for revenge scenarios and the like, the reality is that Christ is asking his followers to remain steadfast because God has triumphed through his Son over sin and death. As the Letter to the Hebrews puts it, "this one offered one sacrifice for sins, / and took his seat forever at the right hand of God." Christ's enemy, death, has been destroyed forever. Since he has "made perfect forever those who are being consecrated," we offer through him our own gifts at this altar. So the **Collect** reminds the gathered assembly that being devoted to God gives us "full and lasting happiness." That is our posture before the Son of Man comes in all his glory: serving with the constancy of faith as we over and over again ask that we may obtain "the grace of being devoted to you" (**Prayer over the Offerings**).

Does the apocalyptic have a place in our culture today outside of the alarmist rhetoric perpetrated by extreme Christian fundamentalists and millennialist militia? Perhaps it does, but the congregation will have to be convinced of it because we are addicted to spectacle that is anything but faith-driven. Special effects, hard-core violence, severed bodies: these are the bread and butter of the entertainment industry. With that in mind, the book of Daniel might make a great movie if left in the hands of people who see the world only in black and white, evil against good. Think of it: the evil forces being defeated by the prince Michael after a period of great distress!

But that movie was meant for another congregation besides the community of faith, which has learned from the apocalyptic that God's power was not meant to be gawked at but anticipated.

I. We wait for that promised day right here at the Eucharist, a sure sign of that eternal banquet that awaits us.

   A. We do so longing for the kingdom because this altar is the place where we are most ourselves, thanks to Christ's eternal priesthood (Letter to the Hebrews).

   B. Serving here makes us constant in gladness with "full and lasting happiness" (Collect).

   C. Our natural state is adversarial because of sin. That is the violence we often associate with spectacle. But our supernatural state is the redeemed self in Christ: that is how we are meant to be, offering ourselves day after day.

II. So how will we face the end of the church year?

    A. There are a lot of options:

        1. Ignore it? But that would be like those who do not heed the lessons of the fig tree and its season (Gospel).

        2. Or keep vigilant. That would mean staying attentive to Christ's words with "constancy," words that will never pass away.

    B. This is what it means to "live and move and have our being" (Preface VI for Sundays in Ordinary Time).

    C. The Eucharist is a constant reminder of the vigil we keep until he comes again, even if "of that day or hour, no one knows, / neither the angels in heaven, nor the Son, but only the Father."

SOLEMNITIES
OF THE LORD
DURING ORDINARY TIME

The Most Holy Trinity

First Sunday after Pentecost

Readings from the Ambo

Deut 4:32-34, 39-40; Ps 33:4-5, 6, 9, 18-19, 20, 22;
Rom 8:14-17; Matt 28:16-20

The book of Deuteronomy evolved over a period of about two hundred years (from the fifth to the seventh century BC), the core of which is the Codex of Law (chaps. 12–26). The Deuteronomic historians position Moses as the sage of memory, the one who holds the history of God's relationship and confronts Israel with the accountability for upholding that divine covenant. That the Lawgiver, Moses, is also the singer of God's works suggests the unique relationship Moses has with the Lord and Israel.

If we were to take the **First Reading** simply at face value, it is a grand monologue of faith. For centuries, of course, it was believed that Moses himself wrote the Pentateuch, and we get a little glimpse into how that identity may have emerged from the initial verses in the selection from Deuteronomy: "Ask now of the days of old, before your time, / ever since God created man upon the earth; / ask from one end of the sky to the other: / Did anything so great ever happen before? / Was it ever heard of?" Moses goes on to recount God's work of salvation in Egypt and other wonders performed "by testings, by signs and wonders, by war, / with strong hand and outstretched arm, / and by great terrors, / all of which the LORD, your God, / did for you in Egypt before your very eyes." Moses recalls his own witness in order to evoke the testimony of others before him. All this God accomplished to "take a nation for himself."

Therefore Moses enjoins the people to keep the statutes and commandments precisely as a response to divine activity, the recollection of which he has given to them as a testimony. Bearing witness seems very much a part of Paul's own correspondence as well, as we see in the Letter to the Romans. But it is not only Paul's faith disclosure that is at stake in the **Second Reading** but also the witness of the Spirit who cries out, "Abba, Father," within us as children of God, which makes us "heirs of God and joint heirs with Christ, / if only we suffer with him / so that we may also be glorified with him." The word Paul uses in Greek is *summarturei*, which means to bear witness to another or testify. We can also see how the word *martyr* (witness) functions in a somewhat poetic fashion: the Spirit cries out literally as a martyr, even as Jesus, the faithful witness, cried, "*Abba,*" on the cross. In a sense, Paul is suggesting that under the conditions of the new covenant established by Christ, our response to God's wonders in salvation history is not limited to keeping the statutes and commandments of ancient Israel, but far greater: the Spirit himself is crying back to the Father as a testimony to God's infinite power and love.

The response of a faithful life does not come easily, even when the Spirit prompts the disciples to do the same. The Gospel of Matthew leaves us with a shaky scene as the followers of Jesus are sent forth: "When they all saw him, they worshiped, but they doubted." That mixture of worship and doubt would find itself entwined in the lives of the disciples themselves and allows a very human reality to be at work, but one that invites the Spirit's participation nonetheless. Moreover, it is these same eleven disciples—already wounded by the missing twelfth disciple, Judas—that, in their imperfection, are able to be commissioned and baptize "in the name of the Father, / and of the Son, and of the Holy Spirit." These disciples, like Moses, will carry the sign of the perfect God even in their own imperfection, much like all the baptized with whom the Spirit dwells as an abiding presence.

Connecting the Bible and the Liturgy

When Jesus says toward the end of Matthew's Gospel that "All power in heaven and on earth has been given to me," he is expressing a Trinitarian reality that will be echoed throughout the liturgical texts for this Solemnity. Indeed, the **Preface: The Mystery of the**

Most Holy Trinity sings of the unity of the one God who has spoken through his Son and given him power in the Holy Spirit: "For with your Only Begotten Son and the Holy Spirit / you are one God, one Lord: / not in the unity of a single person, / but in a Trinity of one substance." Later, the Preface again praises the Trinity in their unity in substance and their equality in majesty.

The expression "consubstantial," newly replacing "one in being with the Father" and used to describe the Son's relationship with the Father in what the first ecumenical Council of Nicaea (325) refers to as *homoousios*, affirms that the Son and the Father are of the same substance. With Nicaea defining the relationship between the Father and the Son over and against Arianism, it would be difficult to exaggerate this creedal expression of faith as more important to shaping Catholic doctrine and liturgy over the centuries. The Son never acts alone but always in unity with the Father and the Spirit and therefore commissions the disciples to baptize not in his name only, but in the name of the Father and of the Son and of the Holy Spirit. Similarly, when the Lord says, "I am with you always, until the end of the age," Christ promises the indwelling of the trinity to all the baptized. Therefore Paul can rightly claim that all those who have been baptized "received a Spirit of adoption, / through whom we cry, 'Abba, Father!' / The Spirit himself bears witness with our spirit / that we are children of God, / and if children, then heirs, / heirs of God and joint heirs with Christ. . . ." And it is also Christ himself, in the unity with the same spirit who also calls out to the Father through his members in the Body.

We mark the sign of God's Trinitarian indwelling as a congregation from the very beginning of the Eucharist as we recall our baptism with the sign of the cross. Later, the **Profession of Faith** gathers the collective will of the congregation into the language of assent and belief in this Trinity, abiding in us all. So it is that the **Collect** prays that the congregation understand the mystery into which they are so deeply immersed, that "we may acknowledge the Trinity of eternal glory / and adore your Unity, powerful in majesty." As a very sign of that Trinitarian unity, the Catholic Christian assembly has gathered at the Eucharist to affirm one baptism for the forgiveness of sins and to cry out "Abba, Father" as a member of Christ's mystical Body in the unity of the Holy Spirit. As Christ offers praise and thanksgiving to his Father in Heaven, this indeed is perfect praise.

Strategy for Preaching

The preacher on the Solemnity of the Most Holy Trinity stands before the congregation as the singer of historical memory, sacred memory. Like Moses represented in the book of Deuteronomy, the homilist asks the baptized assembly implicitly about the God they have come to worship: Have you ever seen anything like this before? Was it ever heard of? Did a people ever hear a voice of God speaking from the midst of the fire? The Christian community has indeed heard God speaking in the midst of the flames before—in Christ—and we live now in baptism as those same tongues of fire settle on those called by the Spirit to live in the indwelling of the Trinity as they celebrate the eucharistic liturgy.

Deepening the faith of the baptized and "naming grace" on this Solemnity seems a clear enough goal, but the question becomes how to accomplish a renewal of the congregation's experience of the Trinitarian God without resorting to an excessive use of abstract language. How, then, to be experiential, but catechetical as well? Concrete, but teach a seminal doctrine of the church? Informational, but take the homily into the realm of witness? Broadly speaking, we know that preaching at the Eucharist intends to evoke a kind of silent faith response, made explicit in the **Preface Dialogue**: we acknowledge what we have heard about God's saving acts in our salvation history and so we come to the altar to offer thanks and praise through Christ, Our Lord. The **Collect** prays that "in professing the true faith, / we may acknowledge the Trinity of eternal glory / and adore your Unity, powerful in majesty." Therefore the core homiletic idea for today is really Christian preaching at its most basic: to recount God's deeds so that the hearer might respond in faith, gratitude, and wonder. We can see that embedded within this core is both doctrine and experience; catechesis as well as mystery.

The key for accomplishing a skillful tactic for this Solemnity is to gather the listeners around the memory of God's saving Word among us. We should recall here that language itself is formative, even as the Word has shaped the people of God by his very presence in history and the indwelling of his Spirit among us. An introduction might focus on a story or an illustration about faith beyond all odds. Since this introduction is really about gathering people, the point does not have to be at all a Catholic or Christian faith achievement;

324 Solemnities of the Lord

it can even be simply the efforts of the human spirit to survive a difficult or impossible situation. What comes to mind here is Viktor Frankl's famous book *Man's Search for Meaning* (1946), the story of those who managed to survive the deadening experience of the Nazi concentration camps during World War II. Or again, Aron Ralston's recent experience of being trapped in the Blue John Canyon and, in desperation, sawing off his arm in order to stay alive. What kept these remarkable human beings going was the memory of loved ones, a hope in the future that never died.

God's indwelling is like that: it is a mysterious force beyond our reckoning that speaks out of the fire of every human person and in a special way in the baptized. Perhaps the homily could then begin a short catechesis about Christian anthropology and the dignity of the human subject. A good reference here might be *Gaudium et Spes* of the Second Vatican Council. When Moses reminds the people of what God has done, the Christian community can affirm this divine reality and more: look what God continues to do in Christ through the work of the Spirit. This is the Trinitarian mystery disclosed in Unity, which the **Preface** for today articulates clearly.

What does the Trinity acting in the Christian community look like? It looks like our parish community, our family, and our life. Here, it would be appropriate to name some local success stories, or the work of the parish. We name local grace not only in the past but right now, giving us hope for the future. Since all of us have had the sign of the cross placed on our heads at baptism, this is an indelible sign that the Trinity never leaves us, a reminder that the work of God happens in us all—here at the Eucharist and when we mission to the world.

The Most Holy Body and Blood of Christ

Sunday after the Most Holy Trinity

Readings from the Ambo

Exod 24:3-8; Ps 116:12-13, 15-16, 17-18; Heb 9:11-15;
Seq., Lauda Sion; Mark 14:12-16, 22-26

The **First Reading** is bound to strike some as utterly arcane as a textual witness for this Solemnity, perhaps inappropriate for *any* contemporary liturgical occasion. After all, such iconoclasts will argue, we no longer sprinkle the blood of bulls all over our altars and, even more, why would we want the contemporary Christian community to associate with a tradition that reckons its history in the midst of such barbaric practices? Haven't we moved beyond such arcane customs?

A counter argument might be made that there have been some attempts to jettison the Hebrew Scriptures after the advent of Christianity, most notably by Marcion of Sinope of the second century, who rejected the deity of the Old Testament in favor of the Christian God revealed in Christ. As we know, the church completely disavows this teaching and sees its own history as intimately linked to the Jewish tradition (despite the long and painful history of anti-Semitism perpetrated by certain members of the church). Moreover, there is something very fundamental going on in this selection from the book of Exodus, which is the final coda of a section that began in chapter 19. We have been following Israel's trek through the Promised Land up to Mount Sinai, where they have now paused to receive God's revelation in the Law of the Covenant or, in Hebrew, *berit*. The present reading is the ratification of that agreement between two parties, made all the more real by its very graphic details. Here, it is blood that affirms the Decalogue (20:1-17), the Book of the Covenant (20:22–23:33). In the section that follows, the cultic ceremony of Exodus 24:3-8 remains a response to God's offer of a covenant sealed with the life of the community—the blood that is sprinkled. "We will do everything that the LORD has told us." Finally, note Moses' crucial role as mediator during this entire sequence, not surprising for the one who has been called from the very beginning of his vocation in chapter 3 to act as a bridge between God and the people of Israel. Moses goes back and forth, to and from Mount Sinai, four times (19:1-8a; 19:8b-19; 19:20–20:20; 20:21–24:8). Moses' role seems quite unique insofar as he seems to claim both a prophetic role and an active cultic, or priestly, role, the latter of which is demonstrated in the First Reading quite vividly and explicitly.

Another reason for seeing the imperative role of the Hebrew Scriptures today is the transition to the **Second Reading** that is quite seamless in this selection for today, especially after the **Responsorial Psalm**; taken together, the readings help to contextualize the role of sacrifice: "To you will I offer sacrifice of thanksgiving, / and I will call upon the name of the LORD." The Letter to the Hebrews appears to have in mind precisely the text we have just witnessed in Exodus 24:3-8. "For this reason he is mediator of a new covenant: / since a death has taken place for deliverance / from transgressions under the first covenant, / those who are called may receive the promised eternal inheritance." Identity of the author of the Letter to the Hebrews is uncertain (for years it was mistakenly attributed to Paul), but the originator of this text lays the groundwork for the doctrine of atonement that will receive fuller attention in later centuries when the sanctifying work of Christ is interpreted in systematic theological detail, first by Irenaeus in the second century and then by Anselm of Canterbury's theory of "satisfaction" in the eleventh. The Christian community's point of departure for Christ's atoning sacrifice has its origins in the covenantal and sacrificial language found in the book of Exodus.

In this regard, the **Gospel** illustrates the work of the blood of Christ, offering himself unblemished to God for our sake. Even a naïve first reading of Mark 14:12 allows us to grasp the parallel Jesus himself seems to make in setting the table for the Paschal lamb and the astonishing correlative he establishes for the ages: "This is my blood of the covenant, / which will be shed for many." We know that he is about to pass through "the greater and more perfect tabernacle."

Connecting the Bible and the Liturgy

As we might expect, the Solemnity today carries with it a direct and unmistakable relationship between the Scriptures and the liturgy. Indeed, the biblical readings for the day are so explicitly liturgical in their references that we would be hard pressed not to find some wonderful alliances between the Bible and the church's public prayer. The task at hand will be only a matter of deciding which texts to choose so that the hearer's faith in the Body and Blood of the Lord will be deepened.

Consider the **Collect**, for instance, which immediately focuses our attention on Christ's gift of "this wonderful sacrament" he has left the church as "a memorial" of his "Passion." Although Mark's Gospel does not specifically reference the memorial character so explicit in the words of institution ("Do this in memory of me"), Jesus alludes to a continuance of the tradition he is establishing when he says, "This is my blood of the covenant, / which will be shed for many." Here, we note the force of Christ's words (mirrored in the atonement language contained in the Letter to the Hebrews), which the **Collect** picks up by reminding the assembly of the very purpose of the institution of this new covenant, "that we may always experience in ourselves / the fruits of your redemption." The **Sequence, *Lauda Sion***, brings the assembly further into a recognition of the participation in Christ's new covenant when it says, "Here the new law's oblation by the new King's revelation, ends the form of ancient rite." The Christian community does not rejoice because we disassociate ourselves from the "arcane" ritual found in the people of Israel under Moses, but because Christ has brought us, redeemed, "passing through the greater and more perfect tabernacle / not made by hands, that is, not belonging to this creation. . . ."

Finally, with Year B's emphasis on the integral sacrifice and atonement of Christ present to us in sacramental form, and highlighting its ancient roots, **Preface I of the Most Holy Eucharist** makes a fitting companion to the biblical texts. (Compare **Preface II** in this regard, which might be more fitting for votive Masses of the Most Holy Eucharist or for use in Years A and C of Corpus Christi). "For he is the true and eternal Priest, / who instituted the pattern of an everlasting sacrifice. . . ." This language echoes the Letter to the Hebrews, of course, in that epistle's recognition of Christ as the eternal Priest and victim. But there is more; Christ also instituted "the pattern of an everlasting sacrifice," meaning the Eucharist is a covenant that is repeated, even as the Paschal Lamb continues to offer himself so that "we are washed clean."

Strategy for Preaching

Homilies on the Feast of Corpus Christi should not be generically used from year to year. Before preparing to preach, it may be useful to scan all the readings for this Solemnity to see what kind of tactic in particular ought to emerge for Year B. As already suggested, the biblical character of this year for this Solemnity stresses the cultic aspect of the origins of the Eucharist, carrying with that aura its christological and soteriological implications as well. Since **Preface I of the Most Holy Eucharist** creates such a strong relationship with the Lectionary readings for Year B, a core homiletic idea may surface from that text and even help to structure the homily. With our mind toward a focus sentence, then, an abbreviated form of the second paragraph of Preface I would read: Christ offered himself as an everlasting sacrifice and so we are sanctified by his Body and Blood.

We could return to the same Preface for a possible structure, but with a caution: preaching should understand and translate this important doctrine in a very pastoral and comprehensible way: Christ is the mediator of the new covenant in his blood for the sake of our redemption. Sacrificial language will need to search out an appropriate analogy and idiom for a contemporary congregation. How do we understand cultic sacrifice? An introduction might explore briefly the historical context of the Hebrew Scriptures as a way into covenant language; there is a modern analogy in the sacrament of marriage that is ratified in the complete self-offering of one spouse to the other in mutual self-giving. Then the body of the homily would continue:

I. Christ gave himself as a gift to each one of us and sealed it in his life blood.

   A. Gospel and discipleship.

   B. Preface I of the Most Holy Eucharist.

C. Catechesis on Grace and Justification (see *Catechism of the Catholic Church*, art. 1987-1995).

D. There will need to be a strong visual illustration to keep this teaching from being too abstract.

II. Christ then left us a new covenant that establishes a pattern for the church—our celebration of the Eucharist.

A. Exodus 24: as a seal of the old covenant, but the new allows Christ to be the "everlasting sacrifice."

B. Letter to the Hebrews.

III. Therefore we might consider this question: what will we do with our sanctification on the Feast of Corpus Christi?

A. Offer praise to the eucharistic Lord (*Lauda Sion*).

B. Thank the Lord for his gift by finding our own self-gift at the altar.

C. Remember: the treasure of the Eucharist is the gift of "unity and peace, / whose signs are to be seen in mystery / in the offerings we here present" (Prayer over the Offerings). We take that unity and peace to the world in which we live.

The Most Sacred Heart of Jesus

Readings from the Ambo

Hos 11:1, 3-4, 8c-9; Isa 12:2-3, 4, 5-6;
Eph 3:8-12, 14-19; John 19:31-37

Can we really imagine Almighty God saying, "My heart is overwhelmed"? Yet this is Hosea's account of God's relationship with Israel, of which the **First Reading** is part of a larger whole (9:1–14:1). In this section, the prophet uses the metaphor of a parent-child relationship to express the enduring and unconditional love God has for his people and, even further, to reveal this Lord as the Holy One of steadfast love who will lead Israel away from slavery into his own heart: "When Israel was a child I loved him, / out of Egypt I called my son." We sense there the divine heart overwhelmed with a kind of nostalgia, recognizing the love that only a parent can have because that special relationship has been present from the beginning and refuses to die.

This Lectionary reading stresses God's mercy, although the full text (11:1-9) points a portrait of Israel as the rebellious child, the one who has made an alliance with Assyria (begun by King Jehu) despite being freed from Egypt's bondage. The larger picture may emphasize Israel's deafness to the call of the Holy, but we also see a God whose expanded heart struggles with the gap forged between justice and mercy, as some commentators have pointed out. These emotions underline the parental quality of God and reinforce the metaphor Hosea has set in motion: that in the end mercy triumphs over justice: "For I am God and not a man, / the Holy One present among you; / I will not let the flames consume you."

That mercy finds its supreme icon in the **Gospel** for this Solemnity, which is John's meditation on the cross of Christ. It is notable that the Lectionary has isolated not the passion of Christ—what we might expect on this day dedicated to the Sacred Heart—but the symbolic aftermath of the crucifixion, particularly its sacramental significance: "one soldier thrust his lance into his side, / and immediately blood and water flowed out." This scene witnesses the life-giving fountain of the heart of Christ, even after his death, the baptismal water for the church, the sacred spring promised to the Samaritan woman at the beginning of John's Gospel. Ironically, in the aftermath of the crucifixion, when justice should have been most obviously the vindication after the Just One's execution, mercy itself overflows. We hear God again say to us: "My heart is overwhelmed."

In some sense, then, we are discovering in the **First Reading** and the Gospel what the Letter to the Ephesians calls "the inscrutable riches of Christ . . . hidden from ages past in God who created all things. . . ." Now we see that living water for which we never need to thirst again. In baptism this very mystery will "now be made known through the church / to the principalities and authorities in the heavens." Appropriately enough for this Solemnity, the heart of God is disclosed in mystery on the cross that yields eternal life. In the cross the Father is glorified in the final work of the Son so that Christ may dwell in our hearts "through faith" and that we, "rooted and grounded in love, / may have strength to comprehend with all the holy ones / what is the breadth . . . which surpasses knowledge," so that we may be "filled with all the fullness of God," and strengthened "through his Spirit in the inner self." The heart of God is incomprehensible, beyond our knowledge, but revealed only in mystery into which we grow through grace to be made strong in that interior world, the landscape of the desert that is the place of our earthly wandering, but out of which God has called us in mercy and love.

Connecting the Bible and the Liturgy

Although each day the grateful church celebrates the love of God in Christ in Word and sacrament, the Solemnity of the Most Sacred Heart of Jesus calls to mind divine charity in moments of sign and symbol in an especially dramatic and poignant way.

The centerpiece of God's love is the cross of Christ, which today receives reverent and deeply felt attention in John's Gospel. The **Collect** earnestly reflects the biblical witness's attention to the crucified Christ's outpouring of blood and water from the Savior's side when that **Opening Prayer** reminds us of the symbolic significance of this moment: "Grant, we pray, almighty God, / that we, who glory in the Heart of your beloved Son / and recall the wonders of his love for us, / may be made worthy to receive / an overflowing measure of grace / from that fount of heavenly gifts." This church is the source of life, the "riches of Christ," as we have noted in the passage from Ephesians, giving us "confidence of access through faith in him." The same inexhaustible treasure of Christ's love occurs in the **Prayer over the Offerings** as well, when the oration asks the Lord to look "on the surpassing charity / in the Heart of your beloved Son." In English there may be some ambiguity with "surpassing charity," a love that exceeds all others. But the meaning in the original has more to do with the ineffability of love. The Latin phrase here is *"ad ineffabilem Cordis delecti Filii tui caritatem"* and the Spanish is *"el inefable amor."* "Ineffable charity" would probably be a better choice here than the one given in the *Missal*, since we are speaking about that kind of love that not only surpasses but also is *indescribable*, indeed, unutterable: that is, the inexhaustible treasure of Christ's love—it is surpassing but it is also ineffable. The very unutterability of the cross of Christ suggests the power of the Word to speak beyond anything we can imagine—even speech itself.

Clearly, the **Preface: the Boundless Charity of Christ** exemplifies this Solemnity at its essence and, as we might anticipate, brings together the biblical readings that underline the liturgical text. Indeed, this **Preface** serves as something of a gloss on John 19:31-37. The cross itself is explained as the definitive expression of love ("he gave himself up for us with a wonderful love"). The symbolic issuance of "Blood and water from his pierced side" becomes "the wellspring of the Church's Sacraments." Finally, the expiation of sin and our consequent redemption is detailed for the assembly, reminding the faithful that Christ on the cross draws all people to himself, "so that, won over to the open Heart of the Savior, / all might draw water joyfully from the springs of salvation." In the end, the liturgy joins the Scriptures in a ubiquitous refrain: we shall look upon him whom they have pierced and witness the heart that has been laid open for our sake.

Strategy for Preaching

The Solemnity of the Sacred Heart, although not a holy day of obligation, holds supreme importance historically and in the spiritual history of the church. Although the historical devotion to the Sacred Heart of Jesus may not have had the kind of popularity this feast has enjoyed in the last two centuries, patristic authors such as Origin and St. Augustine wrote about the heart of the Savior poured out for his people. In the Middle Ages, St. Bernard and St. Gertrude would be more explicit in their devotion until, by 1856, Pope Pius IX made the Feast of the Sacred Heart obligatory for the whole church. Undoubtedly, the devotion to the Sacred Heart of Jesus occasions the divine absurdity of God's love in Christ. The feast became popular—as did artwork for the home depicting the Sacred Heart—in a time when rationalism was in the ascendancy throughout the West.

As far as preaching is concerned, the **Preface** used for today constructs an outline that may be shaped into a homiletic core idea: Christ's love for us was shown on the cross, the fountain of our salvation. This focus sentence is also something of a theological summary of the work of the Redeemer, a mega theme for Christianity that preaching might return to again and again. As such, the Preface stands as an instruction—not through a poetic series of propositions but simply as a joyous singing of God's love during the liturgy (a celebration itself made possible by the very mystery that the Preface articulates). That is the Heart of Christ laid open in the sacrament.

A proposed outline might look something like this:

I. Introduction. Examples of love we witness in ordinary life: parents for children, spousal devotion, a teacher for students.

II. God's love in Christ is a wondrous, sacrificial offering on the cross. (Preachers should rightly ask the next question: what does this look like?) It looks like this:

   A. Hosea text: "My heart is overwhelmed."

   B. Illustrations: Jesus used to depict the heart of God, such as the Father in Luke 15, or the shepherd searching for the lost sheep and leaving the others behind.

   C. This is crazy love or what the French call *l'amour fou* and is irrational and excessive. Might point to what some might say are the excessive colors depicting pictures of the Sacred Heart as the only way to capture such mad love.

III. And out of this abundance or excess pours out blood and water, the wellspring of our salvation, symbolized in the sacramental life of the church.

    A. Baptism (water) new life.

    B. Eucharist (blood) eternal life renewed.

    C. Excessive love also never dies because at the Eucharist we ask to "be made worthy to receive / an overflowing measure of grace / from that fount of heavenly gifts" (Collect).

IV. So that we might all draw water joyfully from the springs of salvation, we might consider how this solemnity will change us by asking these questions.

    A. How do we draw water and renew our relationship with Christ each day?

    B. Do we allow God to deepen "our inner self" (Ephesians) by recognizing God's love for us?

    C. How do we respond in gratitude for what we have been given?

    D. Image: giving over our heart to Christ at the altar where his own blood has been poured forth, a renewal of our baptism, an offering in spirit and in truth.

Our Lord Jesus Christ, King of the Universe

Last Sunday in Ordinary Time

Readings from the Ambo

Dan 7:13-14; Ps 93:1,1-2, 5; Rev 1:5-8; John 18:33b-37

Fittingly enough the biblical readings for today in the B cycle are full of powerful language that remind us of Christ's triumphal reign. The selection from the book of Daniel is part of a larger context (chaps. 7–12) that focuses on the consequences of the reign of Antiochus IV Epiphanes (175–164 BC). Chapter 7 begins with a record of what would become several visions, this one as it appeared to Daniel in a dream. As we might expect, the history of the past is presented as if these were the future. In the brief selection for today, Daniel sees a symbol of the fifth kingdom as the Son of Man who "received dominion, glory, and kingship; / all peoples, nations, and languages serve him." There are some who see this Son of Man as a representation for Israel or a type of angelic figure coming to deliver those who are in bondage and in distress. As we know, Jesus is identified as the Son of Man in the Gospels (cf. Mark 14:62), and Jesus himself tells an apocalyptic story about judgment in Matthew's Gospel where the judgment of the nations appear "[w]hen the Son of Man comes in his glory, and all the angels with him" (25:31).

Though written in a time of great tribulation and difficulty for Judaism, the book of Daniel speaks to us about envisioning the Son of Man as an immediate presence, the *now* of God's power. Indeed, it is this very in-breaking of the Son of Man and his kingdom that becomes the voice of the apocalyptic for us in the twenty-first century. We are no longer keeping vigil for the Son of Man; he is here in our midst. This reality completely escapes Pilate who is standing before the King and misses the Truth. Pilate instead becomes entrapped with titles and witty semantics and legalisms. Instead, Jesus stands before him as the revealed truth embodying God's power, which is not of this world. Only those of faith can grasp the in-breaking that is before their very eyes. "For this I was born and for this I came into the world, / to testify to the truth. / Everyone who belongs to the truth listens to my voice." The book of Revelation affirms Jesus as "the faithful witness, / the firstborn of the dead and ruler of the kings of the earth" who is not bound by time. God's future is now. "Behold, he is coming amid the clouds." The word that is used here in Greek is *erchetai*, an expression that simply means "comes"—very much in the present tense (in English translated progressively). This use of the present (rather than the future) underscores the in-breaking that is now, as if the author himself is part of this very moment of God's crashing into our time; that is, God's Kingship, over which we have no control, not even enough to anticipate its future. We are in the now-time of God's reign. No wonder the **Second Reading** closes with the phrase, "'I am the Alpha and the Omega,' says the Lord God, / 'the one who is and who was and who is to come, the almighty.'"

Connecting the Bible and the Liturgy

The last lines of the Second Reading cannot but be a reminder of another triumphal moment in the church's liturgy, well-known to the faithful as the **Blessing of the Fire and the Preparation of the Candle** at the start of the Great Easter Vigil, or *Lucernarium*. In a sense, the blessing of fire and the enkindling of the new paschal candle is something like this Solemnity of Christ the King: we stand in the middle of a God who makes us holy in a new fire of the present moment because he is not bound by earthly time. As the presider makes the signs of the Alpha and the Omega on the paschal candle and then inscribes the numerals for the current year, he says, "Christ yesterday and today; / the Beginning and the End; / the Alpha / and the Omega. / All time belongs to him; / and all the ages. / To him be glory and power; / through every age and for ever." This newly lighted paschal candle becomes the visible presence of the risen Christ, making the night radiant with his glory;

it is a burning reality that Christ is living now among us at the eucharistic liturgy.

The promise of the risen Lord given to the church at the Easter Vigil restores us to lost innocence and claims us as the King's own. Along these lines, the **Collect** for the Solemnity of Christ the King also allows for the congregation to move ever so gracefully into the experience of Christ's reign. "Almighty ever-living God, / whose will is to restore all things / in your beloved Son, the King of the universe, / grant, we pray, / that the whole creation, set free from slavery, / may render your majesty service / and ceaselessly proclaim your praise." Though we may have had associations of kingship with a monarchical structure that was restricting to an American sense of democracy, it is clear that the celebration of Christ as ruler of all things is a liberating presence: it was "[f]or freedom Christ set us free," Paul tells us in Galatians 5:1. So, this celebration of Christ the King is a liberating feast, jarring us loose from earthly powers and sinfulness. All the more so do we know this freedom when we come to the Eucharist; it is here that the Lord has come to be fully present in the breaking of the bread and the prayers, as we hear in the **Prayer over the Offerings**, "As we offer you, O Lord, the sacrifice / by which the human race is reconciled to you, / we humbly pray / that your Son himself may bestow on all nations / the gifts of unity and peace." This is a King who gathers all the nations into the peace of God's kingdom, not at some distant moment in the future, but now: "His dominion is an everlasting dominion / that shall not be taken away, / his kingship shall not be destroyed." All time belongs to him.

Strategy for Preaching

Fans of children's literature will fondly remember the White Rabbit at the beginning of chapter 1 of Lewis Carroll's *Alice's Adventures in Wonderland* (1865), whose appearance we first encounter with the busy creature scurrying about and muttering, "Oh dear, oh dear! I shall be too late!" As we later learn, the little fellow is also the executioner for the Queen of Hearts, with whom he has a very important rendezvous and cannot afford to be tardy.

We really do think that time belongs to us or to those to whom we surrender our power and safety, don't we? We give our time over to our jobs, our families, or our compulsions. Time is a way of making ourselves feel like we have a place in the world, that we can order and slice up our day, can control that which has been given us. I know of one priest who once narcissistically said to his people after he was late that "the Mass does not begin until I get there." Nice. It would be good for such people to learn who really owns time and to whom we belong. That is the real encounter with this Solemnity of Christ the King. We are truly surrendering to Christ what we already know by faith: that he has sanctified us and reconciled us to the Father, collapsing all time in his very presence. So, the core homiletic idea for today could be something like this: we are already present to the Christ in his kingdom that has claimed us at this very moment.

As already suggested, the paschal candle and its inscription for the Great Vigil of Easter begins to lay out the dynamics of the reign of God. The preacher might recall this inscription for the congregation as an introduction, visualizing for them the "Alpha and Omega."

I. But what does it mean that all time belongs to the King of the Universe, Jesus Christ?

   A. A story would be useful here about someone we know who made good use of time before death.

   B. Crisis in the book of Daniel for the Jewish people who faced the cruelty of oppression with the reality of hope in the Son of Man.

II. We face a different kind of persecution: an unawareness of God's presence.

   A. Time becomes more and more important to us not as stewards of God's creation but as supposed owners, stealing time from others and God.

   B. Quotation from one of the mystics such as St. Teresa of Avila, Br. Lawrence of the Resurrection, or St. Thérèse of Lisieux who have their own way of speaking of God present in the here and now.

   C. The Gospel for today in which Jesus speaks to Pilate about a kingship not of this world.

III. The Eucharist and this Solemnity brings home the reality of God in our lives now.

    A. Our ongoing sanctification and redemption (Collect).

    B. Our participation in the sacrifice of Christ as "priests for his God and Father."

    C. Through our offering Christ bestows on us the gifts of unity and peace.